FIGURE SKATING

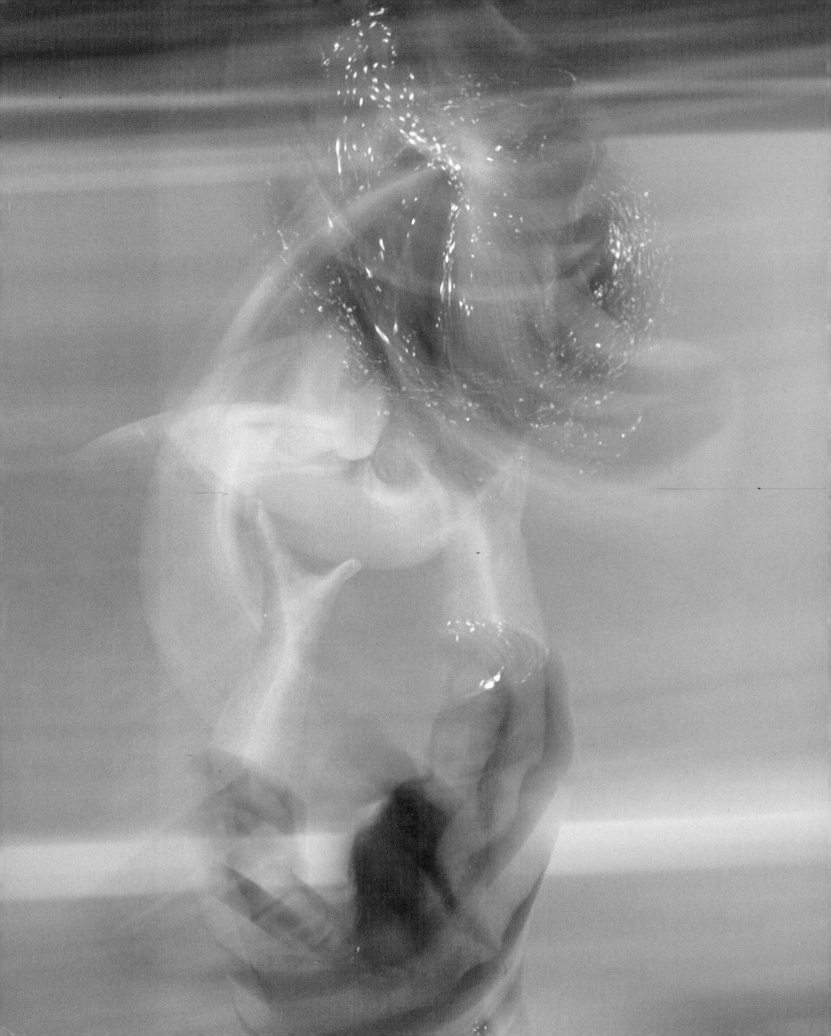

FIGURE SKATING

A Celebration

Beverley Smith • **Edited by Dan Diamond** • **Foreword by Elvis Stojko**

M&S

Canadian Cataloguing in Publication Data

Smith, Beverley, date.
      Figure skating: a celebration

Includes index.
ISBN 0-7710-2819-9 bound   ISBN 0-7710-8105-7 pbk.
1. Skating. I. Diamond, Dan. II. Title.

GV850.4.S55 1994 796.91'2 C94-931890-6

Designed by Kong

Updated paperback edition published 1995

The support of the Government of Ontario through the Ministry of Culture, Tourism and Recreation is acknowledged.

Printed and bound in Canada on acid-free paper.

McClelland & Stewart Inc.
The Canadian Publishers
481 University Avenue
Toronto, Ont.
M5G 2E9

2 3 4 5 98 97 96 95

For Wayne, who has always been there, through thick and thin

CONTENTS

ACKNOWLEDGEMENTS

Over the years, many people have lent a willing, helping hand in my quest for knowledge of the sport of figure skating; thank you all.

In the writing of this book, many people have happily answered the call of a writer working to unforgiving deadlines; their help has been instrumental. A special thank-you goes to Toller Cranston, who freely gave of his time and talents at a time when he was under a heavy touring and painting schedule; his support and encouragement gave a tremendous boost to the project. And to me.

In no particular order, I would also like to thank:

Bernard Ford, for his knowledge, intelligence, and wit about the subject, in particular ice dancing;

Louis Stong, who has always been generous and helpful in imparting information, any time, any place, whenever I needed it;

Peter Dunfield, who helped put historical events in perspective and who was extremely helpful in opening doors to Japan, its fascinating culture, its skating folklore, and its people;

Sandra Stevenson, a walking encyclopedia of skating and a true friend;

Ann Shaw, who unselfishly sent me her rule books, when she really needed them herself;

Jackie Stell-Buckingham, who bent over backwards to keep me up-to-date on rule changes and who unravelled the intricacies of skating's testing and judging systems, as well as the sport's technical demands;

Frances Dafoe, who was more than helpful in every way and was willing to give of her time for the book;

Acknowledgements

Sheldon Galbraith, an enthusiastic, knowledgeable, endlessly fascinating Hall-of-Fame coach, whom I could talk to all day – if I didn't have a book to write;

Frank Carroll, who had great tales to tell and thoughts to impart, and who took the time to do both;

John Nicks, who smuggled me into the restricted area of a rink so that we could have a quiet chat about pairs skating;

Barb McCutcheon, who lent an endless amount of moral support – and otherwise – during the writing crunch;

Brian Williams, who always kept his word and opened some broadcasting doors;

Sally Stapleford, for her willing, long-distance help from England;

Courtney Jones, whose amusing anecdotes and generous support helped make the project a lot of fun;

Michael Cosgrove, for his willingness to open up his private skating library;

Barbara Graham, for taking the time to fax me vital information during her whirlwind, globe-trotting tours;

Sergei Tchetveroukhin, for his candid insights into the Soviet system;

Sandra Bezic, for her frank perceptions and kind support;

Margarite Sweeney-Baird, for putting things into technical perspective;

Maria Jelinek, for her help in many ways;

Jane Garden, for her astute insights on judging and on skating in general;

Brenda Gorman, for always being at the ready to open channels and impart information;

Ellen Burka, for her historical perspectives and forthright analyses;

Pat Kennedy, for her tireless and cheerful editing, and all the rest of the enthusiastic staff at McClelland & Stewart. Working with them has been a pleasure.

Beverley Smith

FOREWORD

by Elvis Stojko

Men's World Champion, 1994

Skating isn't a job – it's a way of life.

You train for months, giving 100 per cent each day, for a competition that will be over in a matter of minutes. You skate through fatigue, injuries, and sometimes disappointment, not because you have to skate, but because you love to skate.

It's the process of striving for excellence – and not the end product of a possible gold medal – that makes it all worthwhile. And finding out who you are and how you react in certain circumstances is as big a part of your development as landing your first double Axel.

The reasons for deciding to pursue skating seriously are as varied as skaters themselves. Some choose ice dancing, because they love to skate to music and learn about the edges of their blades. Others choose to skate as part of a pair. For the woman pair-skater, there is the rush of freedom while performing a difficult throw triple jump or the thrill of flying high above her partner in an overhead lift. For her partner, satisfaction comes in the show of physical strength required to do the difficult technical movements that can astound an audience.

Others prefer singles skating because of the intensity and the amazing feeling you get when completing a difficult triple Axel or quadruple jump. Singles skaters love to soar through the air and challenge themselves to top what other skaters have done.

Competition is our meeting ground. Many of us have been skating against each other since we were in our teens, and our common history has broken down international boundaries and helped form friendships that may last a lifetime. When a group of skaters gets together at an international event, we are all curious about each other. Most skaters speak some English or French, and through talking, we soon discover how similar we are.

(Figure skating is one of the few sports that uses music, but the artistry in other sports is similar to that of skating. Turn down the sound on your television the next time you watch football, basketball, soccer, or hockey, and then add your own classical music. Watch the flow of the action and the smoothness of the plays. To me, any sport played at the elite level is a kind of art, and great athletes are artists in their own right.)

For the people who watch figure skating, our jumps appear to defy the law of gravity. But rather than defying this law, we are actually ruled by it. Jumping – the result of a combination of speed, timing, power, distance, flow, and finesse – is like being on a roller coaster. Momentum swiftly hoists you up and then plunges you down, before you can catch your breath. The difference is that a roller coaster doesn't produce its own power the way a skater can, using the knees to control both speed and force.

There are two types of jumps in skating: toe-assisted jumps, which take off from the picks or toe of your blade, and edge-assisted jumps. In either type, it's important to combine the right amount of speed with the right amount of power. If you have speed only, you won't get the spring. With power only, you're working against the flow of the jump. When all of this comes together, and your timing is right, you just float up. It's an incredible feeling.

It's like when children learn to write. At first, they break the pencil because they're pushing too hard. Eventually, they find the right pressure and can control it. Once they've mastered the technique, their writing starts to flow, and the pencil caresses the paper.

It's the same on the ice. The way the foot touches the boot and the way the blade caresses the ice creates lines. How deep you want these lines, the amount of pressure on your blade, and the edge you use are your decisions. There are many combinations of these factors, but once you know where your center of gravity is and you know how much pressure you need to perform a certain jump, you become one with it.

When I teach someone to skate, they often try to work their blades to make themselves go forward, instead of allowing themselves to surrender to the blades and the way they flow. Again, it's like writing: you don't work the pencil, you let it glide across the paper.

Mastering the techniques to be an elite figure skater takes years of training and knowing your body, inside and out – how it reacts in different situations. But for me, just 20 per cent of my sport is physical; the other 80 per cent is mental.

I enjoy the physical activity, but the search to be a better person is equally, if not more, important. When times are tough, you give 100 per cent, not only because you want to win, but because you want to prove to yourself that you can stand up to the challenge.

At the moment of competition, you can feel a range of emotions. You can be nervous, scared, or unsure, or you can get pumped and be happy and excited. But what is most important is how you perceive those feelings. The flow of energy generated by your emotions, no matter what they are, is the same. You have to surrender to this flow and control its use.

Before the technical program in a competition, you can experience an adrenaline rush that lasts all day. Just before you go out onto the ice, your stomach is twitching, you've got butterflies, and the adrenaline is pushing so hard that you can't feel your muscles. You're so pumped with energy that you often feel tired. But I've learned that the body always follows the mind. I don't try to control my body; I try to control my mind.

Compared to the intensity and pressure of competitive skating, performing as part of a skating tour is like the glamorous world of show business. Touring teaches you a lot about people, other skaters, the business of figure skating, and yourself. You also get the opportunity to entertain large audiences and to see firsthand how much your skating may touch others.

Before I won in 1994, I used to wonder what it would be like to be world champion, but now that I'm there, I'm more interested in what's next. Again, it's the process, not the product, that interests me. The process is to keep getting better at what I do. Skating is an open road for me to travel down in the next few years.

This road has been paved by many great skaters. When I started, I looked to Alexander Fadeev and Scott Hamilton for their quick footwork; to Brian Orser, the stylist and the Baryshnikov of the ice; and to Brian Boitano, the powerful, unstoppable jumping machine. Each had a unique style and each was a distinct kind of champion.

I know, too, that I have my own style and that I am a different kind of champion. My biggest natural talent isn't my skating or even my jumps. The gift that God gave me was drive. My drive for skating and for knowledge of myself is intense. I believe that you don't always need a gold medal around your neck to be successful. Success is more a measure of who you are; it's being yourself and recognizing your individuality. It is also being able to interact with people and to be with people you love and who love you in return.

For my future, I hope to compete through the 1998 Winter Olympics in Nagano, Japan. For the sport in general, trying to guess where skating will go artistically is as difficult as predicting the personality of a newborn baby. The future of the sport is so wide open that we can only wait, watch, and be amazed.

For instance, technically, there's a possibility that quadruple Axels can be landed, but this will require improved equipment. Stronger and lighter boots and blades could also make even a quintuple jump a reality.

∽

Skating means so much to so many different people. For the spectator, it's big tricks, music, costumes, and skating personalities; it's power and grace combined with art and athleticism. For the athlete, there is the thrill of a good performance and the personal satisfaction of coming through when it counts. My first experience with this was at the 1990 Canadian Championships in Sudbury, Ontario, when I was seventeen. I skated a clean long program, and everyone was standing during the last minute. They had to turn up the music, and the crowd went absolutely nuts. Going into my last spin, I couldn't even hear myself think. I was tired, but the adrenaline was pumping through me.

Five thousand people had just reacted to something that only I did. I wasn't part of a team. It was only me. All my hard work and training had paid off. I had connected with them, and the feeling was incredible.

Recently, I was asked if it made me feel powerful to get the kind of reaction I did that day in Sudbury. "No," I said, without having to even think about the answer. "It doesn't make me feel powerful. It makes me feel happy."

Figure Skating Today: An Introduction

Oksana Baiul as the Black Swan during the 1994 season.

The world of figure skating is a rich and wonderful tapestry, full of color and woven in remarkable ways.

Its threads are lavishly infused with human triumph and tragedy, magnificent spectacle, enormous pressures, high risks, shattering defeats, big paydays, rampant adulation, intrigue, and a colorful spectrum of personalities that live all these things out.

Sometimes this world seems larger than life; a life of beautiful make-believe, of glitter and theater, of starry dances to the tune of success and television rights. But the dance has picked up speed, particularly during the 1994 Olympic season. Can the dancers keep up?

A swirl of media attention was bound to hover over figure skating, already a television plum, at the 1994 Olympics in Lillehammer, Norway. Indeed, figure skating had already become the favorite child of Olympic winter sport, with its blend of intriguing characters, close-up, heart-on-your-sleeve emotional drama, judging controversies, and high entertainment value, particularly for women, a market that advertisers desperately want to reach.

But from the moment that a little dose of hard reality – in the form of pugilistic, single-minded Tonya Harding – entered the picture, the profile of figure skating exploded. The media seized hold of a tale that featured ambition over fair play and, like a dog with a bone, wouldn't let go of it for months. Not weeks, but months.

"The Tonya Harding thing is historical," says 1976 Olympic bronze medalist Toller Cranston, speaking of the conspiracy that was intended to maim the landing knee of Harding's rival Nancy Kerrigan, one of the favorites to win Olympic gold. "Everything about it is odious and wrong."

The Harding–Kerrigan saga speaks to the ultimate story of greed, of the forsaking of human kindness, empathy, and fair play for Olympic glory and the supposed $10-million payday that a gold medalist, particularly an

American female, is expected to reap from success at the Olympic Games. In some quarters, winning is everything.

However, the irony of what Cranston calls a "pathetic charade" did skating a lot of good. The charade created a jackpot that was no mirage. "The Tonya Harding incident caused skating to go through the roof," says her former agent Michael Rosenberg. "Skating is now one of the two or three most popular sports in the world."

Harding became notorious the world round. Even Japanese newspapers covered her exploits daily. She focused enormous attention on a sport that was already starting to fascinate everyone who watched it. In the dusty corner of newspaper offices, even male baseball writers began to debate the merits of Oksana Baiul versus those of Kerrigan.

Skating, for perhaps the first time, became the topic of choice among sports-minded men at a gymnasium or a cluster of dark-suited businessmen at a luncheon. Even controversial Canadian broadcaster Don Cherry joined the fray when he launched an invective during his hockey program against Olympic judges who placed Russian Alexei Urmanov ahead of Canada's Elvis Stojko at the 1994 Lillehammer Olympics. It is a sport that sparks public debate and opinion. It is a sport that spawns the instant expert. Its controversies are an asset.

Even in the United States, where the exploits of Harding and friends were largely deplored, mothers with little girls in tow signed up for skating lessons in large numbers. "Our basic skills [membership] has definitely gone up," says United States Figure Skating Association (USFSA) president Claire Ferguson. "Tonya sure helped us. All these little kids are showing up. Their parents are dragging them there."

Since the Lillehammer Olympics, professional tours and shows have been selling out more quickly, according to Tom Collins, who organizes the U.S. tour of world champions that takes place after every world championship. (The first sixteen shows sold out in four days.) During one spring tour, a "Stars on Ice" show in Toronto proved so popular that organizers added a second night to the stop in the city. Tickets for the 15,000-seat Maple Leaf Gardens sold out in about a week for the first show. The added show sold out in about two weeks. Also since the Lillehammer Olympics, where throngs of non-sport media descended to glean every nuance of a sensational saga, some professional skaters have asked for, and succeeded in getting, twice, sometimes three times, the previous going rate for appearances in tours.

Tonya Harding, whose exploits brought worldwide attention to the sport

Rosenberg has said that, since the Olympics, the fees for most skaters have increased by 50 to 75 per cent, and by "gigantic" proportions for the top handful of skaters. The top ten skaters on the money circuit can make more than $1 million a year from shows, tours, professional competitions, and endorsements, he says. The top three skaters earn between $3 million and $4 million a year. Depending on the athlete and the market in which he or she skates, a performer can earn from $300 to $30,000 a night.

Before Kerrigan even had the Olympic silver medal around her neck, she had already signed a reported $9.5 million in various deals over the next two and a half years. Oddly enough, Kerrigan is in high demand, even though she has never won the world title. Ironically, she is the beneficiary of a tawdry incident.

The high profiles and earning potential of skaters like Kerrigan stem from television interest, which is booming. "In the 1990s, so much of big-time sport is television-driven, both from an exposure point of view and financial," says Brian Williams, a sports commentator for the Canadian Broadcasting Corporation (CBC). "Look what's happened with baseball salaries. They went up when television went up."

Because of the Harding–Kerrigan soap opera, the Columbia Broadcasting System (CBS) in the United States expected healthy ratings from the Olympics, and they got them. Its Olympic broadcast in which the women's event was shown was the sixth-highest-rated television show ever, the most-watched television show in the United States in eleven years, and the third-most-watched sporting event in U.S. television history, trailing only the 1982 and 1983 Super Bowl events.

It's not surprising that CBS decided to telecast its figure-skating programs during prime time. For the past ten to fifteen years, figure skating is perhaps the only non-team sport that has been deemed worthy of prime-time slotting outside of an Olympic schedule.

"There aren't a lot of sports you can put into prime time," says Peter Sisam, the former vice-president of sports for the Canadian Television Limited (CTV) network and now vice-president of broadcasting for the International Management Group, a sports and athlete-management agency. "Tennis doesn't even go into prime time. But figure skating does."

In fact, viewers the world over have demonstrated a desire for more television coverage of skating. The total hours of broadcast time from the 1991 world championship in Munich hit 139.46 hours – not including Eurosport coverage. During the 1993 world championship in Prague, networks

Nancy Kerrigan, who actually benefited from the Harding– Kerrigan soap opera

committed themselves to 214.11 total hours of coverage, an increase of about 50 per cent in only two years. More than forty-four networks showed the 1994 world championship in Japan. Organizers of the Prague event issued more than 1,050 accreditations for media.

"Figure skating has captured people's imaginations," Williams says. "It's a sport that I believe is almost made for television. You can capture the . . . artistry and athleticism of it up close. In a football game, you don't see their faces. Figure skating is big-league."

And in a strange way, judging controversies can enhance the appeal of figure skating. "People argue about the judging," Williams says. "It sort of involves them in a way that they're not involved in, say, a hundred-meter dash, something that's not subjective. I'm not sure figure skating even realizes how big this is."

The CTV network, which has long held figure skating in high esteem in Canada, hit its best skating ratings at the Lillehammer Olympics (2.5 million viewers on the night of the women's long program). Even without Harding or Kerrigan at center ice, CTV achieved a rating of 2.3 million viewers for the less-controversial-but-star-studded men's long program that included two previous Olympic champions and a four-time world champion.

In Canada, where figure skating has grown from a very popular sport to a wildly popular sport, the Harding–Kerrigan phenomenon alone did not attract eyes in record numbers to television sets. Even during the 1993 Canadian championship in Hamilton, Ontario, 2.3 million people watched the epic battle between Kurt Browning and Elvis Stojko in the men's long program.

The live audience in Hamilton also set figure-skating attendance records in Canada. The Canadian Figure Skating Association (CFSA) estimated local organizers would sell only about 6,000 seats and would set up a curtain to hide the vacant seats. Instead, the 17,000 seats of Hamilton's Copps Coliseum sold out for three consecutive nights for the first time since it was built in 1985. More than 113,000 people passed through the gates during the championship, two and a half times more spectators than have ever been seen at a national championship.

The sellouts marked a turning point in Canadian skating. The success of the Hamilton event prompted the CFSA to consider placing championships only in major Canadian centers with large arenas.

Television had turned both Browning and Stojko into recognizable stars, which in turn sparked high ratings for their own television ventures.

Kurt Browning, four-time world champion

The one-hour CBC special "You Must Remember This," centered around Browning and his portrayals of Humphrey Bogart and Gene Kelly, attracted 2.7 million viewers – and, of course, the higher the ratings, the higher the price for commercial spots.

The world figure-skating championship in Japan was expected to be a ratings disappointment, with viewers perhaps weary of countless hours of Olympic (and pre-Olympic) skating coverage and because of the horrifying dropout rate of some of the sport's stars, who made the Olympics their last amateur stop of the year. Even so, the U.S. National Broadcasting Company (NBC) ratings for skating, tape-delayed by half a day, twice outpointed live National Collegiate Athletic Association (NCAA) basketball on CBS with its American viewers.

Canadian viewers showed no signs of overdosing on skating coverage, either. The CBC's most popular program proved to be the exhibition of world champions, which traditionally takes place on the final day of the world championship. The three-hour program attracted 2.473 million viewers in English-speaking Canada. A two-hour program in Quebec attracted 899,000 pairs of eyes. Altogether, skating coverage of the gala reached 10,174,000 Canadians – about one in three – who watched the telecast for up to fifteen minutes.

Most notably, the women's long program, without any of the Olympic medalists from Lillehammer performing, attracted 1,791,000 viewers over three hours, outdrawing the popular "Hockey Night in Canada" that followed on a Saturday evening.

Because of the influence of television, showbiz has become a much more important part of the figure-skating mix. A memorable image serves a skater well during exhibitions. Philippe Candeloro of France – the ultimate showman among the current group of world championship competitors – has left a lasting impression with his Rocky Balboa routine, in which he leaps onto the ice after a comic run through the aisles past spectators, while sporting a pair of boxing gloves, with the American flag draped across his shoulders.

At first, his exhibition number astonished officials from the French skating federation, who were less than pleased that their skater did not use a French flag. The routine also did not go over well with American audiences when he tossed the flag at spectators during performances at a world tour through the United States in the spring of 1993. Now he folds the flag carefully or drops it softly on the ice.

Philippe Candeloro,
the amiable Godfather

Still, he's one of the few skaters who sends his teenaged female fans into rapture when he rips the flag off and exposes his naked torso. The routine has become folklore. Candeloro's image has become unforgettable, if controversial, always certain to spark some kind of response.

"I'm sure they have applause meters along the side, because whoever gets the highest applause gets the best offer [from tour operators]," says Canadian coach Ellen Burka, disturbed by what she sees is a trend of skaters "milking the audience for encores," particularly in exhibitions. "Candeloro milked the audience with his body.

"Everybody's trying to get the audience as long as possible, as loud as possible, because it means money. That's what it's all about, money. Nothing to do with skating any more."

The hitch to all the fanfare, however, is that, in the end, the skaters have to skate. That's not as easy as it sounds. With each new generation comes a wave of skaters who try to push the boundaries of the sport, if not artistically, then technically. The men's event at the 1994 world championship in Japan was "a technical onslaught," according to four-time world champion Kurt Browning, who retired from the amateur (the International Skating Union calls it the eligible) ranks before the contest.

"It wasn't just one or two guys competing against each other," he says. "It was five or six guys doing six, seven, eight triples in their programs, with triple-triple combinations. And Elvis threw in a quad, almost landed in combination. "I'm blown away. I've never been able to watch a men's competition before. I've always been in it. Now I understand why people love figure skating so much. I'm speechless."

But the triples and the quads don't come overnight. They are done, after countless efforts, by those unafraid of falling and failing. Behind the blinding spectacle is the somber truth: it takes fifteen years to learn how to do a triple Axel, the most difficult of triple jumps, with its three and a half rotations, Stojko once said. It takes fifteen years to perfect all the building blocks of skills, to hone the edges – backward, forward, inside, outside – to feel instinctively the split-second timing, to harness the explosive burst of power that launches a skater airborne and ignites him or her to turn, turn, turn, and descend to unfold a tightly wrapped petal of a body into open-spread arms and a long, extended free leg. And it's done in the blink of an eye, with effortless dispatch – and all the while the skater is moving with breathless speed on razor-thin blades across an unforgiving medium, ice.

Only the best can do the triple Axel, the hallmark of virtuosity, linking together three major physical forces – movement across the ice, elevation off the ice, and rotation – from the fleeting moment of takeoff. It is as if skaters have wings on their feet. The higher they fly, the better. But skaters fall more often than they succeed.

For all its beauty, figure skating is the most brutal of sports. In a national or world championship, there are no second chances. Dan Jansen of the United States missed his Olympic moment in one speedskating event in 1994, but he had another chance to make up for it. Not so in figure skating, speedskating's ruthless, beautiful cousin. In this vein, the skater's experience goes beyond the pale, far from the simple fare of ordinary life. What average worker would have to face the pressure that Canada's Kurt Browning did at Lillehammer in 1994, when he mouthed the words "I'm sorry" to thousands of spectators and millions of television viewers after he suffered a bruising defeat, his second Olympic disappointment, the chance of a lifetime gone forever? Not only did Browning feel he bore the responsibility of having let down a nation, but it seemed that he had fought long and hard for naught. A two-year training commitment was washed away with his tears in the two minutes and forty seconds of his disastrous technical program, in which he finished twelfth, making it impossible for him to crawl out of the deepest competitive hole he had ever fallen into.

A moment's lapse of focus, a single moment of doubt, a sprig of hesitation can interrupt the chain of dynamics in a calamitous way, particularly in a short, technical program with its exacting mark deductions. A missed jump or a faulty edge becomes a lost opportunity, devastating when lucrative professional dollars are on the line, when TV viewing of skating is at its height worldwide, when media attention is intense, and when spectator interest, at least in some countries, has never been more fervent.

When a skater is surrounded by spectators, he or she is never more alone than when they lose control for a fraction of a second, and the moment is recorded forever by an intimidating row of gaping, 300-millimeter camera lenses.

"Every time you step on the ice, you take a chance," Browning said after he lost his focus while attempting a double Axel on home ice at the 1994 Canadian championship in Edmonton, Alberta. "That's what makes champions. When you take those chances, sometimes it pays off. I took a chance trying to do a really big double Axel. I was trying to go for that 6.0, and I got the 5.0 instead. Usually it pays off."

Pressure? It's no wonder 1987 world champion Brian Orser of Canada used to turn on the shower in the men's dressing room to drown out the reading of a competitor's marks before he skated. The 1982 world champion

*Elaine Zayak,
the 1982 world
champion, at
sixteen. She rose
to the top quickly
after doctors
suggested she
take up skating
as therapy.*

Elaine Zayak of the United States tried another tack; she used to flush the toilets.

Browning almost floundered under pressure in the last year of his career; he came close to quitting days after he won his fourth world title in 1993, unsure that he could face the music one more time in the wild year leading up to the Olympics. "You know what it's like when you come home from a trip and you relax and you get sick?" Browning said. "That's what it felt like. I finished. I won. And then I just went, 'I don't know if I can do this any more.'"

A serious muscle spasm just before the Prague championship brought back memories of the back problems that led to his downfall at the 1992

Olympics in Albertville, France, where he finished sixth. Those memories haunted Browning more than anyone knew. Early in the week in Prague, Browning was so frustrated that he was in tears a couple of times.

"It wasn't the pain, but being scared that I would get caught out there with your proverbial pants down. That I'd be caught out there in competitions not being able to do it.

"It's almost like you're stranded out on center ice, and you know you shouldn't be there . . . anywhere but in front of people and judges. It's such a naked feeling. That's what I felt at Albertville. You feel like you don't deserve to be there, and you're pretending that everything is okay."

And these words are from a finely tuned athlete who can do things most other skaters can't. Success breeds enormous pressure, enough to shake focus, since a champion constantly feels tugs and pulls from every direction. At home at Skate Canada, his only international competition leading up to the 1994 Olympics, the popular Browning couldn't find a moment to himself.

"Sometimes I feel a lot more pressure at the practices, almost like I'm being used," he said, speaking of the hundreds of people watching his every move and gasping at every slip. "Everywhere I turned, there was a Canadian or someone who was interested in getting an autograph.

"It's a catch-22 situation. You need them. You want them. You work all your life as an athlete to get them. And then you have to pretend that they're not there, to focus and do your job."

The 1992 Olympic champion Victor Petrenko of the Ukraine had another cross to bear at the 1994 Olympics. According to his agent, Rosenberg, he had forfeited $750,000 in revenues from his newly established professional career to take advantage of an ISU rule change that allowed him to return to amateur competition. It's just impossible to commit to exhausting tours or shows when one has to train for an amateur competition. But the gamble didn't pan out. Like Browning, Petrenko faltered under the bright lights and failed to relive his Olympic memory.

The sacrifices are high and long-lasting. Even one-time Canadian track star Dave Campbell quit figure skating as a youngster to take up 1,500-meter running because "figure skating is tough," he said. "It takes too long to get anywhere."

It means setting aside a normal life for a single goal. Browning didn't get to open his Christmas presents until after the Canadian championship in January. He had been busy training thousands of miles away and couldn't get home.

"I don't know if it's skating, but sometimes you feel like your emotional growth has been stunted," said David Liu, a university graduate who skates for Chinese Taipai, the name used by Taiwan in international sport competition. "We're in a field where we've always been young people, and also we don't really get to see outside of this bubble that we're in."

Skaters aren't the only ones who make sacrifices. Parents forfeit time, the luxury of sleeping in late, a new car, or a new outfit in order to shoulder the enormous cost and commitment their children face. Being a figure-skater's parent "comes on you gradual, like being choked with smoke," Browning's father, Dewey, said in *Forcing the Edge*, Browning's autobiography.

So why do it? In the modern age, perhaps it's the hope of a payday. Perhaps it's glory. In the days before television, it was all for the love of the sport. Sonja Henie explained why in her autobiography *Wings on My Feet*:

> A life on ice may not seem very special to other people. A little cold, perhaps. To me, however, it is new excitement over and over.
>
> If you are not a skater, you probably can't imagine what I mean. I could try to tell you by saying it's a feeling of ice miles running under your blades, the wind splitting open to let you through, the earth whirling around you at the touch of your toe, and speed lifting you off the ice far from all things that can hold you down. It's a sense of power, of command over distance and gravity, and an illusion of no longer having to move because movement is carrying you.

A History of
Competitive Skating

Jackson Haines, the father of modern freestyle skating, was an international celebrity, the equal of a Pavarotti in Europe. Although his skating was thought to be too slipshod and go-as-you-please, he made popular the basic skating principles of using the head, body, arms, shoulders, free leg, and hip, as laid down in ballet.

THE ESTABLISHMENT YEARS (PRE-1940)
. . . .

*S*ome people still talk about Jackson Haines as if they saw him on television last week, but the truth is that Haines died in 1876, at the age of thirty-six, after catching pneumonia riding in a sleigh across Russia during a blizzard. But his "international" style lives on in the Robin Cousinses and the Katarina Witts and the Sergei Grinkovs of the modern skating world. For the American-born Haines was the father of freestyle skating, with all of its rhythm, emotion, and life.

Haines was never really appreciated in Britain, where the world's first figure-skating club had been formed in Edinburgh, Scotland, in 1742. The sentiment was the same in Haines's home, in the United States, where, during the 1860s, skaters copied the style of the British, who skated stiffly and mechanically, arms pinned to their sides, top hats perched carefully on their heads, and all the while thinking scientific thoughts about their accurate tracings. Their style was difficult, complicated, and precise.

But Haines would have none of that. His arms were made for moving, and his pulse was made for racing. Trained as a ballet master, he wanted to dance on ice.

"He was very amazing," says Canadian coach Ellen Burka, who guided the careers of her world-champion daughter Petra Burka, 1976 Olympic bronze medalist Toller Cranston, Canadian champion Tracey Wainman, and, at least until he was fourteen, 1994 world champion Elvis Stojko. "[Haines] was the first interpretative skater. He skated to music and performed like a dancer because he was a ballet dancer. He took his ballet moves onto the ice. He must have had a very flexible body to do the things that he did."

The British and Americans thought Haines was quite out of control and completely without taste, but the Austrians, with their love of theater and music, took him to their hearts when he made up waltzes, marches, mazurkas, and quadrilles to music and played them all out on the ice. Haines was also a prime example of the sacrifices common in figure skating; he left behind a wife and three children in the United States to spend eleven years dashing about Europe, giving exhibitions and even teaching a few things about blades to Czar Alexander II.

When he became a star in Europe, skaters in the United States started to copy his style. There was much to copy. Haines invented the sit spin, and, from ballet's arabesque, came his spiral, a move that 1995 world bronze medalist, Nicole Bobek, does to perfection, with her free leg stretched out impossibly behind her as she glides on one foot across the ice.

Another ballet position prompted Haines to fashion the spread-eagle, a move done to the ultimate by 1988 Olympic champion Brian Boitano, who glides on two feet at an acute angle to the ice with his legs spread apart and toes pointing outwards. Haines also devised a rudimentary form of the camel spin, in which the free leg is extended parallel to the ice surface, founded the disciplines of pairs skating and ice dancing, and was the first skater of note to have worn a blade attached securely to the sole of his boot (rather than attaching the blade with straps or clamps).

Haines stirred up interest in figure skating in all the countries he visited: Austria, Germany, Russia, and Hungary. He is credited with single-handedly reviving and stimulating the passion for skating in Scandinavian countries, which would flourish during the late 1800s and up to the Second World War. Within fifteen years of his death, skating in Europe had become well organized on local, national, and international levels.

With the memory of his lyrical performances still dancing in their heads, the Viennese organized an international skating meet in 1882, in which contestants had to perform twenty-three compulsory figures (variations of figure eights), a special figure (a seemingly endless tracing done on one foot that produced a wondrous design, of the competitor's choosing), and a four-minute long program. The winner, fittingly enough, was Leopold Frey of Austria, a student of Haines. Finishing third was Axel Paulsen, the Norwegian who invented the one-and-a-half-rotation jump that bears his name and was first displayed at the Vienna meet.

But clearly, the advancements made by Paulsen showed that the test of a figure skater had already intensified. During early skating history, in the 1600s and 1700s, skaters gained membership to clubs by skating a circle on one foot, then on the other (the earliest notion of compulsory figures), and finally by demonstrating the ability to jump over three stacked hats (free-skating with a flair). Succeeding at those tasks brought skaters in line with some of the best. It wasn't until the mid-1800s that anyone even thought of skating backwards.

After the first skating club opened in Britain, other clubs popped up all over Europe – especially in the countries that Haines had passed through – and in Canada and the United States. The British also founded the world's first national skating association in 1879, but it was more to straighten out disputes in rules, times, and prizes awarded in speedskating, which enjoyed a far greater popularity at the end of the nineteenth century, than "fancy skating." Indeed, speedskating was so popular that it attracted heavy betting on races, which produced irregular results and the need for a governing body. Even though it was the sport of the masses, the upper class controlled its organization.

While speedskating was the major sport of the working class during the late 1800s, figure skating, only in its infancy, was the domain of the aristocracy and the privileged few throughout the world. When the International Eislauf Vereinigung (IEV), now the International Skating Union (ISU), was formed in 1892, its purpose was to make standard the distances for international speedskating competitions. But it also entertained proposals for rules from the little-known figure-skating enthusiasts, focused mainly on a list of school figures, versions of figure eights and loops that tested a skater's technical balance, and control of inside, outside, backward, and forward edges. While the British proposed a list of forty-one versions of figure eights and loops, the Germans and Austrians added variations that brought the list to more than eighty. (Compulsory figures were dropped from competitions after the 1990 season.)

One of the ISU's roles was to define the rules concerning amateurs, including limiting prizes awarded in competition. Its first act was to ban anyone who was not strictly an amateur skater from ISU events. For this reason, Axel Paulsen was never seen in a sanctioned world competition. The ISU excluded him because he had received money in speedskating races.

The International Skating Union was formed with six founding members: Austria, Germany, Britain, Hungary, the Netherlands, and Sweden, with the Dutch, lovers of speedskating, prompting its formation. Currently, the union has its headquarters in Davos, Switzerland, and still sets rules for both speedskating and figure skating. In figure skating, the union sanctions all non-professional competitions, including the world championships, and its rules are used for Olympic figure-skating events. Currently, there are fifty member countries affiliated with the international body, including new skating nations such as Greece, Israel, and Mexico that rarely, if ever, see snow. The breakup of the Soviet Union and other countries has also greatly expanded the number of members currently under the ISU banner.

The first world championship, for male singles skaters only, was held in St. Petersburg in 1896, but those early events were not given world-championship status until 1924, when the ISU gave them its blessings retroactively. Some of the earliest versions of the annual event had only a handful of competitors in them, all from countries that Haines had inspired.

Ulrich Salchow of Sweden finished second in the second world championship, but his influence on the sport was yet to come. He won ten world titles from 1901 to 1911, more than any other male in skating history, and invented the Salchow jump, a rather simple jump launched from a backward edge, which he unveiled in 1909.

"When as a young man I first saw Salchow, I was impressed by his lithe strength and control," wrote early-twentieth-century British skater, Captain T. D. "Tyke" Richardson in one of his many books, *Ice Skating*. "Later on he became mannered and pedantic, which one can well understand after such tremendous success. He was, moreover, a man of forceful personality and character, which was given full scope when, in the many years between the two wars, he continued to exert unchallenged influence on the sport as president of the International Skating Union, and whether one liked his rule or not, it must be admitted that he was the last of the great presidents."

In 1913, the world first saw a Lutz, a very difficult jump in which a skater takes off from a long-running backward edge, which was created by Austrian Alois Lutz, who never competed in a world championship.

In 1910, Werner Rittberger of Germany, who finished second three times at these new world championships – twice to Salchow in 1910 and 1911 – invented the loop jump, a demanding jump in which the skater takes off and lands on the same foot. Ironically, Rittberger, whose loop jump is considered more difficult than a Salchow, could never defeat the inventor of the easier maneuver.

One of Salchow's fiercest competitors was Nicholai Panin (also called Kolomenkin) of Russia, who finished second to the Swede in the 1903 world championship. Panin skated under a pseudonym because he was of Russian nobility and, in his culture, it was considered unsuitable for one of his class to partake in athletic competitions.

Salchow's greatest, but most controversial, triumph occurred in the 1908 Olympic Summer Games in London, England, the first time skating had been part of the Olympic movement. (The Winter Games were not held until 1924 in Chamonix, France. Figure skating was the first of any winter event to be included as an Olympic sport.)

Salchow won, but Panin had been primed for victory. Earlier that season, he had handed Salchow his first defeat in six years, and at the London Olympics, he had won the special figure, a separate event, which was discontinued after the 1908 Games. But when three judges ranked Salchow first after compulsory figures, and only two thought Panin best, the Russian withdrew in protest, saying the judges had conspired against him.

Panin made his mark in other ways. After the Communist revolution, he gathered together all of the best skaters in the country in one school. These skaters eventually passed on Panin's knowledge as coaches and laid the foundation for the development of Soviet skating. But figure skating was only a minor sport in Russia for decades – until the sleeping giant awakened during the 1950s.

Rinks with artificial ice were well established by the time of the 1908 Olympics. After the first opened in England in 1876, they popped up quickly in other countries around the world. The third world championship in 1898 in London was held on artificial ice.

Salchow tried to defend his Olympic title in 1920, the only other time figure skating was a part of the Summer Games, but he was forty-two years old and finished fourth to a younger man, Gillis Grafstrom of Sweden, winner of world titles in 1922, 1924, and 1929.

Grafstrom was made in Haines's image. The Swede was widely regarded as the finest interpretive skater of his era. To see him trace even a figure was poetry. In shirt and tie and jaunty white fedora, Grafstrom whipped all the opposing forces of his body into a curving equilibrium and turned and carved ice at will. He skated with a soft flexing of his knees, with a gentle, controlled blade. A Fred Astaire on skates, he also possessed a wonderful flexibility and inventiveness. The flying sit spin, the inside spiral, and the sit spin done with a change of foot were all his ideas. He was also the first to show a "modern authentic conception" of an Axel with more graceful execution, according to Richardson. These advantages helped him to win three Olympic gold medals, the last in 1928, at age thirty-four, when he ignored a badly swollen knee. Although his last appearance at a world championship was in 1929, Grafstrom was still skating in 1932, when he won a silver medal at the

Olympics in Lake Placid, New York, despite the fact that he completely lost his focus and began to trace the wrong figure. The reign was over, but the memories weren't.

He was a poet, painter, etcher, and by trade an architect. "Competition and honours to be given meant little to him," Richardson wrote. "He just loved skating. Entered for a championship, if he didn't feel like it, or if the weather was bad, he would shrug his shoulders and say 'No, I don't think I skate,' much to the joy of the others who didn't have a chance."

The first women's world championship was held in 1906, but only after Madge Syers of Britain had caused some consternation among the male ranks of the ISU when she applied to enter the men's event of 1902. Because there were no rules that could dismiss her application, she was allowed to enter, and subsequently finished second to the great Ulrich Salchow, striking a blow for women's liberation as she defeated two men, one from Germany, the other from Britain. Salchow was so impressed with Syers' effort that he reportedly gave her his gold medal. Many thought she should have won.

The following summer, the ISU immediately passed a rule that banned women from competing in the event against men. Its reason? A woman's long, bulky dress prevented the judges from seeing her feet. Syers had skated in the fashion of the day, a skirt that fell to her ankles. And she may have been lucky. As late as 1851, a woman was stoned to death in Germany for venturing out on the ice to skate.

The ISU didn't get around to staging a sanctioned women's competition until two years after Syers' venture, but Syers didn't sit still in the meantime. She won two British championships in 1903 and 1904, once defeating her husband, Edgar. She continued on to win two women's world titles in 1906 and 1907 and became the first female Olympic figure-skating gold medalist in London in 1908, the unanimous choice of five judges. With her husband, Syers also won an Olympic bronze medal in the 1908 pairs event, which had just been admitted as a discipline in both the world championships and the Olympics. In 1917, Madge Syers died of influenza. She was only thirty-five years old.

. . . .

"Rumour, nay more than rumour – a good deal of expert opinion – thought she should have won [the 1902 world championship against men]." – British skater and author Captain T. D. Richardson, of Madge Syers, who created a sensation when she entered the men's competition in 1902. She finished second, and immediately thereafter the ISU banned women from skating against men.

In 1920, another woman fell afoul of the ISU's unspoken policy. One judge warned American skater Theresa Weld that it was too "unsuitable" for a woman to be doing jumps because her skirt would fly up to her knees, and this was improper. If she persisted, she would lose points. Weld threw caution to the wind and landed a small Salchow jump to win the free-skating portion and the overall bronze medal.

Syers had started a revolution in skating: the female skater, wrapped in glory, took the sport to the masses in a way that Haines had never dreamed. First there was Charlotte – and she was known as only that. And then there was Sonja Henie, who changed everything about the sport forever.

Charlotte Oelschlagel made her name not in the world or Olympic arena but in ice shows that played from Berlin to New York. The daughter of a wealthy furniture manufacturer in Berlin, Charlotte was a child prodigy who, at the age of seven, played harp, lute, and mandolin in appearances with the Berlin Philharmonic Orchestra.

She took up skating to improve her health after a nervous breakdown, and, in spite of her family's objections, became a show skater at the age of ten in theatrical ice productions at the Berlin Eis Palast. One of them was a musical comedy called *Flirting at St. Moritz*, with more than a hundred performers in its cast. And she was its star. She was unforgettable, with her long tresses cascading down her back.

In 1915, American producer Charles Dillingham signed Charlotte to a $5,000-a-week contract to skate at the New York Hippodrome, the largest theater in the United States at the time. The contract was originally for six weeks, but Charlotte proved so popular that she stayed for three years, skating for audiences of six thousand twice daily.

Charlotte also starred in the first skating movie, *The Frozen Warning*, a silent thriller about First World War espionage. The plot hinged on the fact that the character played by Charlotte was able to trace the message SPIES into the ice with her blades to warn her unsuspecting countrymen of sinister intrigues.

Sonja Henie, Queen of Ice and Queen of Shadows

But Charlotte had more than star quality; she also had skating ability. Maribel Vinson Owen, an Olympic bronze medalist, skating coach, and the first female sportswriter for the *New York Times*, wrote in 1951 that Charlotte sparked such admiration that "there are many who swear that she was the greatest woman skater who has ever lived, years ahead of her time, limited not by ability but by invention, from doing all the double jumps of today." She was also a master of the camel spin and Axel jump, and she and her partner-husband Curt Newmann invented a version of the death spiral, a rivetting move used in pairs skating in which the man pivots on the ice while holding the woman's hand as she encircles him in a laid-back position.

Because of Charlotte's legendary quality, dozens of new rinks and hotel ice cabarets opened in the United States during the 1920s. Her most notable routine was that of "The Dying Swan," and she was coached by Russian prima ballerina Anna Pavlova, who simultaneously danced the number on a stage set up on the ice as Charlotte skated.

Charlotte died in 1984 after a life of intrigue and adventure. But her career had set the stage for the next skating hero, who just happened to worship Pavlova and wished, too, to bring dance to ice: Sonja Henie.

Before Henie was born (fittingly, in a freak spring blizzard in Norway in 1912), skating was a worldwide pleasure of the aristocracy, a marvelous toy of the privileged few, who celebrated its victories and delights largely among themselves. Over the years kings and queens, princes and princesses, and lords and ladies had taken to the ice, among them various Dutch monarchs, Charles II and James II of Britain, Russian Czar Peter the Great, Louis XVI, Marie Antoinette, and Britain's Prince Albert, husband of Queen Victoria, who were all fascinated by the "pretty art."

But Henie brought skating to the masses, attracting unprecedented media and spectator interest in Europe and North America. She changed the way women skaters dressed. She changed their boots. She changed their style. She changed their future. She changed everything.

She became the best-known (and richest) figure skater of all time. When she died in 1969 of leukemia at age fifty-seven, she is said to have been worth more than $47 million. She was also a Hollywood legend, with eleven movies to her credit, filmed between 1936 and 1948. She won ten consecutive world titles, equaling Salchow's record, and three Olympic gold medals.

Henie first made history with her youth and her garb during the first Winter Olympics in 1924, when she finished only eighth and last – although one judge gave her a first-place mark. In a competitive event that had always been undertaken only by adults, Henie was an anomaly at eleven years of age, and, until Cecilia Colledge of Britain came along at the 1932 Olympics, she was the youngest to compete at the Games. (Colledge, age eleven in 1932, was eight months younger than Henie had been when she launched her Olympic career. Colledge later became the first woman to do a double jump, a Salchow.)

Because Henie was so young, she could also get away with wearing knee-length skirts that would not have been thought proper for her competitors, who still trundled about in voluminous, ankle-length skirts. The shorter skirts, Henie found, enabled her to try moves previously attempted only by men.

Henie won her first world title in 1927 on home ice at Oslo, Norway, when she was only fourteen years old. Her mother planned her costume, a "revolution," she said, from the clumsy dresses in vogue. It was white and "tight fitting, with no folds or furbelows to confuse the picture of my movements," Henie wrote in her autobiography *Wings on My Feet*. "If I never remembered anything else I ever wore, I would remember that trim white velvet dress with its bell skirt."

Afterwards, Henie tended to wear circular skirts with beige bloomers and beige skating boots at a time when women were wearing black boots, like the men. When her competitors copied her, Henie switched to white boots. In the

"Sometimes I wake up in the morning feeling like a lottery winner. . . . Whenever I take a good look at the situation, it seems to me I'm so lucky it's almost indecent. Like having more money than you know what to do with. Except that I know what to do with my luck." – Sonja Henie in her autobiography Wings on My Feet

fifty-some years since Henie competed, women the world over have skated mainly in white boots.

Throughout her competitive years, Henie took ballet lessons and began to hatch the idea of combining her two passions on ice. She figured her dance patterns on ice contributed to her win at the 1928 Olympics in St. Moritz, Switzerland. "Until the Olympic Winter Games of 1928, figure skating had been rather stiff and pedantic in its competitive form," she wrote in her auto- biography. "The free-skating programs, the half of each contestant's perfor- mance that is left to his invention and taste, had been little more than a series of school figures and minor stunt figures strung together on an abtrusive thread of navigation from one spot on the ice to another." American coach Frank Carroll, who met Henie in the year before she died, agreed. "Skaters in that day were so klutzy," he said.

But in St. Moritz, Henie changed all that. Her choreography "gave form and flow to the sequence of orthodox spins and jumps," she wrote. "As a mat- ter of history, good skaters in all countries since then have come to build their free-skating programs to a large extent on dance choreography."

Henie, the daughter of a wealthy furrier from Oslo, was never a modest, shrinking violet. She was skating's first well-known character. Once, during an exhibition in Toronto, she received a bouquet of roses with her million- dollar smile, but offstage she angrily threw them to the floor and trampled them with her skates. "Orchids for Sonja!" she cried.

She also caused whispers when she arrived in the United States for a series of exhibitions in 1929 with ten pairs of skating boots and sixteen skat- ing dresses, all cut shorter than the North American style. She sometimes showed up at early-morning practices wearing jewels. Some objected to her display of opulence.

One of her pageants was a four-hour marathon with a hundred skaters in front of 17,000 spectators at Madison Square Garden in New York, one of the two largest indoor arenas in the world at the time. Everywhere she went, large crowds gathered. Even at home in Oslo, she could attract 10,000 to a nation- al championship, and in a couple of formal exhibitions held to give her expe- rience at Bergen before the 1928 world championships, a total of 35,000 people showed up. At the Olympics in 1932 in Lake Placid, scalpers sold standing-room tickets for her performances at $5 a piece, a steep price con- sidering the event took place during the Depression.

At fifteen, Henie got her first taste of mob behavior, when a crowd gath- ered around her as she arrived at the rink in Göteborg, Sweden, for an exhibi- tion. The crowd nearly squeezed her to death, she said. "On our way back to the hotel, the pressure of the crowd on our automobile windows shattered the glass, and later, smashed the plate-glass windows of our hotel," she wrote. "The militia brought order."

Her Hollywood career only served to enhance the interest in skating on the North American continent. Haywood Hal Broun wrote that Sonja Henie was the "greatest single box-office draw in America." Her "Hollywood Ice Revues" always played to packed houses. Organizers turned people away by the hundreds to shows sold out long in advance.

In the early days of the tour, the Sonja Henie Junior Olympic Club was formed, and within a few weeks, forty thousand members, all children, signed up for skating lessons, according to Henie's autobiography. Scores of young girls all wanted to be like Sonja Henie, and her post-amateur career in the United States spurred an interest in the sport in North America to unprecedented levels. To this day, the sport flourishes in the southwestern corner of the United States. Skaters such as Brian Boitano, Kristi Yamaguchi, Tai Babilonia, and Randy Gardner all came from California.

Although Henie spurred interest in figure skating among her adoring fans in North America, Norwegians were not always enamored of her activities, particularly when they involved Nazi leader Adolf Hitler. Henie made a lasting impression on the Führer at the 1936 Olympics in Germany when she gave Hitler the Nazi salute and in a loud voice shouted "Heil Hitler!" Hitler tossed her a kiss, but the next day Norwegian headlines screamed, "Is Sonja a Nazi?"

Although Henie's parents had no use for Hitler, they accompanied her on at least two occasions when she was invited for lunch at his mountain hideaway near Berchtesgaden. During one visit, he gave her a large photograph of himself in a silver frame and wrote "a lengthy inscription" underneath his picture, according to a less-than-complimentary biography written after her death, *Queen of Ice, Queen of Shadows*.

The book – written in conjunction with Henie's brother Leif, whom Henie had disinherited – told of the German occupation of Norway. Henie's friendship with the Nazi hierarchy became clear when German officers, intent on using the family's grand estate as a headquarters, turned on their heels and left immediately after they spotted the Führer's photograph in its silver frame in the parlor. Throughout the war, they never harmed the Henie properties, and Henie never spoke out against the Nazis during the war.

But for the rest of her life, Henie seemed to fear the Norwegian disapproval of her war activities – or lack of them. Perhaps feeling guilty that she had not responded to a request for $50,000 from the Norwegian war underground, she apparently engineered an announcement – in May 1945 – by a Norwegian journalist who said she had given him $45,000 to aid in the war efforts. However, according to the book, there are no records of the donation.

Toward the end of her touring career, which took her to Europe in 1953, Henie vigorously protested the idea of skating a homecoming show in Oslo because she worried that the Norwegians still disliked her for her lack of war aid. When she was finally persuaded to perform in Oslo, she was met with thunderous applause and welcomed "with wide open, loving arms." Tears ran down her cheeks.

From her first charge onto the ice to her last, Henie left a lasting impression on skating. When she left amateur skating, there were more female competitors at the world level, and they tended to be younger. While only five women competed at the world championships in 1925, thirteen took part in the 1932 event. During Henie's day, the women's event usually attracted more entries than any of the other disciplines. "She set the model for figure skating," American coach Frank Carroll says. For years after Henie's image swept the world, Carroll noticed dozens of "old women in public rinks all running on their toes, just like her."

Carroll's teacher was Mirabel Vinson Owen, who finished second to Henie in the 1928 world championship and third in 1930. She told him a great deal about Henie. "She said Sonja was an absolutely fabulous skater," Carroll recalled. "She skated much faster than other people skated. She was away ahead of her time. Even if she skated today, she would have been a champion easily, because of her ability and dance and personality."

For Henie was, Carroll said, a talented, all-around athlete. It is said she could have been an Olympic champion in any sport she chose. No one could surpass her in a foot race. No one could beat her in tennis. She had the perfect body, strong. During her movie career, directors grumbled about making her legs look less muscular. But Carroll's last memory of her is far different. She arrived at a club one day, he said, in a midnight blue Rolls Royce, with a pair of Norwegian elkhounds on a leash. She was dressed in a blaze of yellow chiffon, with a yellow scarf draped around her neck, and on her finger the biggest yellow diamond he had ever seen. "It was like a knob that covered two of her fingers," he said. Everything matched perfectly, all yellow, all exactly the same hue.

But he noticed that her legs were thin. She was ill and had been told that she was suffering only from anemia rather than leukemia. To the end, she spoke of doing a television special. She died in the arms of her third husband, Niels Onstad, on a plane flying from Paris to Oslo on April 12, 1969. But the legend lives on.

THE RISE OF THE NORTH AMERICAN SKATER AFTER THE SECOND WORLD WAR

• • • • • • • • • • • • • • • • • •

Before the war ravaged many corners of Europe, figure skating had been dominated by Europeans: Austria's Karl Schaefer (in 1925, the first skater to do a double-loop jump), French pairs Andrée Joly and Pierre Brunet; Hungarian pairs Emilie Rotter and Laszlo Szollas, German pairs Ernst Baier and Maxi Herber. Even a couple of popular Sonja Henie clones, Cecilia Colledge and fellow Briton Megan Taylor, won world titles just before the war. But when the fighter planes bombed the land and political strife took its toll over the six years from 1939 to 1945, the sport was devastated in continental Europe.

In many countries, some athletes faced starvation. Rinks disappeared, and so did the coaches. In more-peaceful prewar times, top American coach Harold Nicholson, who trained Sonja Henie, had moved to England to be close to the major teaching opportunities in Europe. But when the war ended, the coaches fled in the opposite direction – to Canada and the United States – just to make a living.

"Nobody skated, nobody," says Ellen Burka, who had been a Dutch national champion and emigrated to Canada in 1951. "Europe was dead for five years. There were no good coaches. England might have had some rinks, but they didn't really have any skaters until the 1950s.

"North Americans were very lucky. They could continue skating, and they had no competition from Europe."

Ice dancing, which finally joined the world championship roster in 1952 and the Olympic fold in 1976, was an exception to the trend of North American domination, particularly because it was a discipline that was adopted wholeheartedly by British skaters, whose rinks were not demolished, as in the rest of Europe. British skaters won thirteen of the first seventeen events, their string broken only by the Czechoslovakian brother-and-sister team of Eva Romanova and Pavel Roman, who reigned from 1962 to 1965. North Americans have never won a world gold medal in ice dancing, unless one counts

Isabelle and Paul Duchesnay, a Canadian brother-and-sister team who spent the most successful part of their career representing France.

Aside from ice dancing, however, North Americans rose to the top as soon as the war was over. Barbara Ann Scott of Canada, at eighteen, became the first North American to win a world title when she triumphed in Stockholm in 1947. Dick Button of the United States followed the next year with higher jumps and flashier technical tricks than the world had ever before seen. People marveled at his Axel jumps, which soared an unprecedented twenty feet (six meters) through the air. He could explode off the ice higher than the rink boards. Both Scott and Button were 1948 Olympic champions. "Button," said Toller Cranston "was imposing, unbeatable Americana, a personality. One couldn't imagine beating him."

In 1948, Scott won her second consecutive European championship in Prague, and the entire village of Davos turned out to chant "Barbarelli! Barbarelli!" when she skated. But not everyone was happy about her success. The North American domination was promising to be so profound that the event was limited to Europeans the next year.

North Americans brought youth and new, more-formidable techniques to the rink, while Europeans were forced to field older skaters. "The war knocked the development out," said Peter Dunfield, who represented Canada at the world championship after the war.

"They lost two generations where they didn't have the youth coming up. So for a while they had to use the people that they had had before the war, older people, and so until they got the youth going, there was a blip, and the Americans had a domination because of that. . . . The Europeans began coming back into the field in the early 1960s. It was almost ten years before they came back. It takes ten years to build a skater."

Not only did North America have the advantage of surviving the war with its rinks and skaters intact, it also had Gustave Lussi, a tall, imposing man with an erect bearing, and Sheldon Galbraith, who brought instruction methods from his days of naval flight training to skating. In a more behind-the-scenes way than a Henie or a Haines, Lussi and Galbraith changed the face of skating with scientific applications, attention to artistry and innovation, and choreography.

Lussi was a Swiss ski jumper who wisely sought other life pursuits after he fractured his skull in his chosen sport. During the 1920s, he moved to Lake Placid, because its mountains and terrain reminded him of his homeland, and began coaching skating. Even before the war, Lussi skaters were

Barbara Ann Scott, the first North American skating gold medalist

"There's no one that we've seen in recent times that spun as well as Barbara Ann Scott did. We even worked on, and she developed, a fast-slow-fast-slow-fast spin. I took a [movie] picture of her under a lightbulb at the Minto skating club [in Ottawa]. Barbara's head stayed under that lightbulb fast-slow-fast-slow-fast. Didn't move. Ever seen a spinner on a Spitfire? The prop turns, but the spinner doesn't move, it stays stable because it's so finely machined. They don't make the precision machinery they used to. And this gal was that kind. She'd spin right there." – Scott's coach Sheldon Galbraith

beginning to make their mark in world championships. One of his first notable pupils was Canadian Constance Wilson-Samuel, who finished third to Henie in the 1932 world championship in Montreal. But Lussi was only just beginning.

Among those who soared under Lussi's instruction – he still continued to give a few tips to young skaters into his nineties – were two-time Olympic champion Dick Button; the 1956 men's Olympic champion, Hayes Alan Jenkins; the 1956 Olympic women's champion, Tenley Albright; the 1956 men's Olympic silver medalist, Ronnie Robertson; and the 1976 Olympic champion, Dorothy Hamill, all from the United States. Lussi also worked with 1962 world pairs champions Maria and Otto Jelinek and 1976 Olympic bronze medalist Toller Cranston of Canada.

The 1976 Olympic champion, John Curry of Britain, also joined Lussi for a short time to solve a problem he was having in landing triple jumps. Although Curry spent three weeks feeling humiliated, falling constantly in front of much-less-experienced skaters at the rink, he made the right decision in consulting Lussi, who stripped Curry's technique down to the basics. The skating scientist discovered that Curry was spinning in the opposite direction to the rotation of his jumps. He advised Curry to do his spins in the other direction, so that both the jumps and the spins were rotating in the same direction. The lesson not only helped Curry rotate like a top when he jumped, but he was also able to incorporate two spins that rotated in opposite directions in his Olympic program.

During summer sessions, Maria and Otto Jelinek learned the fundamentals of jumping and spinning from Lussi. As a result, they were the only pair capable of doing double-Axel and double-flip jumps during their 1962 championship routine. They could do any double jump they chose. And their spins were better than those of their competitors. The Jelineks also set a trend by showing off very innovative pairs moves, such as overhead lifts in which the man turned several times while holding his partner in the air. Before the Jelineks' innovation, the male partner did not turn during lifts that were simply up and down movements. "Even now you can tell if somebody has taken from him or from his pupils, who are now teaching and using the same method," Maria Jelinek says. "He had his own little system . . . and even people who tried to imitate him couldn't really do it. To all his pupils, he was a bit like a god. They looked up to him."

Dick Button was one of those who did. As a young boy, he was told by a teacher to give up skating because his body type just wasn't designed for it.

Tenley Albright,
a high achiever

But Lussi unravelled the mysteries of physics to him, and Button became the first skater to do a flying camel spin, a double Lutz, a double-Axel jump, and the first triple jump ever seen in skating, a triple loop. He won both the 1948 and the 1952 Olympics, without question, without peer.

"[Button's] jumps were very athletic and strong," says Donald Jackson of Canada, who also took instruction from Lussi after winning the 1962

The charismatic Maria and Otto Jelinek finished second to world champions Barbara Wagner and Robert Paul at the 1960 Canadian championships in Regina. The crowd booed the world champions as they stepped onto the podium and lit matches as a measure of respect for the Jelineks' outstanding performance.

world-championship title. "He did them with sheer power and determination. He used his brute strength to get around the jumps. He was sophisticated. He had control. He just ripped it out."

What Lussi gave to his students was a "very solid, basic foundation," Button says, "so that still today, I remember exactly what I would have to think about in doing any of the moves that we did.

"[Lussi] gave us something to think about. Except for those times when emotion or excess of energy or competitive pressures got in the way, most of the time you had a solid technique and were consistent. All of these people today are not consistent, not because they haven't done it enough, but because their basic technique is not strong."

So absolutely did Button trust his mentor that he claimed that if Lussi had ordered him to jump from a window, he would have done so without a moment's hesitation, but he would have made sure his toe was pointed and his head was in the right position.

Swiss-born
Gustave Lussi
(center)
revolutionized
skating when
he moved to
North America
to coach. One
of his first
star pupils was
Dick Button
(right), the
unbeatable
two-time Olympic
champion from
the United States.

"A great trainer will instill absolute trust in his students – a kind of blind faith and an unquestioning obedience." Dorothy Hamill wrote in her autobiography *On and Off the Ice*. And so he did.

"He was crazy, intelligent," says Button, who used to live with the Lussis in Lake Placid. Once, while the high-flying Button was training, Lussi stopped him, rushed out onto the ice with a chair, and stood on it to measure the distance from the ice to the ceiling. He did it, he said with a twinkle, to prevent Button from hitting his head on the ceiling when he jumped.

"He had a way that you just did what he said," Maria Jelinek recalled. "You didn't question it, and it worked. He would say something, to do it some way, the arm or the leg, or don't look like this or think this way, and you did it, and it worked. And you were amazed. We had a lot of faith in him."

Lussi's forte was his questioning, analytical, lively mind. He transferred his knowledge of body movement from ski jumping to figure skating and adapted it to need. "It was very systematic the way he thought," Jelinek said. "He thought out all these things: Why does this work? Why do you go up or down? He figured out the best way and applied it to his kids . . . And he could adjust from one student to the other. He didn't use the same thing with everybody. It depended on how the other person reacted. He was a very special guy."

To this day Maria Jelinek remembers Lussi having an influence in every area of his pupils' lives. He always questioned everything and made it fun. Spins and jumps weren't the only things he taught his skating students. He shared his love for the outdoors – he was a very good fisherman and hunter – and his passion for making things. He built dams on a nearby creek. From his house in Lake Placid, he strung up a pulley that went clear across a lake to the other side. "You held onto it and went sliding across, holding on with your hands, to the other side."

When he took his skating students fly fishing at his creek, he would tell them, "'You watch, that hook is going to land right there.' And it would land right there," Jelinek says. "We were all pretty amazed and impressed."

Lussi realized he had a "jewel" on his hands, he said, when Ronnie Robertson, an American skater, walked into his school. He knew the young Robertson could take his theory of spinning to its height. And, according to Robertson, who trained with Lussi for the last three years of his amateur career, Lussi was unusual in that he was the only teacher who taught a theory about spinning.

Lussi revolutionized Robertson's career. Under his instruction, Robertson competed in two world championships and one Olympics, where he won silver medals in all three behind Hayes Jenkins.

Robertson became the king of the spin. He could revolve 240 times a minute, spinning so fast and with such centrifugal force that, if he held his arms out, traces of blood would ooze from the pores of his fingertips. Naturally, it was much more comfortable, effective, and intelligent to hold the arms in against the body during a Lussi spin.

A truly great spin is far more energy-draining than a quadruple jump, Button says. And a truly great spin lasts a lot longer than a triple jump. It takes great strength to hold all the forces together.

Science aided athletics when Lussi hatched an idea to reduce the friction on the blade so that a skater could spin longer. That meant grinding the toe

Ronnie Robertson, who won the Olympic silver medal in 1956, was said to be the fastest spinner in skating history, with his ability to rotate up to 240 times a minute. "When he spun, you'd see his face and the back of his head at the same time," said Canadian coach Louis Stong. Even tests in the NASA antigravity chamber failed to make him dizzy.

pick of the skate down to next to nothing, allowing the skater to glide more. Lussi had Robertson spin up on the front part of his skate, just behind the toe pick, on an area that was only a quarter to an eighth of an inch (0.6 to 0.3 centimeters) wide. Spinning on that area would cause him to travel the least amount of distance, enabling him to spin in the least amount of time.

Lussi always had his pupils practice spinning for half an hour to an hour every day. It was important not only for spinning but for jumping. "Lussi felt a triple jump was just a spin in the air," Jackson says. "You could see who were his skaters on the ice. They stood out. They did the best spins in the world."

Jenkins was a master of the flying sit spin. Button had his flying camel spin. And Hamill was famous for her own camel spin, called the Hamill Camel, a maneuver in which she dropped her body into a sit spin from a camel spin.

Nowadays, there are hardly any good spinners, according to Button. United States champion Scott Davis is one of the world's best, but "he doesn't know how to finish the spins," Button says. "He gets the speed started, but he doesn't know how to fulfill it and make it finish off as well. It's as if he stops it in the middle. Scott Hamilton does the same thing. He gets a wonderful center, good speed, and then doesn't follow through. One of the reasons is that it's very energy draining."

Because arms were very important to Lussi, the ISU had to keep rewriting its rulebook. In the years before the war, a skater was forbidden to raise the arms above the waistline. That prevented anyone from doing explosive jumps or ballet moves. Lussi didn't agree. And Lussi was surely a master of the artistic school, as well as the technical. He had a feeling for music and choreography and devised certain moves, like hops and little steps, that would mirror the music's mood. Every arm movement was significant. Long before a skater took the first bow, each movement would have been precisely set.

Canadian coach Sheldon Galbraith, the only coach to train world champions in three disciplines – including Barbara Ann Scott, Donald Jackson, and pairs skaters Frances Dafoe and Norris Bowden and Barbara Wagner and Robert Paul – was part of the same North American freestyle movement, in which careful attention was paid to technique, precise movements, and choreographed programs.

Scott was not a disciple of the big jump, but she was definitely part of the beginning of the scintillating freestyle moves. "She jumped smaller than anybody I ever saw," Canadian coach Peter Dunfield says. "She was barely two inches off the ice when she jumped. She was a very quick, tight jumper. But

Sheldon Galbraith, a ground-breaking coach

Wearing her famous hat, Barbara Ann Scott (right) made a triumphant return home to Canada with her coach Sheldon Galbraith (left) after she won the 1948 Olympic gold medal in St. Moritz, Switzerland.

Wearing her famous hat, Barbara Ann Scott (right) made a triumphant return home to Canada with her coach Sheldon Galbraith (left) after she won the 1948 Olympic gold medal in St. Moritz, Switzerland.

she was a very fast spinner. And besides, she was the first that really had programs that were choreographed and skated well with the music.

"She did things that other North Americans were doing, like choreographing their movements to the music more precisely. Sheldon Galbraith was probably at the forefront of that because he was really a disciplinarian on precise movement with the precise beat, and you do it that way every day, and you do it until it's perfect."

According to Frances Dafoe, Galbraith was the first skating coach that understood how to train an athlete as well as coach one. From his experience as a U.S. navy pilot, he understood the need for high-altitude training, particularly because Winter Olympic Games were often staged at high, mountain sites, but he had a very difficult time persuading the CFSA that his athletes must train at a high altitude three weeks before they competed. "They wouldn't believe there was a problem," Dafoe says. "They thought it was all in our heads."

Above all, Galbraith believed that skaters had to be fit and know their routines, without thinking, in every muscle. He understood that better than anyone. For three years, the Canadian-born coach had skated with his brother, Murray, in the "Ice Follies" as a shadow pair, in which two skaters skate the same solo routine without touching, in exact unison. Under the regimen of professional show business, Galbraith and his brother skated their routine thirteen times in one practice session. Each program was three minutes, forty seconds long.

"They hired a piano player to play our music, and we were to rehearse this while they had the choreographer there," Galbraith says. "They're paying the piano player, and they don't care about what your needs are, and what your cares are, and what your pains are. You're getting paid, and you do it. It's blood, sweat, and tears.

"That was my basis for how to train. You work it till you've got it, until it becomes second nature, not till you understand it, because it's not going to be a verbal discussion. It's going to be a performance. First come the bruises, then come the blisters, then come the calluses."

Galbraith, who also taught flying in the U.S. navy, became intrigued with the navy's techniques for training its men to recognize aircraft and battleships back in 1943. The trainees were given glimpses of a movie image of a ship for a fraction of second and were expected to retain it and recall it equally quickly in tense situations.

Because Galbraith figured time was of the essence in an athlete's life, too, he thought movies would be a valuable training tool for skaters. By 1946, when he began to train Scott, he started filming her programs with an eight-millimeter camera. When the film was developed, he showed it to his students to speed up their understanding of skills. The only trouble was that, in 1946, it took eleven days to process the film. Eventually, Galbraith was able to have it processed the same day.

"We only had black and white at that time, and rinks weren't properly lit to take pictures," Galbraith says. "These films brought about a much more rapid rate of learning. It solidified what the conception should be and what adjustments could be made."

He also showed his students films of other skaters, particularly professional skaters, to give them an inkling of what novel ideas could be developed in skating. "They'd make much more of an effort to broaden the scope of their skills," he says.

As a result, his first prize pupil, the petite Scott, could "outskate almost all of the boys," Galbraith says. "That didn't include Dick Button, unless they

With the U.S. flag stitched to his sleeve, Dick Button exhibited sheer power and strength in his jumps. In 1948, he became the first skater to land a double Axel and, in 1952, the first to land a triple jump – a loop.

got into school figures. With figures, Button had no chance with her. She was fabulous."

Even though Button is credited with being the first to land a double Axel in 1948, Scott could also do them at the time. However, because she slightly "cheated" her landings, Galbraith did not allow her to include one in a program. "The quality of her performance had to be perfect, in that she wasn't a high jumper, although certainly an adequate one."

Galbraith was as versatile as Lussi, searching for new ideas for any aspect of skating. The Canadian coach revolutionized skating, says Frances Dafoe, who recalled Europeans commenting on a "musicality" they had never previously seen when they watched her performances with partner Norris

Bowden. Dafoe and Bowden won two world titles and a Olympic silver medal in pairs skating in 1956.

"We used music a great deal," she says. "Normally the music was played, and everybody sort of skated straight ahead, and the music was background, and then you hit the highlights."

They had Galbraith to thank for these changes. He invited an orchestra leader to the Toronto Skating Club to explain the phrasing of the music and how skaters could interpret it. Indeed, the industrious Galbraith broke paths for others to follow, technically, artistically, and methodically. It was no surprise that, shortly after Dafoe and Bowden dazzled the world with their novel pair moves, the Soviets arrived with their own eight-millimeter cameras. And then along came a musical, lyrical Soviet pair that changed the direction of figure skating for the next three decades.

THE SOVIET INVASION

. . . .

During the 1950s, they were already there, movie cameras pressed against their cheeks, one eye a-squint, and they were filming everything in sight at international skating competitions. They were the Soviets, and they saw a beautiful sport that they wanted to know everything about. They left no stone unturned.

The Soviets entered the international sports arena in 1956, but postponed their Olympic figure-skating performances for another four years while the sport developed in their country. It grew quickly because scores of indoor rinks popped up in large and small towns across the country as part of a reconstruction plan after the Second World War.

The Russian presence on the world and Olympic scene had been missing since 1914, when the best finish of a team of one woman and two men was a modest sixth. In those early years, there had been only one Russian pair who had competed at the world championships – at the first one in 1908 (A. L. Fischer and L. P. Popowa won a bronze medal) – then none were seen again until the husband-and-wife team of Nina and Stanislav Zhuk arrived in 1958. By this time, they were all called Soviets. And they were good.

The Zhuks won silver medals in the 1958, 1959, and 1960 European championships in their first foray into the big leagues. And as the first Russian/Soviet entry into a world championship in forty-four years, they finished eighth of fifteen couples in 1958, while another Soviet pair, Ludmila

Belousova and Oleg Protopopov, finished thirteenth. Both Belousova and Protopopov, who eventually married, were descendents of the St. Petersburg school started by Panin, whose dream was the creation of artistic images.

With these tools in hand, the Protopopovs were to become giants of the sport, as they introduced an artistic style of pairs skating never before seen. They led an almost complete and utter domination of pairs skating by Soviet skaters in the years that followed. In the thirty years since 1965, when the Protopopovs won their first gold world medal, Soviet pairs have won the event twenty-six times. The Protopopovs won their first of two Olympic gold medals in 1964 – before they won a world title. Soviets (or Russians) have won every Olympic pairs gold medal since.

The reign of Soviet pairs in world championships has been interrupted only five times, twice by Canadian skaters (Barbara Underhill and Paul Martini in 1984; Isabelle Brasseur and Lloyd Eisler in 1993), once by an American pair (Tai Babilonia and Randy Gardner in 1979), once by a couple from the German Democratic Republic (Sabine Baess and Tassilo Thierbach in 1982), and once by Radka Kovarikova and Rene Novotny of the Czech Republic in 1995.

The Soviets brought passion to ice dancing and dominated it, too, from the beginning. Although the German Democratic Republic completely dismissed ice dancing from its extensive sport program in its early days because the discipline was not an Olympic sport until 1976, the Soviets, with their love of ballet, music, and dance, embraced it wholeheartedly. In 1970, although the Soviet ice-dancing school had been backed by only five years of international competition, it created two blazing skating stars in Ludmila

Ludmila Pakhomova and Alexander Gorshkov created an entire gallery of unforgettable images in their ice dances, which took skating in a new direction. In 1974, they invented the tango romantica (shown here), now one of the compulsory dances. Pakhomova, who had been married to Gorshkov, died of leukemia in 1986.

Pakhomova and Alexander Gorshkov, winners of the Soviets' first ice-dancing world medal. In the same way that the Protopopovs had an undeniable impact on pairs skating, Pakhomova and Gorshkov brought something new to ice dancing and redirected its development. Four-time world ice-dancing champion Courtney Jones of Britain calls the Soviet contribution to ice dance "sex on ice." "The English couples skated as if to say, 'Keep me at arm's length.'

But the Russians brought drama," says Jones. "They wanted you to get as close as you can. They want you to say 'I want to eat you for breakfast.' I'm all in favour of sex on ice."

Pakhomova and Gorshkov so dominated ice dancing in their time that they won the world title six times in seven years, losing it only once in 1975 – when Gorshkov was ill and could not compete. In the twenty-six years since 1970, Soviet or Russian ice dancers have won twenty times. In almost every year since 1974, two Soviet ice dancers, if not three, have stood on the top of a medal podium at one time. Soviets have dominated pairs skating in a similar way, with more than one team on the podium in most years since 1965.

The only year that Soviets or Russians did not win the Olympic ice-dancing gold medal was in 1984, when a British couple made the world sit up and take notice of their glorious edges and engaging style of artistry. Their names were Jayne Torvill and Christopher Dean. They also won four consecutive world titles.

Eventually, the Soviets also made inroads on the men's event, but without ever dominating it. The first Soviet male singles skater to make it to the world podium was Sergei Tchetveroukhin, who won two silver medals (1972 and 1973) and one bronze (1971), but who was always unable to defeat Czecho-slovakian Ondrej Nepela. Since then, five gold medals have been won by Soviet males, including Sergei Volkov in 1975, Vladimir Kovalev in 1977 and 1979, Alexander Fadeev in 1985, and Victor Petrenko, a Ukrainian who skated for the Commonwealth of Independent States when he won in 1992.

In all the years since the Soviet Union reared its head in international skating, none of its women had ever won world or Olympic gold medals. Suddenly, in 1993, a few short years after the Soviet Union fell into pieces, Oksana Baiul won, but for Ukraine. Her Olympic crown followed in 1994. When asked why the skating power had never produced outstanding female singles skaters, pairs champion Stanislav Zhuk, who became one of the country's best-known coaches, jokingly said, "Because I don't coach them."

Eventually, he did coach Elena Vodorezova, who won the first world medal of any kind for a Soviet woman, a bronze, in 1983. She was unable to fulfill her potential, however, because she developed arthritis. Later Anna Kondrashova (1984) and Kira Ivanova (1985) won world silver medals. Both were outskated by Katarina Witt of the German Democratic Republic, which had produced a flurry of top female skaters in the 1970s.

Zhuk became a well-known coach of skaters from every discipline but dance, and he taught explosive, technical exploits. The antithesis of his style was centered around the pairs school from St. Petersburg, or Leningrad as it was known during the 1960s. And the Protopopovs flew as the school's first ensign. The world had never seen anything like them.

When they won their second Olympic gold medal in 1968, Ludmila was thirty-two years old and Oleg was thirty-five. Wherever they went, they received standing ovations, as the pair brought ballet to ice with beautiful lines in a disciplined style, often evoking the love between a man and woman. They performed Liszt's "Liebestraum," or "dream of love," with such magic that the music became their music.

When countrymen Natalia Mishkuteniok and Artur Dmitriev used the same music to win the 1991 world title in Munich – and the Olympic gold medal in 1992 – Oleg Protopopov objected to their interpretation. "They have good technique, but I didn't understand what they wanted to express. Because I didn't feel the dream of love. Because Liebestraum is a very deep philosophical thing. And this is a shadow . . . [Dmitriev] didn't show that it was his dream, because I didn't see a woman. I saw a very strong girl who do the same as the man. But pair is a contradiction between a man and a woman. She should be graceful, he strong. And together, this is one piece of the love. If she will be stronger than me, I do not know who I am, sorry."

The Protopopovs' contribution to skating was "emotion and beauty," according to Canadian skater Toller Cranston. "It was quality of emotion, not just emotion. . . . They were brilliant, so incredibly phenomenal, and also mad fanatics about their skating."

"They stamped their personalities on competitive pairs skating, and their musical interpretation was by far the best up to that time," says John Nicks, who won a world pairs title for Britain in 1953 with his sister, Jennifer, before he eventually became the coach of 1979 world pairs champions Tai Babilonia and Randy Gardner and 1995 world bronze medalists Jenni Meno and Todd Sand of the United States.

The Protopopovs also exploded the myth that skaters were past their peak at nineteen or twenty. Oleg didn't start pairs skating until he was about that age. "He was a prime example that, if you keep yourself in shape, you can go on into your twenties and thirties," Nicks says.

There was one strange irony about the Protopopovs; they were so outstanding that no one dared to copy them at the time. It was almost as if the pairs to follow conceded that the Protopopovs were one of a kind, and they could never be their equal. Instead, the new generation tended to lean in the direction of the new stars of the 1970s, Soviet pairs skater Irina Rodnina, who

When Alexander
Zaitsev was
first paired
with Irina
Rodnina, he was
so in awe of her
that he would
stutter when
he spoke to her.
Eventually they
won six world
titles and two
Olympic gold
medals. They
married and
had a son,
but later
divorced.

won ten consecutive world titles and three Olympic gold medals with two different partners, Alexei Ulanov and Alexander Zaitsev.

"It was all about virtuosity and strength," Cranston said. "It was overpoweringly virtuoso. But you could not beat them at their own game. You could only offer an alternative. But everyone was trying to be like them. They were super-duper power machines that were unbeatable. Only someone like the Protopopovs could have toppled Rodnina and Zaitsev, because they offered something different."

Rodnina and partners were coached, at first, by Zhuk, who had been the polar opposite of the Protopopovs when he and his wife skated: all risk, wild speed, and cascades of difficult tricks. There were no halftones and fine shades in Zhuk's school.

The only skaters who gained a brief moment in the sun in the reign of Rodnina were Babilonia and Gardner, who won a world title when the tiny Soviet wonderwoman took a year off to have a baby. "All of a sudden you saw this beautiful skating again," Cranston said. "They were lovely and gorgeous, but that flame flickered for a moment and went out."

But an offshoot of the drive to technical prowess in pairs skating was already established by Zhuk, their first coach, before the retirement of Rodnina and Zaitsev. While the skaters' careers were winding down, Zhuk was already putting together "flea-and-gorilla pairs": the tall, muscular man and the tiny, childlike female. There was a distinct advantage to this strategic pairing. A tall, muscular partner could much more easily hurl and lift a tiny partner during athletic pairs moves than could a male whose partner was the same size.

The first well-known couple of this ilk was Marina Cherkasova and Sergei Shakhrai, who won the 1980 world championship after both Rodnina and Zaitsev and Babilonia and Gardner had retired. When Cherkasova first appeared on the scene, she looked like a preschooler. The trend was criticized at the time, Nicks said, because the Soviets were bringing girls that were so immature in appearance and feeling to high-level international events. But the trend took hold.

"When the Russians set the mode, most of the other countries realized they had to follow suit," Nicks says. "That's the reality of pairs skating today."

The trend reached its zenith with Ekaterina Gordeeva and Sergei Grinkov, who won an Olympic gold medal in Calgary in 1988, when she was only sixteen and he was twenty. Two or three times, early in their career, they did quadruple twists; Gordeeva, at 4 feet, 9 inches (148 centimeters), was more than a foot shorter than her powerful partner, Grinkov, at 5 feet, 10 inches (180 centimeters). And at the time, she weighed only about 79 pounds (36 kilograms), a little more than half of what her partner

Marina Cherkasova and Sergei Shakhrai were the first pairs skaters to use an extreme height and weight differential to their advantage; they were the first to land a quadruple twist in 1977, but the partnership dissolved after Cherkasova began to grow.

weighed, at about 150 pounds (68 kilograms). At eleven, when Gordeeva was first matched with Grinkov, she weighed only between 48 to 53 pounds (22 to 24 kilograms).

As the technical tricks became more demanding, and the danger and the difficulty of finding appropriate partners increased, fewer pairs skaters entered world championships. During the early to mid-1980s, it was common to see only about thirteen pairs competing. In 1981 and 1989, post-Olympic dropout years, the numbers tailed off even further to eleven.

At the same time, the other disciplines were growing; entries were increasing to an almost unmanageable level. To cut down on the numbers, the ISU instituted a rule that said a country could send as many as three skaters per discipline in dance, men, and women to a world championship only if one of its skaters had earned a medal in that discipline at the previous world championship.

But because the number of pairs skaters was dwindling, the ISU retained its rule to allow a country to send three pairs if one of its pairs in the previous world championship had finished within the top-five placings. Keeping the rule allowed the few countries that did have pairs skaters to send as many of them as possible to world championships. (In 1981, only seven countries sent pairs to the world championship. In 1989, only six fielded pairs.) At the 1994 world championship, a record twenty-eight pairs entered the competition, nine of them from former Soviet countries. Aside from former Soviet countries, as many as thirteen countries sent at least one pairs entry to Japan.

The Soviet domination of pairs skating found an echo in ice dancing; as seen earlier, the entire discipline was transformed by Pakhomova and Gorshkov, who were an exciting turning point in the smooth, "dancey" school of thought that had concentrated on technique and timing in a precise, British way. Pakhomova, the daughter of a Soviet pilot who shot down twenty German planes in the Second World War, was the key to the couple's success.

"She was a great artist, and the first of the greats because she influenced the greats that came after her," Toller Cranston says. "She was number one. There was nothing like her. Her husband [Gorskhov] was like a maître d'. All he did was present her. He didn't skate well. But she was so dazzling, it was like this huge firecracker that kept spewing fairy dust that hypnotized the crowd, and he was all but invisible."

Her artistry was original, deeply felt. And every Soviet or Russian dance couple since has skated with the same flavor: drama on ice, all choreographed professionally. Their coach, Elena Chaikovskaya, was trained as a dance

·················

Ekaterina Gordeeva and Sergei Grinkov, as close to perfection as skaters get

choreographer. So was Pakhomova. Like Pakhomova and Gorshkov, the best of the dancers that followed came from the Moscow school.

Soviets Irina Moiseeva and Andrei Minenkov took up the torch with equal style, and probably better technique. The year that Gorshkov missed the world championship in 1975, the couple that came to be known in the western world as Min and Moe won their first world title. When Pakhomova and Gorshkov retired, Moiseeva and Minenkov again won gold.

In this pairing, Minenkov, the diligent technician, was overshadowed by his beautiful and creative wife, Moiseeva, but both showed the influence of the Bolshoi ballet in their skating. Both of them impressed a young Torvill and Dean when they first encountered the Soviets in a competition.

"We felt so small in the dazzling company," Jayne Torvill said in the biography *Torvill and Dean*. "When we got to see Moiseeva and Minenkov on ice for real, they were not only better than we had imagined, but they seemed so strong and powerful and so big. . . . As it was, they looked fabulous, particularly Irina, beautiful and balletic, and I couldn't have conceived that anybody in the world, let alone us, would ever beat them. We were quite bowled over by them."

TELEVISION AND THE SHORT PROGRAM

Figure skating had been popular in various pockets around the world, particularly with Sonja Henie before the Second World War and Barbara Ann Scott after the war. Just as Henie's career began to wind down, Scott arrived to fan the flames further and make skating a topic of household conversation. Everywhere, skaters pressed to get a chance to see Dick Button tour in the United States. "But in my time, figure skating was still a minor sport," Button says. "I remember the neighbors saying 'You do what?' Now people are apt to say 'Wasn't [Brian] Orser's jump interesting the way he landed it?'"

The difference between Button's day and Orser's day was television, which first made a tremendous impact at the 1960 Olympic Winter Games in Squaw Valley.

"Television changed everything," Ellen Burka says. "That was the number-one thing that changed the world. Television made a star out of skaters. And now it's so exaggerated, it's all televised and everybody knows who the skaters are."

*Petra Burka,
the first woman
to land a triple
jump (a Salchow)
in competition,
distinguished
herself with her
athletic prowess
and consistent
performances.
"She was a dynamo,"
Canadian coach
Louis Stong said
of the 1965
world champion.
"She had lots of
energy. She started
all the triple
jumping among
the women."*

Still, at the time that Canada's Petra Burka became the first woman to land a triple Salchow jump and win the 1965 world championship, figure-skating events weren't widely televised throughout the world. "You read it in the papers and people happened to be at the competition, but you didn't know what went on," Burka says. "A person could win a gold medal and nobody would be at the station to say hello when they came home.

"The crowds in Europe were fantastic, enthusiastic. At my first worlds in Prague, people were just longing to see people from the west. They were standing outside, nearly pushing the doors in just to get in to watch a practice. But nobody was a star. Nobody made money."

Gradually, televisions permeated the market, just in time for the Peggy Flemings of the skating world, who were eventually able to command sizable professional fees when they retired from amateur competition. Fleming earned an estimated $500,000 in the first year of her professional career and created the first television skating special.

Janet Lynn, who won no gold medal at the Olympics or the world championships, won the heart of the world while smiling through her tears in defeat. Everyone forgave her for her miscues. Although *Sports Illustrated* had predicted Lynn would make $100,000 a year when she left the amateur ranks, the young skater signed a three-year contract with the "Ice Follies" for $1,455,000. She signed it with a nineteen-cent ballpoint pen.

Skating was also a minor sport in Japan – until its TV networks became involved and the country developed a few stars, such as 1989 world champion Midori Ito. When the Japanese public network, NHK, discovered that the Tokyo Broadcasting System (TBS) held the rights to all of the competitions seen in the country, it jumped into the fray by staging its own event, the NHK Trophy, now one of the most popular international competitions for skaters. Within the past five years, Japanese organizers have been able to sell tickets to people other than the mothers and fathers and a few interested friends of skaters.

Television also helped to clean up the sport. Up to the 1950s, political gamesmanship among judges had been rampant in figure skating, even at the world-championship level. The political intrigue intensified during the 1960s, when the Soviets became firmly entrenched in the sport and Soviet satellite countries jostled and traded and bartered marks with them. Through television, however, spectators could see whether a skater actually performed badly or well, and the marks became public in a more immediate way.

With the help of television, the introduction of the short program for singles skaters in 1973, and the subsequent lessening of the value of figures, the 1970s became a free-skating bonanza for skaters. The swing away from compulsory figures also had a dramatic effect on the development of artistic programs, particularly those of Toller Cranston of Canada, John Curry of Britain, and Janet Lynn of the United States, which were more pleasing to television viewers and network executives, who feared that uninspiring, machine-like programs would be difficult to sell to audiences and advertisers. (The short program, in which a singles or pairs skater must perform a fixed number of required elements, has undergone several name and format changes over the years. For a brief time, it was called the original program, then the technical program. As of July 1, 1994, it will again be called the short program.)

At a time when his competitors wore the "monkey suit," John Curry began to experiment with men's costumes and adopted plain garb. In 1975, ISU officials warned him against wearing a simple blue costume with a spiral, a white vapor trail running across his upper body, because it had influenced the judges against him, even though other skaters were wearing spangles and beads.

Cranston and Curry burst onto the scene at about the same time in the 1970s. They were the same age, and both broke ground for other male skaters, allowing them to show more artistry in their skating. But they accomplished this in very different ways.

Curry's style was fashioned by his lifelong worship of the Royal Ballet in England. When he asked to take dancing lessons as a boy, he was met with a resounding no. But when he saw an ice show on television and asked to take skating lessons instead, his parents agreed. "Skating, being a sport, was approved of, whereas the dancing idea had been treated with grave mistrust," he said in his autobiography, *John Curry*.

"If we didn't have Toller Cranston, what would we have to talk about?" Kurt Browning once said of the larger-than-life Canadian personality and artistic trailblazer, whose unusual body positions and skating flair changed the sport forever.

Curry eventually got his ballet lessons, and they showed in his graceful arm movements, leg extensions, and body posture, his soft touch on the ice. And he was expressive. His winning routine to Minkus's "Don Quixote" at the 1976 Olympics was so exquisite that it daunted others who thought of using the music for years to come. "I have always tried not to put ballet steps onto the ice, but sometimes I do things in a balletic way – if I am lucky," he wrote. "I always knew that if I had one thing to say in life, and one thing only: I believe that skating can be expressive."

Before Curry died of AIDS in April 1994, he saw the evolution of his artistic aims. Although hordes of male skaters didn't run out immediately to take ballet lessons to follow Curry's example, expression and artistry became an important part of the skating package. Fine examples of Curry's delicate touch on ice are shown by Paul Wylie, the 1992 Olympic silver medalist from the United States, and David Liu, the artistically pleasing U.S.-based skater who represents Chinese Taipei. Both were Curry students.

Cranston, on the other hand, took only one dance lesson as a five-year-old tagalong behind his sister. Although he was obsessed by the idea of dancing as a child, the dream lasted only thirty minutes. "I was an immediate failure, unable to keep time with the other children, mixing left foot with right, bored to distraction with the exercises at the barre," he wrote in his autobiography, *Toller Cranston*. "I was devastated and never went back."

But Cranston had other tools to work with: a body that could be stretched and molded into seemingly impossible positions and an artist's soul that understood movement, color, and music.

"John Curry was truly a great skater," Cranston says of his archrival. "It wasn't that he was creative, but he was a real artist and interpreted skating on a level of refinement and sophistication that was uncontested. Still, today, his Olympic performance would have an effect."

Cranston took Curry's direction a step further. Cranston's skating made an emphatic, glorious statement; Curry, beautiful in a pale, delicate way, was restrained and polite by comparison. While Curry interpreted the prim Royal Ballet, Cranston was more like the Bolshoi, skating in a passionate, furious minor key.

"Toller had a body that was so stretchable," his coach, Ellen Burka, says. "Some people are born like this. He was the weirdest skater, but I developed the weirdness in him. He had incredible body movement."

Even at forty-five, Cranston could stretch a free leg to impossible heights, his vertebra sliding perfectly and nimbly into unusual curves. He could still do the highest Russian splits ever seen, heels soaring above his head. His flexibility is envied by younger skaters.

"His style was his own," Burka says. "It's a different style altogether. His own invention. And what incredible spins he had."

Cranston had such an unusually long stretch that Burka urged him into contrasting the move with a bent knee, a position frowned upon at the time in Canada. "He had problems being accepted in Canada," she says. "It was only after he went to Europe, and they went overboard about him, they raved about him, that it was okay at home."

European audiences and skaters took Cranston to their hearts. During his last amateur performance, an exhibition after the 1976 world championship in Göteborg, Pakhomova rushed out onto the ice, half-dressed, to watch. "The highest compliment one skater can pay another is to watch. It's the acid test," Cranston says. "It was very touching for me when I heard about it."

They all ran out to watch Janet Lynn, too, the best skater never to win a world championship. She won bronze medals at the 1972 world championship in Calgary, Alberta, and at the Olympic Games, beaten in both by Beatrix Schuba of Austria. Schuba, a much-less-compelling free-skater,

"I started really loving the freedom of being on the ice. I'd be practicing and some music would be playing and I would just start skating to music. And soon I'd be lost in myself, moving along, not caring what I looked like or anything, just doing what I felt on the inside, and being creative." – Janet Lynn in her autobiography Peace and Love

placed only ninth in the Calgary free-skate, but won gold on the basis of her utter dominance in compulsory figures. (Schuba's triumphs actually sparked a move to introduce the short program and lessen the emphasis on compulsory figures.)

However, even with the help of the short program, which should have enhanced her chances, Lynn won only a silver medal at the 1973 world championship, behind Karen Magnussen of Canada. The American skater fell a couple of times in the short program.

"The best woman I ever did see was Janet Lynn," Cranston says. "I never saw anything like that. She mystified all the skaters of her age, and yet she was a person who had no mystique off the ice. . . . But on the ice, she became ethereal, magical. She wove a spell.

"Ellen Burka used to say – and it's true – she had million-dollar teeth. It wasn't that they were perfect teeth, but she had a smile that was worth a million. It electrified you. It was a scandalous smile. People ran to see her, all the competitors on the world tours."

Curry choreographed a number for Lynn at an exhibition at Madison Square Garden to the music "The Blue Danube." "To this day, I have never seen anything like it," Cranston says. "It was achieving a sort of perfection, like intercourse between skater and music. They became one. It was the definitive performance of females that I've ever seen. It was kind of spiritual. It is what you are supposed to be and what you're supposed to do."

Lynn, a pixie-like gamine with short, blonde hair, completely conquered the silent Japanese crowd at the 1972 Olympics in Sapporo. In their culture, their silence is their greatest expression of honor. The film log of Winter Games events that the organizing committee toiled over showed only one figure skater. It was Lynn, even though she did not win, and the film log showed her entire long program.

"Janet Lynn captured the heart of the Japanese people with her movement," Canadian coach Peter Dunfield says. "This was the epitome of skating in the minds of the Japanese. I was with Janet Lynn when she went back to Japan the year after, because she did a pro tour. I have never seen such mass press hysteria as she created. She was the one person that really got people emotionally involved with figure skating in Japan."

And just about everywhere else, too, particularly with the helping hand of television.

From Backyard Rink to Olympic Podium and Beyond

Today's rising skaters enjoy a star turn at center ice as champions from earlier eras look on. Front row, left to right: Lloyd Eisler and Isabelle Brasseur, Natalia Mishkuteniok and Artur Dmitriev, Oksana Gritschuk and Evgeny Platov, Maia Usova and Alexander Zhulin, Lu Chen, Victor Petrenko, Oskana Baiul, Kurt Browning, Nancy Kerrigan, Philippe Candeloro, Surya Bonaly, Scott Davis, Elvis Stojko, Alexei Urmanov.

Top row, left to right: Sergei Grinkov and Ekaterina Gordeeva, Elizabeth Manley, Isabelle and Paul Duchesnay, Dorothy Hamill, Brian Boitano, Katarina Witt, John Curry, Toller Cranston, Scott Hamilton, Robin Cousins, Marina Klimova and Sergei Ponomarenko, Denise Biellmann, Gary Beacom, Dick Button, Jayne Torvill and Christopher Dean, Brian Orser, Elena Valova and Oleg Vasiliev, Ludmila and Oleg Protopopov.

Painting by Toller Cranston.

omewhere, in the thousands of rinks around the world, toddlers and younglings are taking their first steps on ice, falling, skidding, smiling, crying. Only a very few of them will one day stand on an Olympic or world-championship podium. It is a long and winding – and expensive – path to take.

For the few who do succeed, a lucrative professional career beckons. With the growing popularity of skating, there are more opportunities than ever for money to be made. While there were only a handful of professional competitions in the early 1990s, there may be as many as fourteen in the seasons following the 1994 Olympics. And new skating tours are popping up everywhere.

It all starts innocently enough, with recreational sessions. That's how Sergei Tchetveroukhin began his career in the Soviet Union. His family had watched the black-and-white flickerings of figure skating on television in that winter of 1956, when skating was, in his country, a novelty. Already, troops of little girls had been flocking to the ice, but there was only one boy in the Moscow club. Tchetveroukhin's mother told him, "Let's go. You'll be the second one."

Tchetveroukhin was ten years old when he first tugged on a pair of skates, already two years behind the normal starting time for his peers. Seventeen years later, he retired from amateur competition, the first Soviet male singles skater to step onto a podium at the world championship and the Olympics.

Today, ten-year-olds are already cracking the technical whip, pushing their way up to juvenile tests, as they are called in Canada. "Our pyramid is so big at the bottom, it's really hard to break through there," Canadian coach Louis Stong says. "You've got to be good. The commitment has to be huge.

"There's always a certain element of society that wants their kids to do well at whatever it is. If we're talking about figure skating, then they get up at five in the morning, six mornings a week, and they skate. If they feel that they're the best ones there, and they're not going to get any better because

Compulsory figures, which were phased out of senior competitions after the 1990 season, are variations of the figure eight, used to develop edge control and body position in skating.

they're the best ones there, they will move their kids to a center where they are no longer the best ones there, but they have to shoot to a higher level. I would say ten-year-olds in Canada generally are doing that."

The push to excel is also in Japan. "As soon as a kid can do an Axel, he's right in there with the top skaters," says Peter Dunfield, the Canadian coach of world champion Yuka Sato of Japan. "It makes the younger ones skate faster right away, out of survival. If they don't skate faster, they're out.

"Their sessions are faster than ours. It's full out for everything. There's no hold-back at all. . . . Our kids are very timid when they first start things. They make up all sorts of intricate entries [to jumps] to give them time to figure out whether they will or not. When a Japanese child starts to jump, they go full bent for election."

Although the stepping stones are similar throughout the world, Canada, with its large skating population, has perhaps the most complex system of all. With smaller populations, in countries with less interest and less-organized clubs, fewer steps are required. Some countries have no test systems, but Britain was the first to set one up.

In Canada or the United States, the progress up the ladder is very graduated and precise, especially in Canada with (as of March 31, 1995) its 195,914 members (not including 4,147 coaches), 1,457 clubs, and a potful of money – from fees, sponsorships, and profits from skating events – to implement programs. Currently Canada has two test streams, one recreational – or at least designed for the average skater – and the other competitive.

Once a recreational skater can twist his or her way giddily around a backward crosscut or a three-turn, there are tests to take. In Canada, they are, in order of difficulty: preliminary, junior bronze, senior bronze, junior silver, senior silver, and gold. And even though the tiny skaters may not yet be in what the CFSA calls the competitive stream, they are also testing their mettle against others at club or interclub competitions. Throughout Canada, there is a competition at one level or another almost every week.

About the time that young skaters are able to pass a senior bronze test, they may enter sectional competitions (Canada has thirteen sections), which serve as "weeding out" events. Some skaters may decide to enter the competitive stream, while others may remain with the average test system. By this time, they are at the juvenile level. Juveniles are usually a maximum of twelve years old, but sections set their own age limits, perhaps allowing a few older skaters to join in the competition.

There is also a pre-novice level (the age limit, set nationally, is fourteen) that currently advances only to sectional competitions, although soon this level may also be part of the Canadian championship. Pre-novice skaters are usually at the stage of taking their junior silver test.

The serious competitive stream begins at the novice level, at which skaters face a different set of tests with more stringent requirements and exacting skill levels than the recreational stream for average skaters. In order to compete at the novice, junior, or senior level, skaters must pass special competitive tests at each level. In the United States, Michelle Kwan passed a senior competitive test when she was only twelve years old, and therefore was eligible to compete at the senior level against seasoned skaters like Nancy Kerrigan and Elaine Zayak.

In Canada, novice ice dancers and singles skaters must be no older than seventeen by a specified date; pairs must be no older than nineteen to compete at the novice level. The junior level has no age requirement, although skaters can compete at the junior level in no more than three seasons. (At world junior championships, the skaters can be no younger than twelve, for women, no older than eighteen, and for men, pairs, and ice dancers, no more than nineteen.)

To skate at the competitive level, it is not necessary to pass tests from the recreational stream. Kurt Browning leaped very early into the competitive stream; ironically, the four-time world champion with the spine-tingling footwork and bragging rights to the first quadruple jump landed in competition never passed his (recreational) gold free-skating test, with its skill requirements lying somewhere between those of novice and junior competitive skaters. Obviously, he didn't have to. To this day, CFSA officials joke that they should just award him the gold test and forget the formalities.

Novice skaters compete first at sectional competitions, but to cut down on the large numbers of skaters in Canada, they must pass through a further qualifying step, the divisional championships (Canada has four divisions), on their way to the national championships. The top four skaters in each discipline at novice, junior, and senior levels in each division advance to the national championships. The USFSA, with 125, 101 members, up 93 per cent from the 1988-89 season, sets up similar qualifying steps (regional and sectional) leading up to the American national championship.

In most cases, a country's national champion – and perhaps even its silver or bronze medalists – qualify for the world championship. Most European nations have one more step to get to a world championship: a top finish at the European championship. For example, although Germany sent three women to the 1994 European championship, it was allowed only two for the world event. The German federation deemed that its top two finishers at the European championship would go on to Japan, regardless of their placing at the German championship.

Because figure skating is not well developed, nor is it a high-profile sport in Asian countries or even in Australia or New Zealand, there are no Asian championships. The Asian Games stage figure-skating competitions, but they have no bearing on world competition. Neither do international competitions that are contested around the world. Events such as Skate Canada, the Nations Cup in Germany, or the Lalique Trophy in France are testing grounds for new programs, but do not serve as qualifying events for world championships or for the Olympic Games. Skaters use them as opportunities to show their wares to high-level judges, who may either be impressed or point out a few technical illegalities in their programs.

The number of skaters that a country may send to a world championship depends on how well its skaters have placed at the previous year's world championship. Figure-skating competitions at the Olympics follow the ISU rule, although the Olympic committee of each country may impose further restrictions on how many athletes it will send to a Games. Each member country of the ISU may send one skater to a world championship. If a country is able to place a skater within the top ten in any discipline, for example women's singles, it may send two women to the following world championship. If a country is able to place a skater competing in singles or ice dancing on the medal podium at a world championship, it may send three entries to the next world event.

Pairs skating has a slightly different requirement: a country is allowed to send three pairs to the following world championship if it places a pair within the top five in the current event.

At the elite level, skaters' needs are many. The sport is becoming so complex and competitive that the athletes cannot do the job alone. They need coaches, choreographers, perhaps ballet or dance instructors, music experts, physiotherapists, doctors attuned to sports medicine, costume designers, and sports psychologists. Most national federations are unable to pick up the costs of skaters' needs. In Canada, the Athlete Trust Fund swelled by 7.4 per cent for the 1994-95 season from the profits of successful national championships. For the first time, during that season, the CFSA contributed $468,600 in financial aid to 900 skaters, including 151 senior and junior national-team skaters who are good enough to be assigned to international competitions in the season leading up to the world championship.

Once, a coach was everything. Gustave Lussi was skating instructor, choreographer, teacher of life skills, and sometimes cook, yet he remained totally objective about his students. Otto Gold, a Czechoslovakian-born teacher who coached Barbara Ann Scott until she was seventeen, was demanding and spare in his praise, but he had a pervasive influence on a young skater's life.

"[In seven years] he told me once that I skated well," recalled Scott in her book *Skate with Me*, saying she became "accustomed" to Gold and thoroughly respected him.

"Usually he concentrated on what was wrong," she wrote. "And if the only thing wrong at the moment was not with me but with ice conditions, say, or temperature or something of the sort, he'd dismiss it with, 'Let's not be fussy.' He wouldn't even let me be fussy about the music I free-skated to. Whatever was on the record player suited him. . . . If I was very low, Mr. Gold would tell me to work harder and give me a little pat on the back.

"He had the blackest eyes I'd ever seen. He could look at you and make you feel just like a sack with a hole in it, and you would wish for a hole in the floor to drop through. And it was amazing how he kept track of all of his pupils, every minute — he knew everything that we were doing on the ice and off it."

Now, many coaches think it best not to become involved in their skaters' lives. But some still do, and their role is becoming very complex. "Now, skating is being run by agents and managers, and coaches have to be able to face that and find their role in it," says Louis Stong, who had to do just that as coach of Canadian champions Kurt Browning, Karen Preston, and Josée Chouinard, all of whom had agents.

Coaching can also be draining at the high levels. Carlo Fassi, coach of Peggy Fleming, Dorothy Hamill, John Curry, Robin Cousins, and Jill Trenary, left the United States a few years ago to pursue a more peaceful lifestyle in his native country, Italy. (He is, however, back coaching in the United States, unable to keep his finger out of the skating pie.) And Stong admits that coaching Barbara Underhill and Paul Martini to a win in the 1984 world pairs championship was draining. "It took an awful lot out of me," he says. "It took full-time devotion. You're always thinking, planning, wondering: Am I doing the right thing? Are they wearing the right thing? Are they skating to the right thing? Are they eating the right thing?"

Sometimes the relationship becomes more than coach-pupil. Canadian coach Josée Picard has often said she thinks of world-champion pairs skater Isabelle Brasseur as a daughter, since she has coached her from the time she was eight years old. Picard struggled to hold back tears when Brasseur skated bravely with a painful cracked rib at the 1994 world championship. It hurt Brasseur to breathe. It hurt Picard to watch.

Others, like Polish coach Barbara Kossowska, take their pupils entirely under their wing. When Kossowska moved to the United States, she took her impoverished prize student, Grzegorz Filipowski, with her to live with her family. There, she taught lessons to help finance Filipowski's career and buy better costumes for him.

Her efforts paid off. When Filipowski won a bronze medal at the 1989 world championship, his dance of joy on the podium was singular, memorable, and endearing. The next fall, he defeated Browning in the short program at Skate Canada. Filipowski is still the only Polish skater ever to win a world medal.

Romanian coach Gabriela Munteanu had much the same relationship with her pupil Cornel Gheorghe. Together they survived the 1989 insurrection against Nicolae Ceaucescu and hid in a darkened rink for three days during the attack. They arrived the following March at the 1990 world championship in Halifax, Nova Scotia, speaking little English and nurturing a four-year-old pair of skating boots, ripped, scraped, soiled, and taped together. Somehow Munteanu had taught Gheorghe to do triple Axels in them.

• • • • • • • • • • • • • • • • • •

Canadian
Karen Preston,
the Grace Kelly
of figure skating

Karen Preston, twice Canadian champion, does a lay-back spin, wearing an unadorned, elegant costume designed by Toller Cranston. Cranston also helped her with choreography for a time.

A group of Hong Kong skaters at the 1987 world championship in Cincinnati, Ohio, had no coaches at all. Chi-Man Wong, at thirty, had been almost entirely self-taught until two years before the event, skating in Hong Kong's only rink, which was all of 30 feet by 70 feet (9 meters by 21 meters). (Currently Hong Kong has three rinks, all one-third the Olympic size of 100 feet by 200 feet (30 meters by 60 meters), and all located in shopping malls.) Edith Poon, Hong Kong's best female competitor, practiced the wrong compulsory figure until she was set straight the week before the competition.

Romanian Cornel Gheorghe has struggled to overcome hardships in his politically beleaguered country. Amazingly, he learned how to do triple Axels and triple-triple combinations in a pair of torn, patched-up skating boots.

Hong Kong's ice dancers withdrew after they arrived with music for their free-dance that was only two minutes, fifteen seconds in length, when it was supposed to be four minutes. And the music for their original dance had the incorrect rhythm. (Each year the ISU chooses a set rhythm to be used in the original dance throughout the season. For the 1994 season, it was the rumba. For 1995, the union has prescribed a quickstep rhythm.) Coaches, particularly English-speaking ones who can read ISU directives, can help enormously in these matters.

If Otto Gold wasn't fussy about the music Barbara Ann Scott skated to, the coaches and choreographers of today are. Canadian ice-dancing coach Marijane Stong was the one who discovered the military-theme music for Brian Boitano's winning Olympic program in 1988, and also suggested that Browning skate to the theme music for *Casablanca*. Neither were casual suggestions.

"She'll take the time to sit there and listen for hours on end," says her husband, Louis, who admits to having three thousand music albums in his Toronto home. "I have gone to bed some nights with her in front of the stereo with the headphones on, and when I got up to leave the next morning, she was still sitting there. All night. She has an incredible stamina for that."

Sandra Bezic, who fashioned the choreography for the 1994 Olympic programs of Brian Boitano, Kurt Browning, Josée Chouinard, and Katarina Witt, as well as a host of professional routines, is also very fussy. "Sometimes I spend more hours editing the music than actually doing the choreography," the former Canadian pairs champion says.

All choreographers work in different ways, but for Bezic the most important part of choreography is the basic idea and the music, which must be well suited to the skater. "It's the key of finding that something special that the skater has that can all be pulled together with a good idea and great music, and music that is well edited and put together." A well-edited piece takes into account the kind of music needed to emphasize a string of technical elements, which are usually set out first; they take into account a skaters' cardiovascular needs and give a program "an emotional ride up and down," Bezic says.

Once Stong came up with the *Casablanca* idea and music, Bezic's job had only just begun. She actually made thirteen to fourteen edits in the music to complete the four-and-a-half-minute routine. She prefers making as few edits as possible, but had to work out nineteen in the long-program music that Barbara Underhill and Paul Martini used to win the 1984 world pairs title.

Sometimes she runs into almost-impossible stumbling blocks. The *Casablanca* soundtrack did not contain any musical phrases suitable for an ending to Browning's routine. Bezic had someone compose and record an ending to the piece that was so in tune with the orchestral make-up of the original, it is imperceptible. These days, the work can all be done on computers.

Once the music is edited, inspiration is needed, sometimes on demand, since out-of-town skaters may spend only five days with her. Bezic hardly ever begins at the beginning to formulate the moves and linking steps between elements and highlights. "I start wherever I'm most inspired," she

Sandra Bezic, internationally renowned choreographer

says. "In *Casablanca*, we started with the cigarette. I always try to find something special in each program, a center point, one special move that is the centerpiece of the program."

The music not only inspires the moves and ideas, it should inspire the costume, too, according to Frances Dafoe, former Olympic pairs silver medalist, who works as a costume designer for the CBC. She also designs costumes for figure skaters. "The most important thing is body line," she says. "If what you're wearing is fighting the line of your body, then it's not right."

And ever since July 1, 1988, costumes have had to be in good taste. The ISU made a rule change to put the brakes on the amateur show that had "gone over the top," according to Toller Cranston, whose apparel in his television special "Strawberry Ice" probably started the trend towards nakedness.

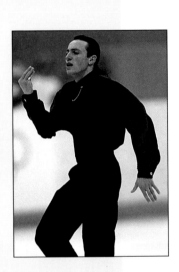

Philippe Candeloro,
star of the future

In the 1982 award-winning television special, which was broadcast in thirty countries, Cranston appeared in a fire-red costume with flames licking up his chest to his shoulder. Above the fire line, it was to have the look of "jeweled skin," although it was created with opalescent sequins, which gave the naked look a shimmer. Dafoe, who designed it, was astonished one day, from her perch on the judges' stand at the 1984 world championship, to see a German pair skating to the music from "Strawberry Ice" and wearing exact replicas of Cranston's costume. Apparently, they had little idea that the real designer of their costumes would also be their judge. Dafoe was amused. (There are no rules governing copying.)

But during the 1980s, the trend slipped madly out of hand. Costumes began to look more naked, more vulgar, more showbiz-like. Amateur judges were under siege from a blitz of plastic sequins and razzle-dazzle. Skaters became "glitter dolls," as Cranston put it. Katarina Witt appeared at a European championship in January 1988 in a high-cut outfit that prompted Peter Dunfield, then coach of competitor Elizabeth Manley, to object, saying, "We're here to skate in a dress and not a G-string. All that's missing is the horse and reins." By the time Witt skated at the Olympics, she had added a ring of azure feathers to cover more of her hips.

The rule was intended to rein in all the excesses, banning exposed areas (skirts must now cover the hips and posterior, and bare midriffs are out); excessive decoration (such as beads, sequins, feathers); theatrical props (Paul Duchesnay once wore a hat that accidently toppled to the ice during a routine, while at the same time, his partner-sister, Isabelle, tossed away a feather boa she was carrying); sleeveless shirts on men (no exposed armpits, please); and tights on male ice dancers. (As of June 1994, the ISU ruled that no male skater in any discipline wear tights in competition.) In short, the ISU frowned upon

Katarina Witt
endured much
criticism when
she appeared
in an earlier
version of this
skating dress at
the 1988 European
championship,
because it was
said to be too
revealing. By
the time of the
Calgary Olympics,
however, she
had added a
few azure feathers
(shown here) to cover
her exposed thighs.

all of those things that served to distract their judges. Men's and women's costumes must be "modest, dignified, and appropriate for athletic competition" at all international, world, and Olympic events, the rule states. In the heat of a serpentine line of footwork, men shouldn't be showing off their chests, either.

A transgression of the rule could spur a judge to deduct 0.1 or 0.2 from the artistic mark. They did just that when they saw Philippe Candeloro of France appear at the 1992 world championship in Oakland, California, wearing rawhide leggings and an elaborate sleeveless tunic ringed and wrapped in fur that went with his Conan the Barbarian routine. Later, he appeared with sleeves attached to the costume.

By the time of the 1994 Olympics in Lillehammer, Candeloro was wearing a simple black shirt and pants, Witt was wearing a plain Robin Hood outfit and a red lace dress she designed herself, and Olympic champion Oksana Baiul, at sixteen, was just learning. She was immersed in feathers and fluff. "An electrified poodle," Cranston called her.

Perhaps the trend of the future will be to ice couture, in the spirit of the elite garb that Nancy Kerrigan wore at Lillehammer. Designed by former skater and current evening-wear designer Vera Wang, Kerrigan's outfit for the technical program was fashioned with white spandex (shiny side inside), stretchy black-velvet inserts, and sleeves made of a synthetic, sheer, stretchy fabric, softly aglitter with rhinestones and pearls at the wrists. Her long-program outfit was inspired by a gown Wang designed for actress Sharon Stone. Somewhere in a yard or two of spandex and flesh-colored sheer fabric, Wang was able to set 11,500 rhinestones.

Had Wang sold the costumes to Kerrigan, the Olympic silver medalist would have had to pay $9,600 (U.S.) for the black-and-white creation and $13,000 (U.S.) for the flesh-colored attire. Priced at $9,600, the costume for the technical program (at two minutes, forty seconds or so) would have cost Kerrigan $60 (U.S.) a second to wear, although she did don it more than once. Wang happily donated them to her.

Both were a long seamstress's yard from the $75 dress Dorothy Hamill wore to win her Olympic gold medal in 1976: a simple pink stretch-knit dress sewn by a friend's mother.

By this point, as many elite skaters discover, the sport gets expensive, time-consuming, and generally all-consuming. Custom skating boots can cost $600 a pair, blades another $400 or $500. The going rate for a top coach in Canada ranges from $40 to $60 an hour, and in the United States from $100 to $135 (Cdn). There are also travel costs to consider – and a skater pays the expenses of the coach at a competition. Parents have travel costs, too. If a skater does not live at home, parents pay for boarding costs. If the skater has to commute a distance to the rink, there are fuel, insurance, and automobile expenses to consider.

In 1991, the CFSA estimated that it costs anywhere from $12,435 to $20,491 (Cdn) a year to field a singles skater at any level from novice to senior. Although the CFSA picks up some of the costs when the skaters make the junior or the senior national team, most of the time parents go it alone. Some parents have been known to spend up to $40,000 a year for a successful skater heading off to international competitions.

Most national federations, however, are not able to pick up as many costs – if any – as the Canadian association does. In the United States, needy skaters get some financial help from the USFSA. Most of the rest are lost without a kind, wealthy patron. Only a handful of the very best attract endorsements.

Some skaters take jobs. Rod Garossino, a Canadian ice-dancing champion, once worked in a lumber store, driving forklift trucks and probing the

Nancy Kerrigan became known for her exquisite, expensive skating dresses taken from haute couture *design. Although the dress shown here was donated to her by designer Vera Wang, it was valued at $9,600 (U.S.).*

vagaries of door knobs. The 1976 Olympic champion John Curry was so destitute that he once took a job arranging meat in a supermarket in England and lived in a small, chilly bachelor apartment, with no money to feed the gas meter. After finishing a discouraging fourth at the 1972 world championships, Curry was approached by an American benefactor, Ed Mosler, who spent a couple of days trying to persuade the skeptical skater that he wanted to help him.

As if financing wasn't enough of a problem, skaters have more things to worry about than ever before. "The pressure on skaters will increase dramatically as the stature of the sport increases," Canadian-team sports psychologist Peter Jensen says. "It's an all-or-nothing sport. And it's always so clear when somebody makes a mistake."

Jensen, an author who also works as a consulting psychologist for other amateur sports, says he knows of few other sports in which a sole athlete is completely surrounded by such large numbers of spectators. If the athlete is a

Canadian skater, there may be as many as seventeen thousand pairs of eyes pondering every wrinkle, gasping at every *faux pas*.

"Skating puts a magnifying glass on them," Jensen says. "While you and I are having a discussion, my attention could wander, I might see something out the window, I might miss something you're saying and ask you to repeat it. But if a skater's attention on the ice wanders for a tenth of a second, everybody knows."

For example, for a few moments in his final year as an amateur, Kurt Browning's attention wandered; his focus went out the window. During the 1993 Canadian figure-skating championship in Hamilton, he looked up into a crowd of seventeen thousand people and saw Paul Martini, who worked as one of his skills instructors, and his concentration was momentarily diverted. "How often is that going to happen?" he said, speaking of a competition that he nevertheless won.

At Skate Canada, he looked up into a capacity crowd and tried to stare at a piece of yellow tape "to make sure I didn't see anyone." But his eye caught sight of someone he knew, and he realized he was looking at his parents, Neva and Dewey. "I shook my head and the music started right then, and I thought 'I'm not going to pull this again. I'm going to try and get focused.'"

Browning won that competition too, but he was not at his best during his long-program routine, in which he fought to land a couple of his jumps and to hold together simpler elements like a spin.

Many skaters retreat into their own worlds, tuning out distractions with a set of headphones as they visualize their perfect programs. Canadian pairs skaters Michelle Menzies and Jean-Michel Bombardier took to wearing a symbol with an arrow pointing straight up, a signal of where they intended to go. And they worked with a motivator to set their directions and to wash away any superfluous thoughts they didn't need in pursuit of their goals while training and competing.

Skating at high levels can be a solitary pursuit. By the time Dorothy Hamill went to the 1976 Olympics, she knew many of her figure-skating competitors. But, in her book, *On and Off the Ice*, she noted that the mood in the athlete's village was strange. "We all went around as if we were in cocoons, not communicating with each other," she wrote. "People seemed to be afraid that if they spoke – if they let anyone else in on what they were thinking – they might somehow take away from their chances for a medal. The path to the Olympic Games is a long and a hard one, and when you are there, you simply don't do anything that might compromise you."

To My Lassie, The finest coach and the Greatest Inspiration I could ever have had. With all my Love, Dorothy

After Dorothy Hamill won the 1976 Olympic gold medal wearing a homemade $75 skating dress (shown here), she signed a three-year $1-million-a-year deal to skate with the "Ice Capades," an American institution established on Valentine's Day 1940, which she bought in 1991.

The use of sports psychologists in skating became more common during the 1980s, but the Soviets have realized their value for decades. Peter Dunfield watched with interest the way that the Protopopovs prepared for competition during the 1964 Olympics in Innsbruck, Austria, from his skaters' dressing-room cubicle directly beside that of the Soviets.

"The Soviets were way ahead of our athletes in the context of mental training," he says. "They did physical training at least forty-five minutes before they would step on the ice before a warm-up. We didn't do that. We did physical training in the hotel maybe for fifteen minutes. . . . They did mental training for an hour. We didn't do very much of that at all. We just weren't in the same league. . . . That's when I knew I had to learn more."

The Soviets were able to develop their preparation techniques because of their central sports ministry. If a major sport, such as track and field, made a discovery in some aspect of training, it would share it, through the ministry, with a minor sport. "In Canada, the leading sports did not share," Dunfield says. "There was no connection between sports until Sport Canada came into being."

During the 1980s, many international coaches enlisted the help of a sports psychologist. Brian Orser was one who benefited from the push. "We're adding one more factor to the pot," said his coach, Doug Leigh. "When you're doing brain surgery, you don't work by yourself."

Canadian skaters often do event simulations, complete with judges, announcers, costumes, exact warm-up times, crowded hallways, bustling dressing rooms, and the incessant snapping of cameras to accustom them to the pressures of competition. Television cameras with bright lights zoom to within six inches (fifteen centimeters) of the skaters' faces.

In the professional world, the pressures are different, and television can become a skater's best friend. The image is all-important. As Hamill skated into her new pro career, she found that "Now I couldn't go out without dressing up. I had to be careful of everything I said. I was required for endless publicity calls, press conferences, and photographic sessions. I lived out of my trunk and seldom saw my family. Home was my hotel room, and my days off were spent on a plane traveling to the next city on the tour."

Almost immediately after Elvis Stojko won his 1994 world title, he plunged into the same world without so much as a minute to breathe. Stojko signed up for at least forty-seven stops on the annual tour of world champions that dipsy-doodled through a record seventy cities in the United States and for the first time stretched, incredibly, into July. It is a tour that almost completely obliterates a social life. (Various independent promoters or agents run professional tours.)

One day in the summer of 1994, Stojko found himself trundling along a Texas highway for four hours on a bus after doing a show, arriving at a hotel at three in the morning, checking in, falling exhausted into bed, and arising in time to have breakfast before heading to the rink at one in the afternoon. Six hours later he was at an airport, headed for the next show. Within a span of fifteen hours, he had skated a show, entered and exited a city, slept, ate, and maybe even smiled a few times, if he had time.

His Canadian teammates, Isabelle Brasseur and Lloyd Eisler, were on the same roller-coaster ride and, in one amazing twenty-four-hour weekend stretch, were scheduled to skate three shows, with Brasseur still nursing a rib injury.

Immediately after his 1994 Olympic disappointment, Kurt Browning stepped into the professional world, leaving the amateur fight to the younger skaters, like Stojko. But Browning knew he was about to face a new lifestyle, even though he had done tours on a temporary basis before as an amateur. "It's not just the fact that the number of shows I'm doing has tripled, but it's all the hard work that professional skaters do besides," he says, speaking of the harried pace of his new life. "It's part of your job to take care of off-ice work, too."

With the skates at home on the shelf, Browning bounced through a sheaf of personal appearances, signing autographs and clowning with people he didn't know. In the weeks leading up to the Canadian "Stars on Ice" tour, Browning was up at half past five in the morning to do a string of radio and television interviews that continued until late afternoon. Hardest of all, he said wistfully, is having to leave home for long stretches. "I've been so used to 'Kurt needs a quiet schedule now, because he's training for worlds,'" he says. "But now I'll be training or competing against Brian Boitano, Scott Hamilton, Paul Wylie, Brian Orser, but I won't have any schedule. I have to train on the road."

Instead of hours of practice a day, Browning may get perhaps only forty-five minutes of ice time to test out his tricks and skates and routines during the tour, and probably only on days when there is a show.

His new life will also make it difficult for him to maintain the health of his wonky back, the one that made him miss the Canadian championship and eventually contributed to his downfall in the 1992 Olympics. While he was an amateur, a daily routine of exercise and physiotherapy kept his problems under control, but now he has to hope he stays in a hotel with a weight room.

A tour skater also cannot afford three bad days in a row, like he or she can in amateur training. "You don't need people talking about you," Browning says. "You don't want that image. You don't want to feel bad about yourself. When you're out there at center ice in front of eighteen thousand people waiting for you to skate, you really want to feel good about yourself."

The attraction for many skaters is money and glory; it's the payday for all those years hunkering down in bone-chilling rinks, falling on triple-Axel attempts, starting from scratch with a new partner, living with doubts, frowning judges, and aching backs, and forever counting pennies.

"The tours are the cake," agent Michael Rosenberg says. "Everything else is just icing. Television specials, endorsements, and personal appearances, pro competitions: that's all icing. The icing can be substantial, but the cake is touring."

Dorothy Hamill didn't discover this lifestyle until her amateur days melted into strictly professional ones; she still lived in the era in which a Barbara Ann Scott (but not necessarily a Sonja Henie) had to return the gift of a car to retain amateur status. During the 1990s, however, ISU rule changes have allowed skaters like Stojko or Browning to make money on tours, through endorsements, and for television specials and still retain their eligibility to skate in world championships or Olympics.

Perhaps the most lucrative television movie deal about skaters centers around the rags-to-riches story of Oksana Baiul, who had been a Ukraine orphan, sleeping on a cot in a rink, before a famous coach took her under her wing. In late 1994, CBS released its made-for-TV movie depicting the life story of Oksana Baiul, the 1994 Olympic champion. Although Baiul, 1992 Olympic champion Victor Petrenko, and their coach Galina Zmievskaya did not act in the movie, the trio were to receive a seven-figure sum for the rights to use the story. Indeed, Baiul could become the modern-day version of Sonja Henie, without the childhood advantages.

Currently, skaters become ineligible for ISU competitions, including world championships and Olympics, only by skating in professional competitions that are not sanctioned by the ISU and which are not governed by ISU rules or judged by ISU-accredited judges. By early 1994, there was only one professional competition, the USFSA's Pro-Am competition, that was sanctioned as a pilot project only, with only American skaters. All of that may change very soon. Within the past few years, a handful of sanctioned international amateur competitions has also been offering prize money.

At its congress in June 1994, the ISU relaxed the rules governing eligible and ineligible skaters even further. An ineligible skater is now allowed to compete at an ISU-sanctioned international event, such as Skate Canada or the Lalique Trophy, if nominated by his or her federation, but are still, however, barred from competing at national and world championships or Olympic Games. And because Pro-Am competitions, which allow eligible and ineligible skaters to compete against each other, were fully sanctioned at the 1994 congress, skaters can expect to see many Pro-Am competitions popping up all over the world in the future. Also, after April 1, 1995, ineligible skaters will not be allowed to regain their eligible status. In figure skating these days, everything is changing very quickly.

Judging

....

At an exhibition at Toronto's Maple Leaf Gardens, Jacqueline du Bief played the part of a statue coming to life, while the sculptor, played by Canadian Sheldon Galbraith, snoozed in a chair. In another memorable performance, she skated in a costume with red-and-white arm bands. When she spun, her arms appeared like a spiraling barber's pole.

Everybody, it seems, hates figure-skating judges.

The nine gurus of skating who file into the hot seats at center stage at any world, international, or national event live a life of isolation, of few washroom breaks, of interminable triple toe-loops and backward crosscuts, of stresses upon stresses. At the 1936 Olympics in Germany, Canadian judge John Machado was taken off the ice, suffering from pneumonia after spending six hours judging the men's figures in a blizzard. (Because of this kind of danger, women were not allowed to judge internationally until Mollie Phillips of Britain persuaded the ISU to lift the restriction in 1947. She became the first female international skating judge.)

The 1994 world championship in Japan posed lesser threats to health and sanity. Ice-dancing judges spent six hours watching a record thirty-six couples skate two compulsory dances each. These are the ice dancers' equivalent to compulsory figures. Skaters must perform specific steps and turns, tracing over them exactly in two or three circuits of the rink (depending on the dance), to, for example, an Argentine tango or a Westminster waltz, chosen before the event starts. Watching repetitions of the same steps skated by thirty-six couples to the same tune can become very monotonous.

After having survived compulsory dances, the judges had to examine thirty-six original dances – a section of the competition equivalent to the short program in singles or pairs events, except that the required element is a prescribed rhythm, such as a polka or a quickstep. (The original dance was once called the original set-pattern dance, which required that the skaters make up their own pattern on the ice to a set rhythm, but they had to repeat the pattern several times around the rink. Skaters do not have to repeat patterns in the original dance.)

Finally, in Japan, the judges had to watch thirty-six free-dances, many of which seemed to have a Hungarian folk-dance echo to them. "If I hear one more Hungarian rhapsody, I think I shall go mad," said Courtney Jones, who acted as an assistant referee.

Although many will say that judging has improved immensely over the past few years (while others will say that a lot of help is still needed to improve its fairness), figure-skating history is rife with tales of controversial decisions, some of them prompting wild protests from frustrated spectators, particularly during the 1950s and 1960s.

One example is the time that French skater Jacqueline du Bief won the 1952 world championship in Paris. There were no television cameras to record the action, but the spectators saw plenty: one judge gave du Bief a perfect mark of 6.0, even though she had fallen twice, once skidding across the width of the rink on her backside. When she won the event over Sonya Klopfer of the United States by only one judge, the crowd erupted noisily, throwing glass bottles and anything else at hand onto the ice. "The judges got away with it because those were the days before television," says Peter Dunfield, who later married Klopfer. "It was so crooked before television, you can't believe."

Du Bief, who had no involvement in the incident, later wrote a book in which she conceded the gold medal to Klopfer, now Sonya Dunfield, who today works as a coach in New York. The two have remained good friends. Du Bief later distinguished herself as an innovative, outstanding show-skater.

There was a similar, perhaps even-more-explosive outpouring of crowd outrage during the pairs event at the 1956 Olympics at Cortina, Italy. For one thing, spectators loved the German pair of Franz Ningel, nineteen, and Marika Kilius, who was only twelve. They grumbled when judges placed them only fourth.

But a second battle was going on between Canadians Frances Dafoe and Norris Bowden, who came to the event with two world titles to their credit, and Austrians Elisabeth Schwarz and Kurt Oppelt. The Austrians won by such a close vote that the accountants had to calculate placings down to the second-place ordinals. The Canadians were short only one second-place ordinal, and the Austrians became the Olympic champions.

"The greatest brokers of political intrigue and wheeling and dealing, which skating was to a certain point at the time, were the Austrians," Dunfield says. "Austrians dealt with skating like they dealt with politics. They were very prominent in the development of skating. They always had great skaters. When they didn't have any skaters . . . it was like Canada had lost all its hockey players. They lost them all because of the war. Their better skaters came to America to be teachers.

"They had no teachers, very poor rinks, and they were into a big rebuilding project, and they could only hang on by their teeth by being really tough

Canadians Frances Dafoe and Norris Bowden, shown skating at Davos, Switzerland, were the first pair to push lifts up into the air above the man's head. The innovative couple won two world titles in 1954 and 1955 and a silver Olympic medal, amid a judging controversy, in 1956.

with the people they could get in competition and really pushing them politically. And that's what happened. Fran and Norrie got caught in that. [The Austrians] worked very hard behind the scenes to make sure the political lines of voting were structured to make sure that Schwarz and Oppelt won.

"The Austrian board of directors for the amateur association was the same board of directors for the . . . Austrian professional show," Dafoe says. "So they needed a few titles."

Spectators threw oranges at the judges and referees after that decision, and the ice had to be cleared three times before the event could proceed.

The world championship that followed for Dafoe and Bowden was even more scandalous. "It was pretty nasty stuff," Dafoe says. They figured they would have a fair shake after the draw on the eve of the competition to determine the order of skating and the judges who would oversee the event. Dafoe and Bowden said they were told seven judges had been drawn and one of them was a neutral judge from Switzerland.

But when the Canadians took to the ice less than twenty-four hours later to compete, Dafoe was astonished to see nine judges on the panel. "They'd added two judges," she says. "We don't know how it was done, but there were nine judges out there, and, of course, the two judges were handpicked. They were friends of the Austrians. It was game over as soon as we saw that."

Although Dafoe and Bowden had had a minor flaw at the end of their Olympic program, at the world championship they came off the ice "having skated the performance of a lifetime," Dafoe says. "There wasn't a flaw. It was as if we had wings on our feet that night."

Still, the Canadians lost a close battle to the Austrians, who were placed first by five of the nine judges. Four judges placed the Canadians first.

After the competition, Arnold Gerschwiler, who trained the Austrians, approached Dafoe and Bowden, and "he was really upset," Dafoe said. "He said, 'This is a terrible blot on figure skating, but I do want to shake the hands of the real champions.'"

That night, after a meeting, most of the coaches at the event asked the ISU to declare the competition null and void. The ISU refused. At the closing banquet, when medals were given out and Dafoe and Bowden were referred to as "the most outstanding skaters," the Austrian team rose en masse and left.

Sometimes the politics of judging extended even beyond the competition venue. Ironically, after Dafoe and Bowden's unpleasant experience, the CFSA suspended both of them, even though they had just announced their retirement from skating. The suspension prevented them from becoming judges themselves, because "they didn't like us saying there were politics in skating," Dafoe said. "They knew we wanted to go on and judge."

Eventually, both became world judges, because their expertise was needed. From the sport's competitive beginning, there had been a lack of judges who really understood what made one skater better than another; in the early days, some became judges because they were part of an old boys' club. Bowden, who had also been a Canadian ice-dancing champion, once sat behind a world-championship judge who had never before marked an

ice-dancing event and gave him tips on what to look for, says Dafoe of her versatile partner, who died in 1991 at the age of sixty-four.

"Our association is very different today. I think it is a fabulous association," Dafoe says. "But at that point in time they could have been a little more understanding."

Sonja Henie also found herself in the midst of a judging controversy at the 1927 world championships in Oslo, in her homeland. Of the five judges, the Austrian and German judges gave first-place votes to Austrian skater Herma Szabo. The other three judges were Norwegian, and they placed Henie first, giving her her first world title. The outcry that followed spurred the ISU into making a new rule stipulating that only one judge per country was to be allowed to oversee a discipline at an international skating event.

Although Henie usually had no trouble in winning first-place points from judges, she also got a little help from her father, the original skating parent, who once chased a skeptical judge down the main street of a town with a broom.

Many would probably liked to have taken a page from Mr. Henie's book during the Cold War, when Soviet and Eastern bloc countries lined up along one voting line and western countries along another. Compulsory figures were a particular breeding ground of strife, because few people actually saw the tracings on the ice. When the ISU gradually lessened the emphasis on figures, many in the skating world were relieved. "Figures were the last bastion of manipulation," coach Frank Carroll of the United States once said.

"[During the 1950s and 1960s is] when the East-West camps really became instilled," Dunfield says. "The Eastern bloc was quite strong because the Soviets dominated the judging. They could really dominate the Czech judge, the Hungarian, Bulgarian, the Polish judge. They were sort of pawns. Anybody who was going to be in judging and travel out of the country, especially during the early Communist domination, had to be a very trusted person. Why were they trusted? They were Communists. If they were Communists, they were dominated by the Soviet Union.

"Therefore there was a very strong coalition there that was glued together because of political ties. Much more so than the West. The West reacted to that, but they didn't initiate it. It was the only way we could deal with it."

Television cleaned up the sport, Dunfield says, but it took longer in the Soviet and Eastern bloc countries. "Initially, none of these countries had TV. . . . Whatever [the judges] did internationally didn't really matter because they weren't accountable in their own country. So when these people came back with these medals, they were really the world champions [it appeared]."

Even in the early days of television, a rights buyer tended to transmit the event only to its own domestic market. Things changed when countries began to pick up central feeds, such as Eurovision. "[Judging improprieties waned] only when they got the broadcasting together and permeated the shield, and countries could really see what was happening. Then they couldn't do it as blatantly as they did," Dunfield says.

It was "a divided world" in those days, Ellen Burka says, and judges did whatever they wanted in compulsory figures, an event that attracted few spectators. Once Burka was told that her daughter received low marks for a figure that a judge said had a couple of "flats" on it – signs that she had skated improperly on the flat of her blade, leaving two tracks on the ice, instead of on an edge, which would leave one track. "Nobody ever saw the figures," Burka says. "Nobody came to watch figures."

Burka found another judge to take a look at the figure, which hadn't yet been swept away. When he found no flats, the embarrassed marker said he was confused by the way the light fell on it, she said.

"Figures was a big field for creations," says Sergei Tchetveroukhin, the first male skater from the Soviet Union to win a world or Olympic medal. "Nobody could see what you do. The judges could do what they wanted. The judges could really screw you up."

Tchetveroukhin acknowledges that judges from the Soviet Union and its satellites used to make agreements on placements, but points out that the Eastern bloc did not always sit in solidarity. Not once did the Czechoslovakian judge rank Tchetveroukhin ahead of Czech star Ondrej Nepela, he says, noting that, historically, a certain animosity existed between the two countries. Soviet and Czech hockey players always tackled their jobs "like enemies."

Certainly, the Soviet skating powers always tried to negotiate, he says. Sometimes it worked, sometimes not. "People are different. Some of them weak. Some of them quite strong. Some of them could be frightened into doing it."

Over the years, the Soviets have often been accused of national bias. At the 1976 Olympics, the ISU suspended a Soviet judge who had placed Soviet skater Vladimir Kovalev first (as well as a Canadian judge who had placed Canadian Toller Cranston first). The rest of the panel had voted for John Curry. Afterward, the ISU took the unprecedented step of suspending all Soviet judges from taking part in international competitions for the 1978 season because repeated suspensions of individual Soviet judges over the previous few years had not worked to stop them from exhibiting national bias.

During the last decade or more, the ISU has set out specific regulations about who is allowed to judge a world championship: a judge must participate in an ISU judging seminar at least once in four years or act as a judge at a world championship or international competition at least once in three years. The seminar includes a formidable set of oral and written tests: candidates must achieve a mark of at least 84 per cent on a written exam and then endure eighteen hours of intense questioning from top international experts from the ISU to defend every mark they give during a live judging competition.

"They deliberately create a high-stress environment with the idea that, if you can't cope with pressure, you shouldn't be judging," says Jane Garden, a Canadian judge qualified to mark at world championships.

There is also a requirement about how much experience a judge must have before he or she can take the tension-packed ISU exams. To be eligible for the first international assignment, a candidate must be older then twenty-three and younger than forty-five, must have judged – to ISU satisfaction – twice in national, divisional, or sectional championships within three years before the nomination, and must have gone to a judges' school organized by their member country.

Some countries have weak judging seminars or schools; Canada's judging seminars, however, are a big production, involving videos that clearly show certain moves, modern teaching aids, and examinations. The ISU offers no guidelines as to what the seminars must include. Some ISU-led seminars may involve an expert instructor covering an extensive amount of information – but he or she may convey it only by reading from a manual.

Most countries don't have a real development program for judges, although, says Jackie Stell-Buckingham, CFSA technical coordinator, some carefully and expertly handpick their international judges. "A lot of countries will use their ex-skaters, like the Jan Hoffmanns (of the former East Germany). They rely a lot on what they know as skaters. They sort of teach them what they need to know to get them to the international level. . . . I have to give countries the credit for picking the right people. A Germany picking somebody like a Jan Hoffman and pushing him up to be an ISU judge, that was a totally excellent suggestion because he's a world medalist and he's a doctor, he's brilliant. They handpick their people pretty well."

European judges also have an advantage over the more-isolated North American judges, Stell-Buckingham says. Although Canadian judges may be better trained, European judges have access to elite skaters more often. "[Canadian and American judges] don't see a lot of international competitions," she says. "But European judges can toddle off to four or five international competitions a year, even if they're not judging, and just watch. Their exposure level to that kind of skating is much greater. They're a lot more familiar with who the athletes are and what that level of skating is looking like these days, what kind of jumps they're all doing, and what their programs are like. They know who the up-and-coming people are that we may not see until they hit a world championship."

Judges don't have to write exams to become "international judges," who judge events other than world championships, such as Skate Canada or the NHK Trophy in Japan. (World judges are always international judges, but international judges are not necessarily world judges, in ISU lingo.)

Under ISU rules, a country may simply nominate a judge to an international competition. The CFSA, however, requires that its judges write ISU-style examinations before being allowed to judge even at international events. This means that by the time Canadians judge a world championship or Olympics, they have actually written the fearful ISU examination twice.

Canada has an extremely regimented system, in which a judge starts by becoming a "primary evaluator," able to judge primary skating tests. Even to get to this level, a potential judge must spend hours at a clinic, taking quizzes, skill-identification tests, and a take-home, open-book examination. They also have to work at being a trial judge, working under a supervisor at live competitions. It can take a year just to become a primary evaluator in Canada. It can take twenty-five years to become an international-level competitive judge in Canada, fifteen if the judge already has a skating background. At each level, the judge is tested with exams, quizzes, and trial-judge assignments.

Currently, there are about eight hundred competitive-stream judges in Canada, about one hundred and twenty of them at the national or international level. Canada has more judges than any country, but then the CFSA is the largest skating association in the world. Every weekend in Canada, a judge can toil and sharpen his or her skills at a high- or low-level competition.

The other problems with a lot of international judges is that they don't get enough actual judging practice, claims Stell-Buckingham. "We can [judge] a competition every weekend here if we really want to, so it keeps you really sharp. A lot of European judges, in pairs and ice dancing in particular, don't see a lot of those, even at the best of times. They can get rusty and out of practice."

What kind of practice do you need? Aside from recognizing various skills, a judge has only ten to fifteen seconds at the most to punch in a set of marks. And a judge must maintain an intense concentration, particularly when judging as many as forty skaters. They do not have the benefit of replays, instant or otherwise. And they must not discuss their work with their neighbors, particularly on the judges' stand. Aside from exchanging a few pleasantries, they must not be seen to chat at all. After all, television cameras may be watching.

Although all world championship judges are required to have taken national seminars, Sally Stapleford, a former British skater and judge who is now chairwoman of the ISU skating committee, says the ISU is mindful that some seminars may not be very thorough. "Canada, America, and a lot of countries that have a good history of skating have seminars that are very thorough," she points out. "But maybe with some of the new members that are starting up, they might not."

China, for example, an emerging nation in the sport, has only one judge who can work at the world-championship level. There are only two or three others qualified to judge other international competitions, Stapleford says. Some potential judges may fall afoul of the ISU requirement that all communications be done in English. The ISU examination is given in English only.

Stapleford says the ISU is working at issuing educational materials to these have-not countries on how to conduct judges' seminars. Still, she says, a judge doesn't get very far in the system if he or she makes mistakes. After each event, a referee makes a report of each judge's effort. The judge may be sanctioned and may have to answer to a letter of reprimand. The judge may be asked to take further education before returning.

During the 1991-92 season, between twenty and thirty judges were suspended for various reasons, says Stapleford. During 1992-93, nine judges met the same fate. In an unprecedented move, six of the nine judges on the ice-dancing panel at the 1993 world championship in Prague were suspended for judging the competitors by reputation rather than by effort, but they were reinstated because proper procedures for their dismissal were not followed. Still, the ISU had made a point.

Perhaps because of the controversies surrounding ice dancing, as of July 1, 1994, the ISU instituted an even-more-stringent requirement for dance judges than for any other discipline. Now, new international dance judges will be put on probation for two years following their first appointment. To continue, the judge must earn a successful judging report for at least one international competition.

Currently, at a world championship, a country may nominate a judge for every event in which it has a competitor, up to a maximum of three. The panel at a world or Olympic event always consists of nine judges, picked from a random draw. The experience and make-up of a panel, therefore, can vary widely. By the luck of the draw, six of the nine judges in the ice-dancing event at the 1994 world championships in Japan came from former Soviet or Soviet satellite countries, a fact that disturbed western coaches and skaters.

"Even if it's being judged well, it doesn't look good," says Canadian coach Eric Gillies, a former world competitor. "And I don't think it's fair. The possibilities are too strong that something can happen the wrong way."

The ISU also has another problem. Nobody wants to be a pairs judge. The pairs discipline is the easiest one in which to make a mistake. It's extremely difficult to focus on two skaters at the same time, particularly if they move away from each other. For a time, at the world level, only about a half-dozen countries had pairs skaters, and few judges bothered to take the qualifications.

A couple of years ago, the ISU lumped the judging qualification for pairs skaters in with singles skaters to ensure it would have enough bodies to make up a pairs panel. That meant that a judge qualified to judge singles skating at the international level was also qualified to judge pairs – even if he or she knew nothing about pairs skating or had never seen a pairs skater.

During the 1994 NHK Trophy in Japan, one of the European judges on the panel for the pairs event had never previously judged a pairs competition. She placed world champions Isabelle Brasseur and Lloyd Eisler second and a Czech pair, who had made some mistakes, first.

It happens a lot, Stell-Buckingham says, adding that judges with singles qualifications tend to judge pairs on their singles skills rather than on their pairs skills. These judges will tend to acknowledge a pair's side-by-side jumping skills, without perhaps recognizing various lifts, which hand-to-hand hold is most difficult, or which version of the death spiral has the most risk.

The situation is improving, however, Stell-Buckingham says, because more pairs skating is developing in countries that have not previously had strong programs in that discipline.

&

For the uninitiated, the marking system is a complex arrangement of points, ordinals, and factored placings. The scale of marks ranges from 0.0 (not skated) through 1.0 (very poor), 2.0 (poor), and 3.0 (mediocre) to 4.0 (good), 5.0 (very good), and 6.0 (perfect and faultless).

Britons Jayne
Torvill and
Christopher Dean
perform their
hauntingly beautiful
signature piece,
"Bolero," which
earned them a
string of nine
perfect marks
of 6.0 for artistic
impression at
the 1984
Olympic Games.

In most cases, judges give out two sets of marks, one for technical merit, the other for artistic impression or, as of July 1, 1994, presentation. (In the past, compulsory dances required only one mark, but a rule change at the ISU Congress in June 1994 allowed judges to award two marks, one for technique, the other for timing/presentation).

Britons Jayne Torvill and Christopher Dean were the champions of the perfect 6.0. By the time they finished their amateur career (the first time), they had amassed 136 perfect marks. If judges hand out a 6.0, it is usually for artistic impression. A perfect mark of 6.0 for technical merit at the world-championship level is extremely rare. Torvill and Dean received a smattering of them; Donald Jackson earned one when he won his world title in 1962, and Elvis Stojko also got one during his 1994 world-championship win.

At the 1985 world championships in Tokyo, a skater from Hong Kong, then a new member of the ISU, put a foot down on his first compulsory figure when he was unable to get all the way around on a single glide and lost his balance eight times. He got a mark as low as 0.1 for his tortuous moment,

Technical marks of
6.0 are rare. Elvis
Stojko earned his
first 6.0 when he won
the silver medal at the
1993 Canadian
championship
in Hamilton.

because the most pessimistic judge couldn't say he hadn't skated the figure. Compulsory figures were phased out after the 1990 world championship in Halifax.

The scale of marks is intended to determine the quality of the performance, a kind of absolute judging. But judges of figure skating also judge relatively. In other words, the most important story that the judges tell through their marks is which skater is better than another in each segment of the event. To do this, the technical and artistic marks from each judge are added together and compared with the totals awarded by other judges to other skaters.

So what happens if, after the marks are added, a judge happens to place two skaters in a tie? A tie is broken in the short program by checking to see which skater has the higher technical mark. But a tie in the compulsory dances, original dance, or the long program is broken by looking to the presentation mark.

Still, marks and the placement of competitors is one of the least-understood aspects of skating. Even though one set of marks awarded to a skater by a judge may seem low in comparison to those of another judge, the marks may still be first-place marks, because the judge has tended to hand out low marks to all skaters.

For example, Russians Oksana Gritschuk and Evgeny Platov received the following marks from the German judge and the Slovakian judge for their free-skating performance at the 1994 world championships in Japan:

Russians Oksana Gritschuk and Evgeny Platov are at their best in the sort of fast-paced rock-and-roll number they used when they won Olympic gold in 1994.

	GER	SVK
Technical Merit	5.7	5.7
Artistic Impression	5.8	5.8
Totals	11.5	11.5
Ordinals	1	2

Although the marks are the same, the German judge actually placed the Russians first, while the Slovakian judge ranked them second.

The placements are called ordinals, and in the long run, ordinals are far more important than the actual marks. Ordinals determine who wins a short program or a free-dance. For example, a skater wins a program if he or she wins a majority of first-place ordinals, or placements. This is what happened during the women's event at the 1994 Olympics, when Oksana Baiul of Ukraine narrowly defeated Nancy Kerrigan of the United States in the long program:

Nancy Kerrigan	GBR	POL	CZE	UKR	CHN	USA	JPN	CAN	GER
Technical Merit	5.8	5.8	5.8	5.7	5.7	5.8	5.8	5.7	5.8
Artistic Impression	5.8	5.8	5.9	5.9	5.9	5.9	5.9	5.8	5.8
Totals	11.7	11.6	11.7	11.6	11.6	11.7	11.7	11.5	11.6
Ordinals	1	2	2	2	2	1	1	1	2

Oksana Baiul	GBR	POL	CZE	UKR	CHN	USA	JPN	CAN	GER
Technical Merit	5.6	5.8	5.9	5.8	5.8	5.8	5.8	5.5	5.7
Artistic Impression	5.8	5.9	5.9	5.9	5.9	5.8	5.8	5.9	5.9
Totals	11.4	11.7	11.8	11.7	11.7	11.6	11.6	11.4	11.6
Ordinals	2	1	1	1	1	2	2	2	1

The vote couldn't have been closer. For a moment, disregard the ninth judge, who happened to be 1974 and 1980 world champion Jan Hoffmann. He basically placed the two women in a tie, with 11.6 points each.

Among the other eight judges, four voted for Kerrigan, four for Baiul. Hoffman's vote had to break the tie. In the long program, the tie is broken by looking to the artistic, or presentation, mark. Baiul won because Hoffmann had given her a 5.9, and a 5.8 to Kerrigan. Only one-tenth of a point separated the two competitors.

However, sometimes judges have a wide variety of opinions about who is the best (particularly if skaters make mistakes), leaving no skater with a majority of firsts. In such a case, accountants calculate who has the majority of first- *and* second-place ordinals and so on, until a winner is found.

One of the most convoluted examples of the ordinal system occurred during the 1979 European championship in Zagreb. No skater among the top three contenders, including Vladimir Kovalev of the Soviet Union, Robin Cousins of Britain, and Jan Hoffmann of the German Democratic Republic, won a majority of first-place votes. In fact, each had received at least two first-place votes from the judges.

Therefore accountants had to take into account the number of first- and second-place ordinals each contestant had. The obvious results were overturned, however, when a fourth skater, Jean-Christophe Simond of France, earned one second-place vote from a French judge. Even though Simond finished fourth overall, that one second-place ordinal he received changed the final order of finish for the medalists.

The ordinals for each skater were as follows:

Vladimir Kovalev, a two-time world champion from the Soviet Union

	URS	GDR	HUN	FRG	AUT	CSR	POL	FRA	GRB
Kovalev	1	2	2	3	2	1	2	3	4
Hoffmann	3	1	3	1	1	2	1	4	2
Cousins	2	3	1	2	3	3	3	1	1
Simond	4	4	4	4	4	4	4	2	3

Had Simond not won the second-place vote, Kovalev would have won the competition, because he would have had seven ordinals that were second-placed or better, while Hoffmann had only six. However, Simond took away one of Kovalev's second-place ordinals, leaving him with a count of only six, the same as Hoffmann. Accountants had to go another route to break this tie; when they took the sum of the ordinals, Hoffman won with a sum of eighteen

Charlie Tickner
of the United
States won
the 1978 world
championship
in one of the
closest finishes
in history,
even though
only two of
nine judges
voted him best.
He won on
a majority
of first- and
second-place
ordinals.

in ordinals, Kovalev, twenty (the lower the sum, the better). Cousins finished third because he had only five first- or second-place ordinals, but, interestingly enough, the sum of his ordinals was nineteen, lower than Kovalev's.

The situation was such an unusual one that it caught the European media unaware, according to British reporter Sandra Stevenson, who attended the event. Because Simond skated last and wasn't expected to break into the top three, and because the event was running late, Dutch television went off the air claiming that Kovalev had won. "Pandemonium reigned in the press room when journalists sought to explain this amazing situation briefly," she wrote.

A similar but slightly less dramatic situation occurred during the 1978 world championship in Ottawa, when three skaters, Charlie Tickner of the United States, Hoffmann, and Cousins, finished in a virtual three-way tie for first place, each receiving first-place votes from judges.

	BRD	CSR	AUT	USA	GBR	GDR	JPN	CAN	FRA
Tickner	2	3	2	1	2	2	2	2	1
Hoffmann	3	1	1	3	3	1	1	3	2
Cousins	1	4	3	2	1	4	3	1	3
Kovalev	4	2	4	4	10	3	4	4	5

Tickner won the title, even though he had only two first-place votes, while Hoffmann had four and Cousins had three. Because none had a majority of first-place votes, accountants had to look at the number of first- and second-place ordinals, and because Tickner had an admirable collection of those, he won.

In singles and pairs events, the short program is worth one-third of the final mark, the long program, two-thirds. Ice dancing is slightly different, because the event is composed of three segments: two compulsory dances (each worth 10 per cent), an original dance (30 per cent), and a free-dance (worth 50 per cent). Once the winners of each segment of an event are determined, the final results are tabulated by the adding together of factored placements that are assigned to each segment. The lower the value of the factored placement, the better. (The use of factored placements has been in place since the 1981 season.) For example, the value assigned to the singles or pairs technical program is 0.5, to the long programs, 1.0. Each amount is multiplied by a skater's placing in each event.

This system sometimes sets up intriguing results. At the 1992 world junior figure-skating championships in Hull, Quebec, Laetitia Hubert of France won the gold medal, even though she won neither the technical (now called the short) nor the long programs. However, she proved to be the most consistent skater. When Hubert finished third in the technical program, she earned 1.5 factored points (0.5 x 3). When she finished second in the long program, she earned 2.0 (1.0 x 2). She won with a total of 3.5 points, the lowest attained by any skater.

Lisa Ervin of the United States won the technical program, but finished only fourth in the long program, leaving her with the following final score: (0.5 x 1) + (1.0 x 4)= 4.5. With that score, she won the silver medal. Lu Chen of China finished only ninth in the technical program, but won the free-skate, earning (0.5 x 9) + (1.0 x 1)= 5.5 to win the bronze medal. If skaters are tied after all sections are completed, the winner of the free-dance or long program is the overall winner.

In ice dancing, the factored placements points are 0.4 for the compulsory dances, 0.6 for the original dance, and 1.0 for the free-dance.

Judges do more than count up the number of times a skater falls on his or her backside during the pressure of a competition. There are jumps and spins and footwork and edges to consider. Generally, the more difficult the content in the program, the higher the base mark a skater gets.

Laetitia Hubert of France won the 1992 world junior championship even though she had won neither the short nor the long programs. She benefited from a marking system that rewards the most consistent skaters throughout the competition.

In a short program for singles and pairs events, skaters must perform eight required elements. If a skater misses an element (or adds one that isn't required), the judge deducts a certain number of marks. For example, if a skater omits a required jump or fails to do the required rotations, the deduction is 0.5. In the past, it has been disastrous if a skater missed a combination jump (two jumps done successively, without a step in between); he or she would face up to a 0.6 deduction. However, as of July 1, 1994, the ISU has reduced the penalty for missing a combination to lessen the stress placed upon a skater during a competition. Currently, the deductions for a failed combination jump are the same as those for an unsuccessful solo jump, spin, flying spin, or spin combination, ranging from 0.1 to 0.4, depending on the seriousness of the error.

If a skater is going to fall during a combination, it is better to do it after the second part, because the deductions are less severe. If the skater makes an inappropriate turn in the midst of a two-jump combination, the loss is 0.2. If a skater lands a solo jump on two feet or steps out of a jump rather than landing it cleanly on one foot, the judge deducts 0.4. The mistake is less serious if a skater touches down with his or her free foot on a jump landing; he or she may lose 0.2. If a skater touches a hand to the ice for support on a landing, 0.2 is lost. A skater is now asked to use a sequence of steps to go into one of the jumps, but if he or she uses only simple crosscuts, the skater is docked 0.2. If a skater does not have a well-defined position in the air on a flying spin, he or she can count on losing from between 0.1 to 0.4, depending on the seriousness of the transgression.

While doing spins, a skater must do six rotations in this section, or, if the spin has a change of foot, five rotations on each foot. Are they quick spins? Are they centered and not traveling across the ice? Do the spins have the required changes of position? Does a flying spin have the correct position in the air?

In a long program, a judge doesn't deduct marks in the same way; rather, he or she gives a skater credit for what is accomplished. A skater will get credit for a quadruple jump, but, in spite of all the hype about them, a correctly landed quad is really worth only 0.1 extra; a jump takes only a fraction of a second to complete.

A judge will look at the way a skater does a jump: Is it high and done in an erect position? Is the takeoff and landing clean? Is it done with speed? Is the technique correct? Is the jump difficult?

Flip Jump

Step sequences can vary greatly in difficulty, too. Does the skater turn in only one direction? Is there a quick change of edges, as well as direction? Is the movement smooth in doing them? Do the steps conform to the music?

In the singles free-skate, the judge looks for a well-balanced program that includes a variety of jumps, at least one jump combination, a minimum of four spins, step sequences, linking movements, and a minimum of two-foot skating.

Jumps, which combine three major forces wrapped up into a burst of energy, are the most difficult highlights of a program. There are two kinds of jumps, those done from edges (Salchows, Axels, and loops), and those assisted by toe picks on the blade (toe loops, flips, and Lutzes).

All jumps are landed with the skater moving backwards on an outside edge. Most are also launched with the skater moving backwards. The exception is the Axel, in which a skater turns forward into the jump, gaining momentum by the swing of the free leg upward. Because it is also landed backwards, the Axel has an extra half rotation. A double Axel has two and a half rotations, a triple Axel, three and a half rotations.

The jump considered the easiest of all is the toe loop, followed in order of increasing difficulty by the Salchow, loop, flip, Lutz, and Axel. A double Lutz is said to be more difficult than a double flip, but when a skater moves into triple rotations, some will say that the flip becomes the more difficult jump because of the difficulty in timing and of placing the right toe pick into the ice at exactly the right moment and position, while the left foot sails along on a curving backward inside edge.

In a toe-loop jump, a skater takes off from a backward outside edge but picks with the left foot. (Some skaters, however, like 1981 world champion Denise Biellmann of Switzerland and 1983 world champion Rosalyn Sumners of the United States, jump from the opposite feet. They are left-footed in the same way that some people are left-handed.)

Toe Loop

A skater gets power for the Salchow jump from the action of the free leg. A skater enters it from a backward inside edge, then swings the free leg forward and up.

A loop jump is unusual and difficult because a skater takes off and lands on the same leg, with hardly any help from free leg or arm action to give the jump momentum. The takeoff is from a backward outside edge, but the knee of the weight-bearing leg must be bent deeply to give the jump an upward thrust.

The Lutz jump is actually similar to the flip, except that, in the Lutz, a skater takes off from a long ride on a backward outside edge. It is a particularly difficult jump because a skater must turn in one direction to prepare for takeoff but, once picking from the toe, launches into the air in the opposite direction.

There are few really good spinners in the world today, but a good spin can be an exciting tour de force, the skater hurling like a top on the flat part of the blade. To prevent dizziness coming out of a spin, a skater focuses on something specific and never lets the gaze wander. Karl Schaefer of Austria, who won world titles from 1930 to 1936 and Olympic gold medals in 1932 and 1936, did the first blur spin, rotating so quickly that it was impossible to discern a particular body part. At the time, critics said the spin was "circus-like," and not skating at all.

There are many different kinds of spins: scratch spins, sit spins, camel spins. The scratch spin is very fast and can be quite dramatic, with legs crossed and hands pushed down. Most spins are done on a backward inside edge. Only a few skaters, like Toller Cranston, are able to spin on the forward outside edge, which gives them a good position for the camel spin.

Flying Sit Spin

Flying Camel Spin

Forward Camel Spin

Salchow

The sit spin is just that, a spin done in a sitting position. Over the last several decades, the sitting position has become gradually lower, and the lower, the better. A change sit spin occurs when the skater switches to the other foot during the spin, a manuever in which it is difficult to regain the speed after the switch. A skater should not rise out of the sit spin when changing feet, and that is not easy to do.

A camel spin was once considered "a girl's spin," until it became a required element in the short program during the 1973 season. It requires that a skater be able to stretch and extend a free leg horizontally to the ice. If the leg is not fully stretched out straight, it will cause the skater's backside to be pushed out in a very unappealing position. The free leg should never be below the head and the back should be arched. Picture a dog trying to catch its tail, and you have a camel spin, Carlo Fassi used to tell his pupils.

Pairs skaters do some of the same elements as singles skaters, but moves that are unique to pairs skating are difficult and often dangerous. A well-balanced pairs long program involves at least three different lifts, including twist moves, not more than two throw jumps, a spin combination, solo spins, and death spirals.

In a death spiral, the woman's descent to her low position must be gradual and controlled, while the man should be in a deep crouch with his knees bent, keeping the toe pick of his skate planted in the ice. He must not rock back off the toe pick, which can sometimes happen as the woman is lifted out of the spiral. The woman should not rest her head on the ice or support herself by touching a hand to the ice. All death spirals must have a minimum of one revolution after the man has attained his pivot position. More revolutions are more impressive. Both partners must exit the spiral on one foot.

There are four kinds of death spirals, depending on the edge the woman uses while she circles around her partner. The Protopopovs invented the forward inside death spiral in 1968 (the woman encircles the man while gliding forward, but on the inside edge of her blade) and presented it to the world in 1969. During this spiral, the woman leans sideways.

The original death spiral – done on a backward outside edge – was invented by Charlotte, the show-skater, and it is still considered one of the most difficult. The woman leans backwards during this spiral.

The backward inside death spiral is easy to spot, because the woman skates with her face and the front part of her body toward the ice. It is called a backward inside spiral because the woman is gliding backward, but on the inside edge of her blade.

The forward outside death spiral is the most difficult and is rarely seen. The woman requires great ankle strength to keep from losing her outside edge while moving forward on it. Isabelle Brasseur and Lloyd Eisler, the 1993 world pairs champions, have done this version in competition.

Often innovative versions of basic moves are created in the professional ranks. Barbara Underhill and Paul Martini, the 1984 world pairs champions – always known for their dramatic death spirals – do a version in which the man holds the woman's outside arm to allow her to drop even closer to the ice. It is an unusual spectacle.

While pairs are doing lifts, judges must see that the woman makes a minimum of two and a half revolutions in the air, while the man, showing no signs of strain, does a maximum of three. Generally, the more changes of hold and position attained, the more difficult the lift is, although Irina Rodnina has said a lift becomes more difficult if the female partner remains absolutely still while the male turns. Brasseur and Eisler are known for having some of the most difficult lifts. They do an impressive one-hand lift, in which Eisler does not just lift Brasseur into position from arm level but, in a dramatic display of strength, picks her up directly from the ice – with one arm, not two.

In the pairs technical program, a judge is to deduct from 0.1 to 0.4 for a failed double jump or lift and 0.5 for an omission, less-serious deductions than in the years before a July 1, 1994, rule change. All other elements carry less-disastrous deductions, ranging from 0.1 to 0.3 for a failed manuever and 0.4 for an omission.

But above all, unison is important in pairs skating. If a pair completes a series of death-defying throws and lifts and jumps but moves out of synchronization, that pair is in deep trouble. Circulars from the ISU even note that

Axel

The 1993
world pairs
champions
Isabelle Brasseur
and Lloyd
"Herbie" Eisler
of Canada
are known
for their
dramatic,
athletic exhibition
programs.
Brasseur is
shown here
in a lift that
is considered
illegal in
amateur
competition
because Eisler
is "carrying"
his partner
as she remains
stationary
in the air.

careful consideration must be given to the selection of an appropriate partner. "If the pair [has] a serious imbalance in their physical characteristics, which would result in an obvious lack of unison, it will be reflected in the mark for artistic impression."

Artistic impression, now called presentation, is a complicated matter. The ISU takes six pages to explain it in its judging manuals. In short, artistry involves the way in which a skater interprets his or her music, the expression, carriage, and style. Overall, a judge is looking for a total package, in which a skater's technical ability is matched by the artistic expression.

Ice dancing is a different story altogether, because it is a discipline with no jumps, spins, death spirals, or throws. Instead, judges compare edge quality, patterns on the ice, positions, turns, timing to the music on steps, and even whether the music is suitable. Ice dancing, states the ISU, must have the character of ballroom dancing, with erect bearing. The music for the free-dance must have a rhythmic beat and melody, thereby canceling out ballet music. Music arranged for the stage or theater is frowned upon, unless it has been rearranged specifically for use on the dance floor. The ISU now says that lack of timing – missing the beat of the music – is a very serious error.

In an effort to distinguish ice dancing from pairs skating, the ISU has ruled that only five lifts are permitted in dancing, and never should a man lift his partner in such a way that his hands stretch above his shoulder line. The lifts must also not display feats of strength or acrobatics. The partner must not be carried. Sitting or lying on the partner's shoulder or back is considered to be a feat of strength and is not permitted.

Speed across the ice is important in ice dancing, as is difficult footwork, done in perfect unison, with flow and glide and coverage of the ice. Edge quality – or the ability to curve about on the ice with blades at extreme angles rather than moving in straight lines – is a measure of skating finesse. So are soft knee-action and strength of stroke.

Both partners should share in the intricate footwork. In original dances, stopping and "excessive show-posing" fail to show an ability to flow over the ice and are restricted, depending on the dance rhythm chosen. Expression is of utmost importance in that most-ethereal of disciplines, ice dancing.

During the original program, dancers may be deducted from 0.1 to 0.4 for inappropriate music selection, incorrect timing, and lack of expression. Judges are to deduct 0.1 to 0.2 for inappropriate costumes. Still, although nobody seems to understand what makes one couple better than another, it is one of the most-watched disciplines in skating.

Pairs Skating

Ekaterina Gordeeva and Sergei Grinkov chose Spanish flamenco music for their original program when they made their amateur comeback at Skate Canada in Ottawa in November 1993. Unfortunately, Gordeeva's costume, made by the Bolshoi ballet, began to unravel during the fast-paced routine.

Pairs skating is not for the faint of heart.

With its spectacular lifts, throws, and twists, it is the most dangerous of figure-skating disciplines. Even the term "death spiral" conjures up images of ruined hearts, broken crowns, and bleak despair when, actually, it is a move of elegance.

Pairs skating is an extremely athletic discipline, but it can also be very beautiful. Some of the world's most treasured skaters have come from the pairs ranks: Ludmila and Oleg Protopopov of the former Soviet Union, Tai Babilonia and Randy Gardner of the United States, Barbara Underhill and Paul Martini of Canada, and Ekaterina Gordeeva and Sergei Grinkov of Russia are each an example of two beings passing unsung messages of harmony through their athletic feats.

Pairs skating first appeared in the annals of blade history during the 1880s. In Vienna in 1888, the world saw the first public exhibition of mixed pairs, a phenomenon that quickly overtook the common practice of men skating in pairs with each other or women in a twosome dashing about the ice. It caused a sensation. Before long, it was clear that unisex skating was not to be as popular as the new mix of sexes.

At first, pairs skating consisted of skaters merely holding hands while carrying out the elements of solo skating. Sometimes it brought nations together. The fourth world pairs championship was won by Ludowika Eilers of Germany and Walter Jakobsson of Finland, when nobody else showed up. A year later, they married, and Eilers changed her name and her nationality. The pair came back as the Jakobssons to show that their 1911 win was no fluke; they also triumphed at the world championships in 1914 and 1923.

Although Austria distinguished itself by producing top-quality singles skaters, in that country pairs skating was a cherished discipline and a specialty. The Viennese were the first to break from the tradition of mere hand-in-hand skating.

Ludmila Belousova and Oleg Protopopov are shown performing a two-handed overhead lift at Colorado Springs, where they won their first world title in 1965. They had married on December 6, 1957. They are still skating today, at ages fifty-nine and sixty-two, and when in their fifties, they learned to ski.

In general, Europeans ruled the ice before the Second World War, and their idea of a pure pair routine was beauty in symmetry, perfection in side-by-side skating, and a spate of single jumps. Twists and throws would have been unimaginable.

"There was a type of little, lifty throws," says Sheldon Galbraith, who coached two postwar world pairs champions from Canada. "The only thing you could compare it with today is if you got a juvenile pair of kids and they tried to do their idea of a pair. It was really very low key."

Andrée Joly and Pierre Brunet of France were two of the sport's most-celebrated prewar stars. Brunet won ten national singles championships and, with Joly, whom he later married, ruled pairs skating from the time they won their first world title on Valentine's Day in 1926. With their precise, classical style, the couple won four world titles over seven years, winning every time they competed. They added two Olympic gold medals in 1928 and 1932.

"They didn't skate every year," Galbraith says. "They skated at a championship and then went into hiding, so to speak, and developed their skills, and others couldn't see them. It isn't like it is today, with television."

In 1940, Brunet moved to the United States to coach and eventually tutored American Carol Heiss, Alain Calmat and Alain Giletti, both of France, and, for a time, Canadian Donald Jackson. All four of his students became world champions.

If Joly and Brunet were the aces of pairs skating before the war, German skaters Maxi Herber and Ernst Baier were its trumps. They were, on the surface, a strange match. When they won the 1936 Olympic gold medal in Garmisch-Partenkirchen, West Germany, Herber was only fifteen, Baier, a thirty-year-old architect from Berlin. Eventually, they also married.

Together, they were the epitome of prewar pairs skating, with their style of shadow skating, in which both skaters perform the same moves in exact parallel while skating several feet apart. Their unison was so outstanding that they could do side-by-side spins with a change of foot in complete symmetry, while other skaters resorted to pairs spins that didn't require such perfect unison. Their performance was also highly unusual for the time because the German government commissioned a top-level composer to write music to suit their style, so that every note complemented their movements. With this intriguing concept of pairs skating, they won four world titles from 1936 to 1939.

Then the war struck, and it changed everything – but slowly.

Skaters in North America were learning the best of techniques from the best of coaches, some of them Canadian, some European émigrés, while skating stood still on the war-torn continent. When the world championships resumed after the war, European pairs skaters recast themselves in the only mold they knew – that of the skaters of prewar Europe. But North Americans were fascinated now with new techniques that were more athletic, challenging, and complex. And in the years before the Soviets began to dominate the sport with the Protopopovs in 1965, the Canadian pairs became an exciting, innovative force that led the sport in new directions. However, the derring-do of the Canadians didn't always sit well with judging panels, which were made up mostly of Europeans.

Canadian pair Suzanne Morrow and Wally Distelmeyer were the first to challenge the status quo at the 1948 world championship and the Olympic Games. Both brought impressive skating skills to the contest; they had swept

Ekaterina Gordeeva and Sergei Grinkov married in 1991 and are the proud parents of their daughter, Daria.

almost every discipline – pairs, dance, and singles – at the Canadian championship that year. (Barbara Ann Scott won the Canadian championship in 1948, but Morrow won three consecutive women's titles in the next three years.)

At the world championship in Davos, Switzerland, and the Olympics in St. Moritz, Morrow and Distelmeyer did a whole array of double jumps, including a double Lutz – all skated at great speed – and were the first to perform a death spiral the way it is seen today, with the woman's head nearly brushing the ice, as the man, holding her hand, pivoted in a circle. Other pairs had tried a few double jumps, but not very successfully. And other pairs had tried a kind of death spiral before, but the woman merely leaned back a little, with the toe pick scratching the ice as the male partner dragged her. "They hadn't perfected the support for the girl, and the girls hadn't supported themselves well in strength development," Galbraith says.

Before the Canadians showed up, death-spiral attempts had been made with a two-hand hold. Morrow and Distelmeyer started out doing them with

two hands and then changed to one hand, another first. The use of only one hand allowed the woman to drop into a lower position. "It just happened," Distelmeyer says. "We thought it would be more spectacular to get into the low position."

Clearly, they offered something new. Still, they finished only third in both events, hexed by an illegal carry lift that happened to be their opening move. "That kind of wiped us out," Distelmeyer says. "I was on one foot and I held her in the air and held the edge very long, right around the rink."

It was their first and only appearance in world and Olympic events.

Galbraith, who did not coach Morrow and Distelmeyer, says the Canadians deserved to win the gold medal in both events that year, at least on North American terms of how pairs skating had developed. "They were not accepted," he said. "The European concept prevailed. The Europeans were doing waltz jumps, Salchows, in symmetry, very nice unison, but much simpler stuff."

But Morrow and Distelmeyer were the first signs of a rising pairs force in Canada that existed until the Soviets descended upon the sport with a sudden rush during the 1960s. Between 1954 and 1962, Canada won seven of eight world pairs titles, including those won by Frances Dafoe and Norris Bowden (1954, 1955), Barbara Wagner and Robert Paul (1957 to 1960), and Maria and Otto Jelinek (1962).

Wagner and Paul, coached by Galbraith, were the last Canadians of any discipline to win an Olympic gold figure-skating medal when they took the prize in 1960. And two of only four pairs that were able to break a formidable thirty-year Soviet domination that had started with the Protopopovs in 1965

ICE CAPERS OF 1941

CLARKSON-NORMAL
ELEVENTH ANNUAL ICE CARNIVAL
POTSDAM, NEW YORK
FEBRUARY 6, 7, 8, 1941

TORONTO SKATING CLUB

1940
25

THIRTY-THIRD ANNUAL
CARNIVAL

America Skates

19 41

OLYMPIC ARENA   LAKE PLACID

PRICE 25¢

Toronto Follies

At the
AUDITORIUM · OTTAWA
February 26th and 27th 1943

Carnivals and other lavish productions were popular throughout North America during the 1940s and 1950s. The Toronto Skating Club was famous for its skating innovations, and the events often attracted skaters from around the world, such as Sonja Henie of Norway, Jacqueline du Bief of France, and Barbara Ann Scott of Canada.

were Canadians: Barbara Underhill and Paul Martini (1984) and Isabelle Brasseur and Lloyd Eisler (1993).

"[Canadians] always skated pairs and singles and fours, always more than one event," says Canadian coach Peter Dunfield. "I think it's because Canadians were always doing carnivals. And if you went to a show, you couldn't just stand on your own solo, you had to do pairs. Some little towns in the north could only afford to bring in two good skaters. So if you got invited to Kirkland Lake, you did a solo, and if you could, you did a pair with a girl that was invited. And if there were four of you, you did a four."

In fact, Canada is one of the few countries in the world that offers fours events at the national championship. With intermittent breaks, Canada has staged fours competitions since 1914. Even David Dore, director general of the Canadian Figure Skating Association, may boast that he is a fours champion. However, immediately after his win in 1964, there was a seventeen-year break until the event was revived in 1982. Several others countries, such as the Soviet Union, Germany, and the United States, had fours skating on a limited basis, but it was largely unknown in other countries.

In the years after the Second World War, Canada bustled with elaborate, popular carnivals at all the major skating clubs, mainly in Ontario. The trend actually started before the war, but continued with a flourish during the late 1940s and 1950s, and then spread to the United States. "Those shows, especially the Toronto Skating Club show, well, you've never seen anything like it," Dunfield says.

"The costuming was extravagant for that era. They had a symphony orchestra playing live. The Toronto Skating Club innovated so many things, with costumes and painted ice. They would work the whole year on the show. So many talented people came out of the club."

Some of them included Dafoe and Bowden, who became the first North Americans to win a world pairs title. The athletic, innovative couple, under Galbraith's guidance, came within one-tenth of a point of winning the 1953 world championship. (Britons Jennifer and John Nicks won instead with "an engaging charm," according to British skating author, official, and competitor Captain T. D. Richardson.) But the Canadians finally succeeded in 1954 and 1955. Dafoe and Bowden finished second at both the 1956 world championship and the Olympic Games, amid judging controversies.

When the petite Dafoe and lanky Bowden arrived on the scene, all pairs were doing the same lifts and moves. But Galbraith had a plan. "I don't think we can beat them at their own game," he said. "So we'll have to have our own game."

Two-time world pairs champions Frances Dafoe and Norris Bowden performed unusual pairs moves that "if not timed to perfection would lead to disaster," according to British skater and author Captain T. D. Richardson. "The striking Axel Paulsen jump of Frances into her partner's arms is one which makes a most sensational curtain to a quick-moving performance full of surprises."

Dafoe and Bowden deliberately did not do any of the accepted lifts and pairs moves. At the time, a woman was raised off the ice in what is now known as a lasso lift, but was never really pushed up into the air. Supported by the man, the women merely did a jump that swung around to the male's back. Dafoe and Bowden made the move far more dramatic. They hoisted it into the air.

Dafoe and Bowden also did the first twist lift, throw jump, catch lift, pressure lift, and another they called an Axel-under-the-arms catch. They would also do a throw, followed by a pivot spin with a lift involved in it, all very complicated and novel. Many of their moves were later ruled illegal, but the twist lift is currently a major part of pairs skating, although the takeoff that is presently used is from a different position.

In the now-illegal catch lift, Dafoe, while executing a full turn, would jump into the arms of Bowden, who was in a spinning position. A copy of the move eventually showed up in the professional routine of Underhill and Martini. Whenever they perform it, the crowd gasps. But Dafoe and Bowden did it first at the 1956 Olympics in Cortina.

"When we went into competition, everybody said 'Oh my god, these people are too athletic,'" Dafoe says. "Because we were so different in many ways, the Europeans particularly were looking at ways to discredit us. But when you look at what they're doing today, it's really a bit of a laugh."

In fact, pairs skating over the last thirty years has probably changed in difficulty more than any other branch of skating, says John Nicks, adding that competitors in his day were strong individual skaters in jumping, spinning, speed, and footwork but were far behind today's skaters in lifts and throws. The performance that brought him and his sister victory in 1953 would not have been good enough to place among the top twenty-four at the 1994 world championship, he says.

While the Protopopovs brought artistry, and the spontaneous standing ovation, to pairs skating, their successors, Irina Rodnina and her two partners Alexei Ulanov and Alexander Zaitsev, dazzled their opponents with their athletics – speed, a variety of novel lifts, and jumps. Rodnina and Ulanov were so spectacular when they first burst upon the world scene in 1969 that they won the world championship, breaking all the unspoken rules of skating seniority that existed at the time. (It was unusual for a skater to win a world title in a first appearance.)

The partnership broke up after a win at the 1972 world championship in Calgary, because Ulanov had eyes only for Ludmila Smirnova, who won the Olympic silver pairs medal with her Soviet partner Andrei Suraikin.

(Top) 1953 world pairs champions Jennifer and John Nicks, a brother-and-sister team from Britain.
(Left) Soviet skater Irina Rodnina became a skating star first with partner Alexei Ulanov, winning four world titles and an Olympic gold medal. The team broke up when Ulanov fell in love with another pairs skater.

Just before the Calgary competition, Ulanov married Smirnova and eventually formed a pairs partnership with her. After her Calgary win with Ulanov, Rodnina left the ice in tears, knowing it was their last performance together.

But her career wasn't over. Rodnina was such a star that the Soviets closed down a rink for a week while she auditioned over one hundred males. The rather inexperienced Zaitsev proved to be the best choice.

Rodnina was the perfect female partner to make a successful pair. She was tiny, at 4 feet, 11 inches (147.5 centimeters), intense, and brave, in spite of crashes and illnesses. Zaitsev, with whom she won six world titles and two of her three Olympic gold medals, was strong and much taller than his partner, at 5 feet, 10 inches (175 centimeters), and he trained by wearing a massive weight belt and by toting around a 71-pound (32-kilogram) weight in each hand.

Without a flinch, they did triple twist moves (a sort of a cross between a lift and a throw, which involves the man catching his partner) and an amazing array of lifts. Brunet, the prewar master of pairs skating, denounced the trend toward athleticism, saying skating had become "a sport for kangaroos."

"I admired [Rodnina] the most of any competitor I've ever seen," Nicks says. "She had such concentration and such determination over such a period of time, with two different partners. That is just an incredible record."

Rodnina was also the first woman to do a double Axel in a pairs routine. It has became a common jump for pairs skaters to do only in the past half-dozen years and is a jump that even now can cause top skaters much grief.

"Their jumps were all very fast and very sure and with great unison," Nicks says. "I think the Russians have certainly brought speed and stroking ability to skating generally. Usually the Russian skaters spend a lot of time on basic skating skills and jumps and footwork and strong, powerful stroking."

Babilonia and Gardner, coached by Nicks, were not blessed with the height and weight differential enjoyed by the trailblazing Soviets and did only a double twist in their final year of competition. The American team distinguished themselves with their elegant style and beautiful lines on the ice, but those attributes did not seem to be enough to match Rodnina's cascade of tricks. Nicks decided to fight fire with fire and sent them to U.S. coach Ron Luddington, who taught them to do throw double Axels and the first throw triple Salchow done in competition. (In 1977, Soviets Irina Vorobieva and Alexander Vlasov, the world silver medalists, attempted the first throw triple Salchow but were unsuccessful.) In these moves, the woman prepares to do an Axel or a Salchow but, instead of jumping, is hoisted through the air by the man in an explosive fashion.

*Tai Babilonia
and Randy Gardner
were the first U.S.
pair to win a
world title in
twenty-nine years
when they skated
a perfect program
in 1979. Later
the pressures
surrounding
Babilonia pushed
her into a drug
dependency. She
conquered it and
reconciled
professionally
with Gardner in
1989. In 1990,
NBC aired a
television movie,
On Thin Ice,
that revealed
Babilonia's trials.*

Rodnina never did throw moves, which cause great wear and tear on a woman's leg, as it absorbs the shock of landing a twenty-five-foot (seven-and-a-half-meter) toss over the ice. Contemporary throws were first done by an East German pair, Manuela Gross and Uwe Kagelmann, who competed throughout the early 1970s and won bronze medals at the 1973 and 1975 world championships. In 1974, Melissa Militano and Johnny Johns of the United States did a throw triple loop, a move copied later by Eastern Europeans.

Rodnina and her partners also may have sparked a later trend in which pairs events became a race of speed across the ice, with countless, undisciplined twists, lifts, and throws, and few other redeeming qualities. However, unlike Rodnina, the pairs that followed embraced throws, particularly if they had a large size-and-weight differential. The smaller the woman, the easier it was for a man to execute these pairs elements.

The best-known of the small-and-tall pair, Marina Cherkasova and Sergei Shakhrai of the Soviet Union, actually upstaged Rodnina and Zaitsev at the 1977 European championship in Helsinki, Finland, by doing the first quadruple twist. This effort earned the "flea-and-gorilla pair" a bronze medal. That same year, Cherkasova and Shakhrai finished fourth at the world championship and inspired other countries to develop similar pairs.

Cherkasova and Shakhrai won the 1980 Olympic silver medal when Babilonia and Gardner were forced to withdraw at the last moment due to an injury, and, a month later, the Soviets won the gold medal at the 1980 world championship over a thin field that lacked both the Americans and Rodnina and Zaitsev, who had taken an early retirement.

However, the success of Cherkasova and Shakhrai proved short-lived when the girl began to sprout. At the outset, Cherkasova, with her toothpick legs, stood barely as high as Shakhrai's armpit. But by the time of the 1981 world championship, they could finish only fourth, because Shakhrai could not adjust to the weight and height changes of his partner. The partnership eventually dissolved.

Their passing left a lasting legacy. Today, the vast majority of pairs skaters have a height differential of between 9 and 14 inches (23 and 25 centimeters) and a weight disparity of about 75 to 80 pounds (34 to 36 kilograms), Nicks says. A height differential even makes some variations of death spirals much easier.

In the early 1980s, the ISU put a stop to some of the acrobatics plaguing pairs and singles skating by specifying certain moves that must be included in free-skating programs. The new rules also stipulated that marks would be deducted if skaters showed a lack of connecting steps between the athletic moves. Those rules were intended to give a strong boost to artistry and good choreography in pairs skating. And the Soviets, with their strong, long history of choreography, excelled.

Elena Valova and Oleg Vasiliev made their first appearance at a world championship in 1983 and won it with interesting and novel balletic positions and fascinating footwork. They did not neglect the athletic side, either.

Elena Valova and Oleg Vasiliev, the once-married couple from St. Petersburg, miraculously finished second at the 1988 Calgary Olympics after Valova "came back from the grave," according to famous Soviet pairs coach Tamara Moskvina. When doctors improperly froze her left ankle to correct an earlier injury, they almost induced gangrene in the foot.

They astonished spectators – and judges – when they landed side-by-side triple toe-loop jumps at a time when a triple jump in a pairs program was unimaginable. Valova's execution of the jump was particularly significant, because female singles skaters had only just started to land triple jumps in great numbers. Pairs skaters tend to do less-athletic singles moves.

Underhill and Martini defeated Valova and Vasiliev at the world championship the following year with less-athletic moves, but they displayed an overall quality of pairs skating that few attain. During their long-lived professional career, which has spanned ten years, some have been moved to call Underhill and Martini the best pairs skaters that have ever lived. "I consider

When Barbara
Underhill and
Paul Martini won
their world title
in 1984, the
crowd burst into
deafening applause
before they had
finished their
flawless program.
Underhill said
she could feel the
vibration of the
noise under her
feet. "We came
from the very
bottom to the
very top in two
and a half weeks,"
said Martini. At
one point, coach
Louis Stong had
even considered
telling the pair
not to compete
at the world
championship
because of their
disastrous practices
that followed a
deflating seventh-
place Olympic
performance.

*As amateurs,
Barbara Underhill
and Paul Martini
were known for
their dramatic
low-to-the-ice
death spirals,
explosive throw
triple Salchows,
and a backward,
upside-down lift.*

what they do as pairs skating," says their amateur coach Louis Stong. "People who get rewarded now tend to be two great singles skaters who happen to be on the ice at the same time."

Stong feels that Underhill and Martini's gifts were the communion between them and the emotions they evoke when they skate. "He was very sympathetic to her," Stong says. "You'll see he turns toward her. They always had eyes for each other. In other words, whenever they could, choreographically, they looked at each other, so that there was this strong sense of communion between them. It's a wonderful thing."

Immediately after the retirement of Underhill and Martini, a phenomenon emerged in pairs skating. This new marvel was Ekaterina Gordeeva and Sergei Grinkov, and their aim was harmony and perfection. They came as close to it as anyone in pairs skating ever has.

In their early days, they were an athletic wonder, landing rare quadruple twists and, eventually, side-by-side triple toe-loops. But always, in spite of the workload, there was the shining face of little Gordeeva, her tiny feet skimming over the ice, weightless, wondrous, radiating glory, as if holding a light for her tall, shy, and silent partner to follow.

World junior champions one year (1985) and world senior champions the next, Gordeeva and Grinkov were expected to launch a dynasty that would rule the pairs skating world as long and unquestionably as Rodnina and Zaitsev. Gordeeva was only sixteen and Grinkov was twenty when they won the 1988 Olympic gold medal in Calgary, Alberta. But suddenly, under

the pressure of being the sport's best and future legends, they began to look human. Although they won the Olympic gold medal in Calgary, they faltered and lost it at the world championship in Budapest, Hungary, a month later. "I was really tired after the Olympic Games, and I didn't want to skate any more," Gordeeva says. Also, she began to grow. "I was sixteen years old, and all girls change then."

Still, for two and a half years more, they pressed on, in spite of health problems – Gordeeva developed bone chips in her foot, which kept her off the ice once for three months, and Grinkov suffered shoulder problems that eventually required surgery – and won two more world championships. Finally, after winning the Goodwill Games in Seattle, Washington, in the fall of 1990, Gordeeva and Grinkov had had enough of competition pressures and decided to turn professional.

Grinkov knew better than anyone else how extraordinary his partner was. So he married her. And when they decided to reinstate as amateurs for the 1994 season, they already had a daughter, Daria, who was less than one and a half years old at the time they went to the 1994 Lillehammer Olympics. Gordeeva had been back on the ice just three weeks after the birth. With Daria to inspire them, they won Olympic gold again.

And at ages twenty-two and twenty-six, they were better than ever. "I think we learned a lot from professional skating," Gordeeva said. "I think we have started to skate like we feel each other better now. That is very important in pairs skating." And they made everything difficult look easy, with complex entrances into lifts and throws and soft sure landings from twist moves and lifts. "We may never see their like again," said an ISU committee member.

For their comeback, Gordeeva and Grinkov skated to Beethoven's "Moonlight Sonata," a musical masterpiece of pale beauty that seemed as if it were written for Gordeeva and Grinkov, with their ghostlike air, the sound of their blades almost inaudible as they traced watery trails. Their perfect unison seemed instinctive, unhesitating, certainly unequaled. Even though they made four mistakes during the 1994 Olympic free-skate, judges placed them first.

"In pairs, unison and unison is what counts," said one international judge. "Unless the performance has unison, judges don't care how difficult the elements are. Gordeeva and Grinkov's unison is superb. No movement is superfluous. The hardest thing to do is not to move, to keep an arm still.

"[Olympic silver medalists Natalia Mishkuteniok and Artur Dmitriev] had an awful lot of extra arm motions that didn't really belong. They weren't doing those kind of things in Albertville [where they won the Olympic gold medal in 1992]. They had been sick and fighting it, and it showed [in Lillehammer]. They know how to do it, but they didn't do it in Lillehammer. They were ragged."

Still, in spite of all their hardships – they were suffering from the flu before the Olympics, and they had a very serious fall while attempting a difficult lift during practice in Lillehammer – Mishkuteniok and Dmitriev won the silver Olympic medal in 1994, impressing spectators with their wild energy and dramatic, innovative moves, some of them showing off Mishkuteniok's unusual flexibility.

With both Russian pairs concentrating on professional tours, the mantle for the future has fallen to Russian skaters again, with the victory of Evgenia Shishkova and Vadim Naumov at the 1994 world championship over

Ekaterina Gordeeva & Sergei Grinkov

"My father always wanted me to dance because he was dancer. He wanted me to be a ballerina. He was a folk dancer. I like to dance, but I didn't want to study in a ballet school. I did some examinations at [the Bolshoi ballet school] but I didn't really want to study this, and I wanted to skate, and it doesn't matter to me how to skate, by myself or not. I was just happy that [coach Stanislav Zhuk] brought us [she and Grinkov] together and that somebody pay attention to me and I wasn't worried that my father was going to take me back to ballet school. I like to dance, but not all my life." – Ekaterina Gordeeva, 1988 and 1994 Olympic pairs champion with Sergei Grinkov, on her early experiences with dance

Natalia Mishkuteniok & Artur Dmitriev

Natalia Mishkuteniok and Artur Dmitriev of Russia are known and loved for their dramatic routines. After they won the 1992 Olympic pairs gold medal in Albertville, they turned professional, without great success. After having quickly risen to Olympic stardom, Mishkuteniok lost sight of her goals, skated without inspiration, gained weight, and almost drove Dmitriev to find a new partner. In January 1993, Mishkuteniok decided to join Dmitriev, who was determined to reinstate as an amateur for the 1994 Olympics, with or without his partner. Mishkuteniok lost nine pounds (four kilograms) and cut her hair and, with renewed enthusiasm, helped Dmitriev win the 1994 Olympic silver medal with passionate, if not quite perfect, performances.

The career of Isabelle Brasseur and Lloyd Eisler was hampered a few times by Eisler's gimpy knees. In 1991, Eisler collided with a goalpost during a pick-up hockey game and incurred so much damage to ligaments that he underwent one and a half hours of surgery and had to wear a leg brace while skating. The following-ing season—the one leading up to the 1992 Olympics— he underwent a second operation on his other knee, which had taken stress because of the first injury.

Canadians Isabelle Brasseur, who was hampered by a cracked rib, and Lloyd Eisler. Brasseur and Eisler, known for their awe-inspiring, high triple twists (early in their career, they practiced quadruple twists but never did them in competition), throws, and difficult, complicated lifts, have also left the amateur life behind.

Shishkova and Naumov, who have long been hovering about the footlights of the medal podium, offer beautiful body lines, innovative lifts, and a pair quality that is stronger than their individual skating abilities.

"Naumov is probably one of the best pairs partners since Paul Martini," Stong says. "He handles the girl beautifully. He's very sympathetic in the way he places her down on the ice. I wish they could skate faster. Their side-by-side jumps seem small, but maybe that's because of lack of speed."

"There are too many changes now in Russia. Conditions for our training are very hard. Too many pairs skate on one rink at once," said Vadim Naumov, who trains in St. Petersburg with his pairs partner, Evgenia Shishkova. Still, Shishkova and Naumov, who is a sports instructor, won the 1994 world pairs championship.

Shishkova and Naumov are one of the few pairs who do side-by-side triple toe-loops. That may impress some judges, but it doesn't impress Stong. Brasseur and Eisler did [easier] double Axels, but that doesn't warrant a placing below a couple who does a more difficult solo move, says Stong, who believes pairs skaters should be judged mainly on their abilities to execute moves that are specific to pairs. Stong was concerned about a rule change made by the ISU Congress in June 1994 that allows pairs to do triple jumps

Isabelle Brasseur & Lloyd Eisler

Isabelle Brasseur and Lloyd Eisler have battled almost insurmountable odds during their career. They fell into a bleak despair and almost quit after they finished only seventh of eleven pairs at the 1989 world championship in Paris. Brasseur, who had fallen on double Axels, took to heart the television comments that she was a frail skater who could not jump. "She believed she was terrible and she was totally in pieces," said her long-time coach Josée Picard. It took her six months to regain her consistency on jumps. However, the pair pulled everything together to win the silver medal at the 1990 world championship in Halifax.

Radka Kovarikova & Rene Novotny

(Left) Czech skaters Radka Kovarikova and Rene Novotny perform a one-handed overhead lift. After being together only four years and training in dismal conditions in Czechoslovakia, the graceful pair won world silver medals. (Above) Kovarikova and Novotny perform a backward inside death spiral. They were an unusual pairs match-up from the beginning. Novotny, at twenty-nine, had already skated with three partners before he approached the tiny Kovarikova, who was only thirteen and had only a few months' experience skating with a partner, doing a few side-by-side moves but no throws. Together, however, they are magic. Kovarikova's shining poise and posture are a perfect foil to Novotny's tall, lyrical grace. They won a silver medal at the 1992 world championship, the first pairs medal won by a Czechoslovakian couple in thirty-four years.

during the short program, thereby emphasizing solo skating skills over pairs moves. It is an unfortunate direction in which to drive pairs skating, he says.

Traditionally, Canadian pairs have been stronger in pairs movements than in solo jumps. Currently, the pairs skaters who are trying triple jumps are Russian, or are from former Soviet countries, from Germany, or from Czechoslovakia. At the 1994 world championship, more than half a dozen pairs attempted triple toe-loops, not all successfully. (At the 1994 Olympics, Gordeeva and Grinkov did not include the jump, while Mishkuteniok and Dmitriev did.) Two of them were Radka Kovarikova and Rene Novotny of the Czech Republic and Mandy Woetzel and Ingo Steuer of Germany, each of whom had won a silver medal at a world championship – the Czechs in 1992 and the Germans in 1993.

Woetzel and her partner Steuer, a twenty-eight-year-old soldier who also surfs and paints, are an athletic pair, whose path to the 1994 Olympics was star-crossed. They were forced to withdraw from Skate Canada in Ottawa during the 1994 season when Woetzel's elbow struck Steuer during a lift, causing him to fall backwards, hit his head, and suffer a concussion. Then, during the Lillehammer Olympics, Woetzel fell flat on her face when her toe pick caught in the ice as she and her partner were doing a hand-in-hand spiral, and she had to be carried off the ice. They finished fourth at the world championship without a hitch, but Steuer, in jest, carried his partner off the ice again anyway.

The Czechs, Kovarikova and Novotny, the only senior pairs skaters in their country for much of their career together, were concerned that conditions in their homeland were so poor that they might have to quit skating, even after they won a silver medal at the 1992 world championship. "Everything is harder and worse now," Kovarikova said. "Our federation isn't able to pay all expenses, and we are students, and we have no money to pay."

But help came from Americans Carol and Walter Probst, who set up an Ice Skating Institute of America, a foundation for helping needy skaters. The foundation pays room and board for the promising skaters to train at Ice Castle International Centre in Lake Arrowhead, California.

"I'm so surprised somebody in America would help us," Kovarikova said. She was also overwhelmed by American food. "There are a lot of vegetables and fruits," she said. "Everything is healthy. We feel it. We feel really different."

Russians Marina Eltsova and Andrei Bushkov have also benefitted from American largesse to train in Colorado Springs for short stints. "Socialism

Marina Eltsova and Andrei Buskhov, trained by the Protopopovs' coach, Igor Moskvin, were squeezed out of a berth for the Lillehammer Olympics with the return of the reinstated professionals, but they finished third at the world championship in Japan.

finish and capitalism start and everything really bad," Bushkov says, speaking of the hardship in his country.

Eltsova and Bushkov missed both the Olympics in 1992 and in 1994 with a run of bad luck. In 1992, they were unable to attend Albertville because Bushkov was recovering from bone chips in a leg, suffered when he fell after Eltsova landed on him during a lift in their performance at Skate Canada. In 1994, Eltsova and Bushkov were squeezed out of a berth at the Olympics when Gordeeva and Grinkov and Mishkuteniok and Dmitriev reinstated as amateurs. But they have to their credit a European championship title in 1993 and a win on a better day at Skate Canada in 1992, and currently they pose one of the greatest threats to win world gold in the future.

At the 1994 world championship, in finishing third, Eltsova and Bushkov lacked the expressive qualities of Shishkova and Naumov, but made up for it with other things, particularly high speed and fine edge quality. Their program was loaded with interesting, difficult elements linked together in unusual ways, including a triple twist that evolved almost immediately into a throw double Axel. As Eltsova lands the double Axel, she and Bushkov link hands.

But Eltsova and Bushkov may be the last of a dying breed: the dominant Russian pairs skater. Ten countries that once made up the Soviet Union sent entries to the 1994 world championship. Seven of them sent pairs. One former Soviet skater, Alexei Tikhonov, now skates for Japan with Jukiko Kawasaki.

"I think the impression that Russian skating is very deep and that they have these dozens and dozens of good competitors is a fallacy," Nicks says. "[At the 1994 world championship], the third Russian pair [was] good but not particularly outstanding. I would doubt whether the homegrown Russian system is going to continue to exist in the way we have seen it."

A promising pair of the future – Jelena Bereznaya and Oleg Shliakhov – now skate for Latvia, but obviously were trained in the former Soviet Union. They come armed with speed and overwhelming pairs tricks – high jumps, including triple toe-loops, and enormous triple twists rarely seen at the world level except from Brasseur and Eisler. Their performance at the 1994 world championship was impressive enough that the largely unknown Latvians elicited a standing ovation from part of the Japanese crowd. There, they finished seventh, but they even received a fourth-place vote from a Canadian judge.

A most poignant statement about pairs development in the world occurred at the 1994 Russian championship in St. Petersburg. Four years earlier in the same city, then know as Leningrad, Gordeeva and Grinkov won the 1990 European championship in front of fifteen thousand people. But at the solemn Russian championship of 1994, in which only eight pairs competed, Gordeeva and Grinkov, probably the most revered of pairs skaters, displayed their wares before no more than five hundred spectators. It may be the end of the era of Russian dominance but the start of a new one, as other countries that have taken up the pairs challenge anew race to fill a potential gap.

Pairs skating will never die in Russia, says Sergei Tchetveroukhin. It may only stumble a little in hard times.

Men's Singles

American David Jenkins, the 1960 Olympic champion, performs a spread-eagle. With tongue in cheek on the subject of his reinstatement to the amateur ranks, Jenkins wrote in the USFSA magazine Skating: "Regaining amateur status will seem a little like regaining my virginity, but I can foresee no stumbling block to my application. Lord knows I haven't been paid to perform in 25 years. . . . I haven't performed at all in 25 years."

If competitive skaters have one thing in common, it is that they lace up their skates faster than anybody, their fingers traveling nimbly from eyelet to eyelet.

But men's singles skaters are, in truth, singular. They are the power and the glory of skating, testing the bounds of danger with their gravity-defying jumps and sanguine display of tricks, making it all look easy with whisper-soft landings and the graceful arch of a back, the turn of a hip, or the stretch of an arm.

For the power, thank Ulrich Salchow, Axel Paulsen, Werner Rittberger, and all who dared jump over three hats piled on top of each other. For the glory, thank Toller Cranston and John Curry.

Power in male singles skating reached new heights following the Second World War with Dick Button, who sprang upwards to the heavens (they skated outdoors in his day) in a way no one had before him. Although Button became the first man to land a double Axel and a triple jump, even his double flips and double Lutzes had more impact than ever seen before. He flew, without wings.

Button, who won five consecutive world titles and two Olympic gold medals, started a gold rush of Americans who dominated the discipline from 1948 to 1959, the year that David Jenkins won his third consecutive world championship. Sandwiched between Jenkins and Button was Jenkins's older brother, Hayes Alan Jenkins, who collected another four world titles from 1953 to 1956. American men swept the Olympic gold medals from 1948 to 1960.

Watching all of these developments from afar was Yuka Sato's father, Nabuo Sato, a Japanese skater born in 1942, whose family had seen all the rinks in his country close down during the Second World War, a time when many Japanese skaters died. In 1953, when he started going to the reopened rinks with his mother, a skating teacher, "We didn't know anything about

what we were doing," he says. His only exposure to skating was the odd news item on television, a documentary in a movie theater, and a few skating pictures that showed in static form what the skating world, particularly the Americans, was doing.

But in 1952, the Japanese skating federation invited Hayes Alan Jenkins and Tenley Albright to come to give exhibitions. The Japanese took pictures of this; eight-millimeter cameras were everywhere, recording treasured information. And from whatever tips Sato could gain, he marveled most at David Jenkins, whose talents he saw on film. "He was like a spring," he said. "He was a jumping machine."

When Sato's coach urged him to try a triple Salchow, Sato didn't know quite what to do. He had never seen one before. Nobody in Japan had. "What's a triple?" he asked.

If Jenkins was a jumping machine, Sato was the speedster of his generation. He eventually did a triple Salchow, but his double Lutz was the fastest at the time. "He went into it faster than anybody else," Peter Dunfield says. "And it was high and long. Very, very exciting. He was a real pioneer, considering where he got to in the world championships and how he learned. He was way ahead of his time."

Sato, a ten-time national champion from 1957 to 1966, managed to finish fourth in the 1965 world championship in Colorado Springs. He should have finished in the medals, but judging politics prevented it, Dunfield says.

The odd male skater played with the odd triple jump at the time, but Donald Jackson of Canada wrote skating history on a chilly rink when he became the first skater to land a triple Lutz, one of the most difficult of triples, at the 1962 world championship in Prague.

He had tried thousands of them in practice, but had landed only five of them properly, cleanly, and on one foot, before the Prague event. About two thousand to three thousand more of them had been close, but not quite right, landed improperly on two feet or with a fall one-quarter turn short of the triple rotation.

"I took a calculated risk," Jackson says. "People said, 'Don't be silly.'"

Jackson was a discouraging forty-five points behind the hometown skater, Karol Divin, after the figures, a spread that was almost impossible to overcome. After all, at the time, compulsory figures were worth 60 per cent of the total mark, and skaters who finished well back at that stage usually stayed there. Jackson needed a string of almost-perfect marks in the free-skating event to make up the huge deficit and win. Even so, coach Sheldon Galbraith told him there was room at the top.

Jackson electrified a crowd of eighteen thousand when he landed his landmark Lutz, but there was more. He did a total of twenty-two jumps, one every thirteen seconds over his five-minute program: two triple jumps (one of them a Salchow), ten double jumps (some of them delayed magically in mid-air, some landed crisply with arms folded, making the feat more difficult), and ten single jumps (some rotated in opposite directions). And Jackson, the first of a long line of Canadian male virtuosos, dazzled everyone with his light, quick footwork, too.

Jackson needed perfect marks to win, and he got them, seven in all, a record that stood until ice dancers Jayne Torvill and Christopher Dean mesmerized judges two decades later. His gritty undertaking prompted Button, acting as a commentator for the American Broadcasting Company (ABC) network at the time, to claim that Jackson's victory was "one of the finest competitive come-from-behind figure-skating performances ever seen."

It would be another twelve years before a skater again landed a triple Lutz in competition. Not surprisingly, triple Lutzes began to pop up again during 1973, after the ISU introduced the short program to emphasize free-skating skills and lessen the value of compulsory figures.

The new short program, with relatively easy requirements in its first year, comprised 20 per cent of the final mark, while figures and free-skating were each worth 40 per cent. The change prompted the most fertile period in singles skating, and one of the first among the new group of skaters to try the triple Lutz again was Soviet Sergei Tchetveroukhin. "I wanted to do the triple Lutz in my last competition in 1973," he says. "I was prepared already. I did it in practice.

Donald Jackson, who had "absolutely perfect jumping muscles"

"But suddenly I got a very bad flu before my national championship. I was okay, but I wasn't good enough to do everything [at the world championship]. So I didn't do it. But I showed it in practice in Bratislava.

"[East German coach] Jutta Muller saw this. So next practice I saw [her student] Jan Hoffmann start to do it. And then a couple months later, we met on some tour. And she told me that Hoffmann [was] now jumping triple Lutz."

The next year Hoffmann won his first world championship with a triple Lutz. "He nailed it," Tchetveroukhin says.

Also, although a triple Axel was not landed in competition until Vern Taylor of Canada squeaked one out at a world championship in 1978, Gordon McKellen of the United States was landing the jumps with three and a half rotations in practice as early as 1974. He also landed one in an exhibition.

"That's why we can say now thank you very much," Tchetveroukhin still says of the gradual turning away from compulsories. "You can see now such great stuff. Figure skating doesn't look boring now. They are jumping now like crazy, but you are also seeing some very nice skating."

The heavy emphasis on figures had been the downfall of many great skaters who either failed to reach the top podium or didn't win a medal at all. John Misha Petkevich of the United States flirted with greatness but never quite reached it. He inspired Dorothy Hamill with his artistry, and the height and vigor of his jumps was astonishing. "He was a god on ice," Toller Cranston says. "He had a power about him that nobody, including Kurt Browning or Elvis Stojko, was in a league with. I actually felt, as a competitor, that I was ready to worship at his feet. He had a kind of incredible body. He was the American dream. He was Hollywood. An incredible virtuoso."

Petkevich twice finished fifth and twice fourth in four appearances at world championships from 1969 to 1972. Even though he had twice finished second in the free-skate in 1969 and 1970, he lost places on the podium because he had been as far down as seventh in compulsory figures.

Cranston himself had even-far-stronger arguments with compulsory figures. In 1972, in his third world championship, he finished ninth in figures, but won the free-skate. Even though he finished fifth overall, his high placing in the free-skate bumped Petkevich off the medal podium.

Cranston won his first world medal – a bronze – in 1974, after finishing eighth in figures but winning both the short and long program. Three times, he was the free-skating champion of the world.

His fifth-place finish in figures at his last amateur appearance at the 1976 world championship in Göteborg plunged him into fourth place overall, even though he had won the short program and finished second in the free-skate to Olympic champion John Curry. It seemed unfair. The flamboyant Cranston rushed out of the rink and tossed his figure boots into a pond, exclaiming he had better things to do with his time.

Robin Cousins of Britain was another skater hobbled by compulsory figures during his career, but also by second-rate knees. Still, he triumphed over both problems to win the 1980 Olympic gold medal, and he did it without a triple Lutz, which he had practised, probably to unnerve his competitors. Incredibly, he never won a world championship, although in three of the events he had won the free-skate. In the 1980 world championship, he won both the short and long program, but finished second to Jan Hoffmann.

But what Cousins brought to skating was a jumping power coupled with an artistic flair honed by his lifelong interest in music and dance. "I always wanted to get into musical theater," he said. "That's what I originally wanted to do. I wanted to be Gene Kelly."

Cousins chose skating because he felt it was a more exciting version of the entertainment and variety shows that he loved on television, but he never let song and dance go. At age thirty-six, he auditioned for and got the part of Munkustrap in the original Cameron Mackintosh production of *Cats* in England. Off went the skates; on went the tabby-patterned tights and furry ears. Cousins has a fully trained singing voice, and he put it to good use in one of his professional skating routines when he skated to a recording of his own voice reading a Wordsworth poem.

"Cousins was athletic and overall a better skater than John Curry," Cranston says. "But he never went the full route of being innovative. He was very clever, and very him, and very good."

Cousins retired from his amateur career after 1980, but the evolution of jumping that followed in the next decade and a half would make him blink in disbelief. The year Cousins won his Olympic medal, Grzegorz Filipowski of

Jan Hoffmann, a two-time world champion for the former East Germany

Toller Cranston

Dorothy Hamill watched in awe as Toller Cranston skated a dramatic exhibition after the 1974 world championship in Munich, where he was revered. "Toller chose to demonstrate the potential of marrying two art forms — opera and ice. He skated to the famous aria from I, Pagliacci, *and as Canio's tragic laugh rang out across the arena, Toller's black-clad shape slowly unfolded. . . . Then in one movement the entire audience stood up and applauded wildly. It was one of the greatest performances in skating history." — Dorothy Hamill in* On and Off the Ice

Robin Cousins's boyhood hero was Gene Kelly. He sang at school and at the church choir and studied dance until skating gained his full attention at age thirteen. During the late 1980s, when injuries interrupted an engagement with the "Ice Capades," he began taking voice lessons. He has been a back-up singer for Roger Daltrey and has performed a major role in Cats in England.

Poland became the first skater to land a triple-triple jump combination. (Both of the triples were toe loops.) The tiny skater was only thirteen.

Mark Cockerell of the United States followed with a similar feat, but Alexander Fadeev of the Soviet Union cranked up the difficulty a notch when he landed a triple Salchow–triple toe-loop combination. During the early 1980s, free-skating routines turned into spark-plug exhibitions, sometimes with few other redeeming qualities. One competitor at the 1983 world championship packed his four-and-a-half-minute routine entirely full of jumps. The only element that was not a jump was a spin that lasted little longer than it takes to brush ice chips off a skate blade.

This trend prompted the ISU to adopt a set of precise regulations for the 1984 season that set out certain skills to be displayed during the free-skating routine. The rules also limited the repetition of other skills, most notably jumps. Currently, a skater cannot repeat a triple jump unless it is in combination with another jump.

Still, the men's event has been a contest of jumping virtuosity. While Vern Taylor was the first to land a triple Axel, Canadian Brian Orser did it with more fireworks; he did it more often; he did it before he even became a senior skater. He became Mr. Triple Axel.

Orser became the second man to land the jump in a competition when he won the Canadian junior men's title, during a memorable routine in which he also fired off two triple Lutzes. It was an extraordinary accomplishment for a skater at that level; almost none of the senior skaters around the world were doing such things at the time. He was a thin slip of a boy from small-town Canada, but he had big ideas. When Orser moved up to the senior ranks, he became the only competitor to seriously push – and defeat – reigning world champion Scott Hamilton of the United States in 1984.

In the era after the 1980 Olympics, Hamilton dominated the men's ranks, chalking up an impressive string of victories nationally and internationally, and winning four world titles from 1981 to 1984 and an Olympic gold medal along the way. For three or four years, he was as unbeatable as Button had been in his time. And because Hamilton was proficient in all areas – compulsories and free-skating – he thrived under the restructuring of the marking system that the ISU instituted for all disciplines, starting with the 1981 season. Under the old system, a judge's points were continuously added together throughout the competition. The winner of the event was the skater who had the majority of first-place votes, based on the total.

Under the new system, which is still used today, the marks are not carried forward from event to event, but the winner is determined on a combination

of the best placings in each portion of the event. This new emphasis prevented a skater from ringing up huge point leads in any one area of the competition. To run this new gauntlet of tests, a skater had to excel consistently in all segments.

This Hamilton could do. He had no triple Axel in his repertoire, but he did have a perfect, precise technique, a light touch on the ice, a flair for spine-tingling footwork, and an expressive, often comedic, air.

He was so proficient in every area of his sport that he could skate just as powerfully hurtling forwards as backwards. Most skaters gather speed with powerful, wide-stroking, backward crosscuts. Hamilton, on the other hand, could race out of a corner forwards and, with only three enormous strokes, gain enough speed to sustain him as he flew through his famous footwork sequences, hardly touching the ice, all the way down the rink. Few conquerors of triple Axels and quadruples can do the same.

Wisely, during his competitive career, Hamilton doffed the sequins and spangles for simple garb, which allowed his winning personality to shine through. He was a champion that the world took to its heart.

But towards the end of his amateur career, Orser made him nervous. "It took ten miles of wind out of my sails when I saw [Orser's marks]," he said after his final long program at the 1984 world championship in Ottawa. "I would have had to be Torvill and Dean to win."

Orser won three of four free-skating matches with Hamilton during the 1984 Olympics and world championship. However, Hamilton, seemingly drained, won both competitions because of his superior rankings during compulsories. But that day in Ottawa, even Fadeev, who was to win the world title the following year, almost defeated Hamilton with an arsenal of amazing feats, including a triple Lutz–triple toe-loop combination. All in all, three men tried a triple Axel at that event. Fadeev had even come close to landing the first quadruple toe-loop at the 1984 Olympics in Sarajevo, but the ISU did not recognize it because the landing was slightly flawed. But one message was clear: jump like crazy or be left behind.

Orser began to put two triple Axels in his program, one of them landed in combination. Others answered in kind, in a way declaring war. By the time of the 1988 Olympics, six men were trying triple Axel–double-loop combinations, most notably up-and-comers like Kurt Browning and Victor Petrenko.

In the time leading up to the 1988 Olympics, the challenges for supremacy were coming from all directions. Josef Sabovcek, a tall, gaunt wisp of a skater from Bratislava, Czechoslovakia (now Slovakia), had an awesome ability to leap high in the air, rotate like a top, and drop back down to earth in an almost surreal manner. He attempted quadruple jumps in competition several times, but never quite succeeded (he came closest at the 1986 European championship, but the ISU ruled he had brushed the ice with the skate of his free leg) – a victim of poor knees, uncertain training habits, and the vagaries of time, place, and chance. Although his best finish was a bronze medal at the 1984 Olympics, his talent was envied, feared, unequaled, and certainly unfulfilled.

Sabovcek and Fadeev weren't the only skaters attempting quadruples. Orser landed them in practice many times, some even in combination. Brian Boitano, who was such a powerful, controlled jumper that he could do a triple Lutz with his arm raised above his head (a move that was later dubbed the 'Tano Lutz), attempted quads in three competitions and never quite passed the ultimate test.

Boitano put away any thoughts of landing a quadruple during the 1988 Olympics and won the gold medal without it, while concentrating more on developing his artistry. The plan worked. He won the Olympics by only one-tenth of a point over Orser, a close ending to the epic "Battle of the Brians."

Brian Orser

Brian Orser, shown as a professional skater (above, left) and in the military garb (above, right) that he wore to win the silver medal at the 1988 Olympics. The 1987 world champion was known for his triple Axel, but skating purists know him just as well for what he did with his feet when he was not airborne. "[In some of his 1988 programs], there was not a step, not one edge that wasn't a clear, pure, and clean edge. He was very, very fluid. He used the idea of painting on the ice, and he took it very, very seriously, to be in love with the ice. If you love the ice, it loves you back. It's just like a relationship; you wouldn't scratch it, you wouldn't hurt it, you wouldn't kick it." – Orser's choreographer, Uschi Keszler

The 1988 Olympic champion, Brian Boitano, as he appeared at the 1994 Olympics, in which he finished sixth (below, right). "The difference between Boitano and [Brian] Orser was that Boitano was so perfect in the air until he lost his timing and reflexes through aging. He had just sensational qualities in the air.... When Orser was on the ground, Boitano was no match for this guy.... Orser is great on the ground and you skate more on the ground than you do in the air." – Canadian coach Sheldon Galbraith

Brian Boitano

Petr Barna, from the Czech Republic, is not only the second skater to land a quadruple jump but is also the only male competitor to receive a perfect 6.0 for artistry for his original program, a rendition of Amadeus, *at the 1991 world championship in Munich. He won the 1992 Olympic bronze medal in Albertville and is married to Czech ice dancer Andrea Juklova.*

But the next generation was even more formidable. Kurt Browning, the slim, gregarious son of a riding outfitter from Western Canada, unleashed the world's first quadruple toe-loop at the 1988 world championship in Budapest, seizing his spot in the sun just as the Brians were dousing their own amateur campfires. In 1989, Petr Barna, of what was then Czechoslovakia, became the second man to land one; in 1991, young Alexei Urmanov of the former Soviet Union became the third.

The quad began showing up in the most unexpected places – such as at the 1992 world junior figure-skating championship in Hull. Konstantin Kostin, a Soviet who later skated for Latvia, finished second in the event, although he fell on a quadruple toe-loop attempt. He eventually did land a quad in competition, but sometimes very little else. Even an unknown skater from China, Min Zhang, landed a quadruple jump at the 1994 Lillehammer Olympics. He failed to qualify for the final at the world championship a month later.

The most amazing quadruple jumps ever seen were probably those done during a sparsely attended practice session at the world championship in Munich in 1991. American Christopher Bowman, a self-described "Hans

Christopher Bowman at his best – in a rowdy, colorful exhibition number to the music of "I Can't Get No Satisfaction," in which he jumps over the rink barriers and dances with a member of the audience. Bowman denied a rash of queries that he had drug problems, which were said to have contributed to beatings he received in Toronto and Pittsburgh. He was a child of Hollywood, who appeared in television shows such as "Little House on the Prairie."

Brinker from Hell," knew that his coaches, Ellen Burka and Toller Cranston, were angry with him for his poor training habits and hearty enjoyment of party life. During the final practice, he skated up to the boards, held up one finger to his disgruntled mentors, and said, "Watch this."

The controversial skater landed three quadruple toe-loops in a row, just to please them and to ease the stoney silence. He had never landed any before, and he has never landed any since. Had Bowman ever trained with any discipline, any skater, including Browning, would have been hard pressed to defeat him.

Bowman won a silver medal at the 1989 world championship in Paris, and then a bronze at the 1990 world championship in Halifax, even though he had astonished his first and longtime coach, Frank Carroll, by improvising his long-program routine. Not surprisingly, he went out in a blaze of glory in his last amateur performance, at the 1992 world championship in Oakland, when he injured himself near the end of his routine and had to be carried off the ice.

But quads will only get you so far. The jump that has been so difficult for many to master is really worth only 0.1 extra point in a long program; an ISU rule forbids judges to put too much emphasis on any one jump. After Browning landed four of them in competition, the last of them in 1990, he put them away to concentrate on other things.

In 1991, while Bowman was clowning, Browning was celebrating. The Canadian won his third world title with an unprecedented three triple-triple combinations, one of them an extremely difficult triple Salchow–triple loop that no one else has mastered to this day.

By the time Browning had won his fourth world title in 1993, his abilities were revered the world over by his peers. Philippe Candeloro admires Browning, and U.S. champion Scott Davis says he has looked up to Browning since he was a young skater. South African champion Dino Quattrocecere mentions Browning in his first breath when asked what skaters he has cherished. In fact, Browning proved to be an exciting link to the outside world for Quattrocecere, who, until sporting sanctions against his country were lifted in 1991, saw no world championships on television. When a relative from Italy sent him videotapes of the events, Quattrocecere's imagination was spurred at the sight of Browning.

Wisely, Browning continued to change his offerings throughout his career, expanding his horizons, pushing the sport in interesting directions, pushing himself, always learning. Strangely enough, when Browning moved

Two-time U.S. champion Scott Davis started skating when he was five years old because in Montana, where he was born, "the winters are cold and long," he said. He landed his first triple Axel when he was fifteen and is considered the best male spinner in the world today.

to Toronto, his new choreographer, Sandra Bezic, set the multiple world champion back to skating basics. But the move wasn't really so strange.

"Before he was even working with [coach Louis Stong], he and I just got on the ice and skated and just did real basics, waltz jumps, and basic spins, just to feel things and just to think about things," Bezic says. "He's such a natural that I don't think he ever really thought about things before. When somebody is so gifted, they don't usually analyze things. But I think the best performers are the truly gifted ones who also understand."

Instead of thinking about triples and high-flying technical feats, Browning began to look to his feet and analyze what he did when he was not airborne. He took more care with his spins, ensuring they were centered and did not travel. These were things, he said, that would not be noticeable to an audience, but they were to him. He took more care with his feet, carving and

weaving large curves, then pulling them back into small, sharp loops with confident, complex edges.

He also began to tap his musical quality, his artistic talent. Even the appearance of his jumps changed, according to the call of the music. Browning could hurl his body into big, high exploding jumps for a dramatic orchestral chord or take gentle, open vaults with silent landings during quiet, expressive notes.

In 1991, he had also skated with Hamilton for the first time, and he made mental notes. "More than anything else, I admire his footwork," Browning said. "I just look at him, and I watch his feet. They just don't really, actually, seem to touch the ice. He has the ability to take a move that's not the hardest move in the world, but he'll sort of press it. There'll be a glint in his eye as if to say 'See that? That's cool, eh?' He can sell. He can be different characters. I can appreciate that, because that's something I work really hard at each time I step on the ice. I want to be someone new."

In 1993, when Browning emerged from months of quiet sessions, with no international competitions, he was new. He bolted out of the chute with a "popping" routine that was far removed from the normal fare of skating performances. Popping is a jerky, spasmodic, robotic style of street dance embraced by youngsters in ghettos, streets, and clubs.

And he popped to music that is not music to judges' ears: a heart-pounding drum solo called "Bonzo's Montreux" by Led Zeppelin. During pauses in the rattling of the drums, Browning would leap into the air and complete a required element. This was his technical program, and even though Browning admitted he was worried the music wouldn't be well-received, all judges but the Russian accepted it at the 1993 world championship in Prague. The Russian judge placed Browning third, preferring American skater Mark Mitchell and Russian Alexei Urmanov, while the other eight rated the Canadian, with his popping moves and non-music, the best. It was a kind of skating the world had never seen before. Later, the Russian judge placed Browning first for his spellbinding *Casablanca* free-skating routine, which has become a classic in figure skating.

If *Casablanca* was any indication, the world of show business was creeping inexorably into amateur skating, and Browning, more than any of the professional-turned-amateur skaters, brought it in with a strong tug. His programs became rather like exhibitions, because his mindset between 1992 and 1994 was tilted in that direction anyway. He had originally planned on turning professional after the 1992 Olympic Games in Albertville, but when he finished out of the medals with a broken Axel and a troublesome back, he decided to continue until the 1994 Games in Lillehammer.

His new technical program for 1994, arranged to Doc Severinson's rendition of the upbeat "St. Louis Blues," went together quickly, like an exhibition number, with some of the moves borrowed from Browning's CBC television special, "You Must Remember This," developed earlier that year.

The music was perfect, Stong said, because it allowed Browning to show off his incomparable edge quality – and the most high-flying, on-the-edge, footwork ever seen. Portraying a "cool, overconfident, overbearing lounge

Kurt Browning

The many faces of four-time world champion Kurt Browning: wistful in his Les Misérables number (left); playful in his rendition of Charlie Brown (center); and wacky in hard-rock numbers (right). "Kurt can do anything. First of all, physically, he's built like a gymnast. The [CBC television special "You Must Remember This"] is really a showcase for his range as an artist, from the comedic flair to the classical. In the "Singing in the Rain" number, it was really tough what he did. It was his footwork, down the sidewalk. Anybody else would be on their butt, and he did it over and over again for a multitude of takes. Skating in torrential rain and performing, all at the same time, and doing it on cue. Nobody else that I've ever worked with can do that." – choreographer Sandra Bezic

lizard kind of guy," Browning constantly switched from edge to edge, varying between sharp cuts to long, flowing curves, the rhythm ebbing and flowing. His complex edge changes also made the takeoffs for his jumps more difficult.

Unfortunately, the program rarely had a chance to bloom. Browning crumpled during this masterpiece of amateur programs at the Canadian championship in January 1994, perhaps because of the pressure of skating in Edmonton, where he had trained for eleven years. The program was also flawed at the Olympic Games, in which he finished fifth.

The 1994 Olympic Games set the stage for battles among the leaders of a new generation of power jumpers and artistic skaters, all searching for a spot in skating history. Currently, at the head of the pack is Elvis Stojko, the 1994 world champion; Alexei Urmanov, the 1994 Olympic champion; and Philippe Candeloro, quickly becoming the rock star of skaters with his charisma. It's a quality that has nothing to do with skating, but it helps to have it.

Also searching for glory are Viacheslav Zagorodniuk, a Ukrainian who has skated in the shadow of countryman Victor Petrenko, the 1992 Olympic champion, but who came out of it when he displayed an arsenal of awe-inspiring jumps to win a world championship bronze medal in 1994; Scott Davis of the United States, probably the best amateur male spinner in the world, who defeated Boitano at the 1994 U.S. nationals but who has been hampered by inconsistency; and Eric Millot of France and Sébastien Britten of

Canada – a skater with a tremendous artistic sense and body line – who have to add triple Axels to their programs to climb into the top group. American Michael Weiss, who landed a couple of clean triple Axels when he won the 1993 world junior championship, has already drawn praise from Boitano and Hamilton.

"I'm not too worried about where the sport is going," Browning said after his retirement. "There seems to be some versatility among the skaters. They're not all jumping beans."

The fun all began at the Olympic Games, where a controversy raged, at least in Canada, about the judges having placed mighty jumper Stojko, with his martial-arts routine, behind Urmanov, with his traditionally classic program. Although Stojko had been criticized in the past for a lack of artistry in his programs, he had improved markedly throughout the 1994 season.

The buzz was that the judges just didn't like Stojko's martial-arts presentation, or his leather-and-chrome techno-hip-hop dance to music called "Frogs in Space," because it was just too avant-garde. And, being the old, stodgy fogies that they were, they liked Urmanov's traditional skate better. Nonsense, said many international judges.

Was Stojko's program controversial? "Martial arts is certainly different for an aesthetic program," said Osborne Colson, a 1936 and 1937 Canadian champion who trained and directed Barbara Ann Scott's first all-Canadian tour. "It's got a fairly different connotation of movement to it. . . . The lines are strong. From watching a martial-arts class, I see that they have a rhythm that you could almost write music to."

But judges don't have a right to like or dislike someone's music, said one Canadian world-caliber judge. "The program is merely a vehicle for conveying skills. It doesn't matter if you like it or not. The winner is the one who has the greatest variety of skills, who can, for example, show a change of speed, who can go from zero to sixty."

However, Canadian coach Sheldon Galbraith, the only coach to train world champions in three disciplines, figures that North Americans have always had a difficulty in knowing how to deal with European judges, who end up sitting in most of the seats on the panel. "You win on expectations being fulfilled," says Galbraith, who surmised that judges disapproved of Stojko's leather-and-chrome outfit for his technical program. "It's just the idea that I'm going to do it my way. Frank Sinatra didn't sing that song when he was trying to go up. He sang it after he got there. You have to ask for their approval."

Victor Petrenko

Victor Petrenko, the 1992 Olympic and world champion from Ukraine, was five years old when his parents took him to a new rink that had just been built in Odessa. By eleven, Petrenko landed his first triple jump and, five years later, at sixteen, his first triple Axel, his technical masterpiece. Quadruples have caused him nightmares in the past. In September 1988, he lost three months' of skating after he pulled a muscle so badly while practicing a quadruple that he wrenched a piece of bone from his pelvis. During his recovery, he couldn't even sit.

(Right) Petrenko's ballet training (he has been taking ballet lessons since he was five) shows up markedly in his amateur programs. He admires Robin Cousins, loves to drive fast cars, and lives in his favorite city in the world, Las Vegas, with his wife, Nina, the daughter of his coach, Galina Zmievskaia. Petrenko also has a younger skating brother, Vladimir, who showed great promise in winning the 1986 world junior championship, but his best finish at the senior level was a tenth at the 1988 world championship in Budapest.

Elvis Stojko

Elvis Stojko's Hungarian-Slovenian parents loved Elvis Presley so much that they named their youngest of three children after him. For several years, Stojko held off on doing a Presley exhibition routine, but in 1993, he secretly had a program choreographed in the United States. He did not unleash it until he won his first national title in January 1994. "I wanted to wait until the right time to do it," he said. Only three people knew of the routine; his parents knew nothing of it until he performed it at the exhibition, wearing an exact replica of a Presley jacket (opposite). Stojko brought different styles of movement to his 1994 performances with his leather-and-chrome biker outfit (below, right) for his techno-hip-hop technical program and his martial-arts long program (below, left), skated to music from Dragon: The Bruce Lee Story, *a movie version of the life of his hero. Some thought the judges disapproved of his unusual garb for the technical program.*

Former competitors Kurt Browning and Elvis Stojko discuss their next move during an exhibition at the 1993 world championship in Prague, in which the Canadians continued their heated rivalry from the national championships and finished first and second respectively.

Browning, on the other hand, says too many people at the Olympics got caught up in "this image versus this image. I think everyone forgot that it's skating as well. Behind all the jumps, behind everything, there has to be good skating. And I'm not sure who displayed that the best."

Various Olympic-level judges and coaches contended that Stojko appeared cautious during his Olympic skate and skated slowly; that his footwork was slow; that he bent over forward from the waist when he landed a triple Lutz, while Urmanov landed the same jump with his back erect; that Stojko's body line in moves like the camel spin did not equal that of Urmanov, who arched his back in perfect form; that Stojko sacrificed the artistry for a section when he bailed out prematurely from a triple Axel–triple toe-loop combination and then (amazingly) rearranged his program to stick it back in moments later.

Many spectators, on the other hand, argued that Urmanov left them feeling bored, that they were taken aback by a recurring posing move in which he flapped his knees in and out, as if he were doing a chicken-sauce commercial during a classical routine, and that his costumes were highly overwrought. But Browning was one who watched from the sidelines and was amazed by Urmanov's unusual performance.

"I didn't actually enjoy his program, but he skated it well," Browning said. "His program moved because I kept waiting for it to slow down, and I kept waiting for a mistake, because that's what I expected. And it just never happened.

After watching Urmanov practice at the Olympics, Browning thought that his program was so "awful" that the Russian had no chance of winning.

Soon after Elvis Stojko became world champion, he discovered the price of fame. While he was quietly toiling at his quadruples in Canada, a wild rumor that he had broken his back in two places while attempting a back flip spread quickly from the Goodwill Games at St. Petersburg to Britain, Canada, and the United States. The gossip varied from Stojko suffering a foot injury to paralysis. There was no grain of truth to the tales.

But Urmanov changed as soon as he took to the ice for the long program, Browning says. "His program artistically was so much better than he practiced." Browning was astonished when Urmanov seemed to hit another gear, another level of being, as he began to present his program and make it come to life. "He was really pushing," Browning said. "I was just going: 'Where is this kid coming from?'"

Urmanov's triple Axel was giant, gorgeous, and landed with perfect flow, said one judge. Even so, the courageous Stojko had the upper hand technically, and all nine judges placed him first. Eight judges placed Urmanov ahead artistically. Overall, six judges thought Urmanov best in the long program.

Urmanov's inconsistency returned when he finished only fourth and off the medal podium at the world championship in Japan, plagued by troubles whenever he set foot on the ice. (He was the first Olympic champion to finish out of the medals at the following world championship.) And Stojko was at his best, deciding at the last moment to attempt a quadruple toe-loop–triple toe-loop combination instead of a quad-double combination. In Japan, Stojko skated with an aggressive command that many said was missing in Lillehammer.

With his world-championship win, Stojko promises to be the star of the future, a major contender in the years leading up to the 1998 Olympic Games in Nagano, Japan. He proved wildly popular during more than forty performances on the annual U.S. tour of world champions in the spring and summer of 1994. "You'd think he was an American," said the tour promoter, Tom Collins, astonished at the popularity of the Canadian in another country. Stojko was also the headline skater of a new tour that passed through seven Canadian cities in September 1994. Skaters preparing for national and world championships are rarely seen in autumn tours.

Stojko comes by his nickname "The Terminator" honestly, because of his undeniable consistency. Bolstered by the spiritual strength that comes through his training as a martial artist – he gained his black belt in karate at age sixteen – Stojko has even practiced quadruple Lutzes and was intending to land one in Prague, on the thirty-first anniversary of Jackson's achievement of the first triple Lutz. He came close in practice.

Karate has helped Stojko in obvious ways, giving him the strength and flexibility to snap his muscular 5-foot, 7-inch (167.5-centimeter) body into gravity-defying quadruple-jump combinations. (He was the first to land a quadruple jump in combination.) It has also afforded Stojko a tough mindset that brushes off pressure and stresses alertness, bouncing back from a punch and maintaining focus.

"It's always to go, go, go, and fight, fight, fight, and never give up," said Stojko, never daunted by his four consecutive second-place finishes at Canadian championships. "It's a way of being."

Despite his masculine image, which perhaps is also spawned by his other hobby, dirt-bike riding, Stojko skates with the softness of an ice-dancer's knee, stroking lightly, his blade caressing the ice. It is no surprise that his stylist is Uschi Keszler, a former German champion, who developed the same style in Orser and in fast-rising ice dancers Shae-Lynn Bourne and Victor Kraatz.

Alexei Urmanov, one of Stojko's major opponents in years to come, will become known for his artistry, but he, too, is an accomplished jumper, becoming the third man ever to land a quadruple jump – and with such outstanding ease that he profoundly impressed Browning. Early in the 1991-92 season, Urmanov fell hard while attempting a quadruple Axel in practice and broke a bone in his landing leg. He was out of action for four months. "This problem created another problem," says his coach Alexei Mishin. "He became afraid to compete. In Prague [when he finished third], he started to believe in himself again."

If Urmanov is following in the lines of hundreds before him with his classical look, Philippe Candeloro is not traditional in any way. "I think he's got a great gift," Browning says. "He doesn't give [a diddly] what anyone else thinks, he just does it. I think that's going to add a lot of fun to things."

Candeloro is the only skater to use the same theme – "The Godfather" – for both technical and long programs during a season. He invented a spin in which he drops to the ice on his knees for several rotations and then bounces back up out of it. It is a move so unique that it has spurred scores of kids at skating clubs around the world to try it too, with much less success. Even Stojko attempted the move, which requires very flexible ankles, at an exhibition after the world championship. Candeloro has also created several moves never seen before in skating, including a series of repetitive hops across the ice from a crouched position and an asymmetrical line of arms and legs and body lean that he often uses as a final bow.

"My favorite program [at the 1994 world championship] was Candeloro's, just because he had so many good, different ideas," Sandra Bezic says. "There weren't a lot of outstanding programs there. It's so hard to come up with something that hasn't been seen or done before."

Margarite Sweeney-Baird, a British coach, says Candeloro is one of the skaters who will take the sport another step forward with his unusual repertoire of movement on ice.

Alexei Urmanov

Alexei Urmanov won the 1994 Olympic gold medal in spite of hardships in his home country. According to his coach Alexei Mishin, the conditions for skating in Russia are "still very bad. We have just one hour, fifteen minutes, in the morning and one hour, fifteen minutes, in the evening [to practice on ice]. I pay for [Urmanov's] costumes and some other expenses. The Russian federation gives only symbolic money. It's very shame to tell. We get $30 to $40 a month. Every year, the ISU pays to every federation a lot of money for skaters which compete in the Europeans and the world. Even in this situation, we have not any real support. We have support from our ice skating club in St. Petersburg, which cover all expenses of the ice. We had not any ideas to stop skating because I am sure if he will get good place, he will get more money finally."

Philippe Candeloro

Philippe Candeloro of France caught the attention of judges and spectators with his novel moves, including an unusual spin in which he descends to the ice, rotates on his shins and knees, and rises back up off the ice. Its creation was an accident, says Candeloro, who admits he fell into the position when he jumped while doing a spin. Because his skate blades do not touch the ice while he is spinning, the ISU does not recognize the move as a required element in a short program. The charismatic Candeloro admits he is not a classical skater, but his best performances have come since he began to work with Russian choreographer Natacha Dabadie, who also designed programs for Igor Bobrin, a 1981 world bronze medalist from the Soviet Union. Bobrin first did the series of straight-line hops that Candeloro has made famous. (Right) Candeloro in the costume that won him the admiring glances of teenaged female fans around the world: his Rocky outfit, complete with boxing gloves and a star-spangled banner that doubles as a shirt.

Veteran coach Frank Carroll is not so enthusiastic. "Skating has become so much more show-business oriented, so much more commercial and showy. The choice of music is more avant-garde. The movements we're seeing on the ice are professional tricks. Candeloro's thing that he does on his knees, and the hops, those are not amateur techniques."

Still, Candeloro has broken loose from the crowd with his combination of tricks and powerful masculine jumps that served him well in the two most important events he faced: the Lillehammer Olympics, in which he won a bronze medal when he was hoping only to hang onto fifth place, and his world silver medal in Japan.

He skated the best programs of his career in those two events, but he has not always been consistent. At the European championship in Copenhagen, Denmark, Candeloro proved an important point; he landed a triple Axel–double toe-loop combination that he had missed in twelve of his previous thirteen technical program routines.

Whatever Candeloro does is not always pretty. He never skates with pointed toe. His shoulders are hunched forward. But he had enough sparkle to cause quiet Japanese girls to flood the ice with many bouquets – so many that they rained on the heads of the judges. A star was born, without a gold medal.

Ice Dancing

The career of
Maia Usova
and Alexander
Zhulin was
often troubled
by unhappy
undercurrents.
More than once,
someone broke
into their Moscow
apartment and
stole music tapes.
However –
even though the
Russian federation
had sternly
stipulated that
pairs skaters
Ekaterina
Gordeeva and
Sergei Grinkov
must train in their
own country if
they wished to
compete as
amateurs in
1994 – it allowed
Usova and
Zhulin to
remain in their
adopted home at
Lake Placid in
the United
States to train.

ven though ice dancing was found in areas throughout Europe and North America during the early twentieth century, its cradle was in Britain.

The ethereal discipline, with its chassés and choctaws, swept Britain with a flourish, particularly from the 1920s on, although not always in the spirit of freewheeling Jackson Haines, the nineteenth-century ballet master on ice.

Swiss skater Jacques Gerschwiler, who taught in Britain during the 1920s, pondered the manner of the stiff-backed English folk, who skated with hands placed rigidly by their sides, and was inspired to develop a style that hinged on accurate technique, power, and control. Gladys Hogg, a British roller-dance champion, was his pupil.

Hogg transposed her skills from wheels to skates and, as an instructor, fostered the best of ice dancing in Britain for years, her pupils often a step ahead of the rest. "Two of the greatest teachers in the world were in Great Britain: Gladys Hogg and Arnold Gerschwiler," says Courtney Jones, a world ice-dancing champion from 1957 to 1960. "Everybody gravitated toward the two rinks [where they taught] for two decades, maybe three. Everybody who is now teaching, all over the world, has, at some time or another, been to Gladys Hogg or Arnold Gerschwiler or to their pupils. They left a legacy behind."

And because ballroom dancing on the floor also became a passion of the British, skaters worked diligently to transfer ballroom-dancing moves onto ice. Grand balls on ice were the order of the day. Rinks dotted London, pandering to the wealthy. During the 1930s, the British invented most of the compulsory dances seen today and held their first dance championship in 1939.

Britons excelled at ice dancing, perhaps because of the set-up of ice time during public sessions, where public skaters had to step aside for a tour of the social dancers. During a public session lasting from seven-thirty to ten in the evening, the fancy-stepping ice dancers would sometimes get two fifteen-minute stints to show off in front of a captive crowd waiting its turn. If you

didn't dance, you didn't get to skate during those intervals. Because adults were involved in social ice dancing, it was the discipline in Britain that was the best organized, and only recently has the practice of dance intervals at public sessions been stopped. Courtney Jones blames the decline of the discipline in his country to the demise of dance intervals.

When the ISU finally sanctioned world championships for ice dancers in 1952, the British were at the forefront and won thirteen of the first seventeen world titles. Winners of the first four titles were Jean Westwood and Lawrence Demmy, whose father was a featherweight boxing champion of North England. Demmy is now first vice-president of the ISU.

Why did a young British man, known to spar in the boxing ring, fall for a sport that the world did not seem to take seriously at the time? "Women," he says. "I was motivated by one particular girl." In England, the rink was the meeting place for young people, and when Demmy spotted a girl he thought was particularly desirable, he thought of skating as a way to get to know her. "I was a very, very quick learner, I can assure you," he said.

Thus was launched the career of the world's first ice-dancing champion, who impressed judges and audiences alike with a winning routine, skated charmingly enough to "Rudolph the Red-Nosed Reindeer." (The trials for the world championship occurred in December, he explained.)

But Demmy had one toe pick in the past and the other in the future. He watched with interest as the sport changed dramatically, and later, as chairman of the ISU ice-dancing committee from 1969 to 1984, he nudged along a

Britons Diane Towler and Bernard Ford broke away from the British mold of skating and reintroduced lifts, speed in footwork, changing dance holds, and more untraditional music. They won four world titles during the 1960s in the days before ice dancing was accepted as an Olympic sport.

few more changes. It was Demmy's idea to introduce the original set-pattern dance (similar to today's original dance) that helped to put more emphasis on free-skating and less on compulsory dances.

In its early days, ice dancing had no restrictions. Sometimes it was almost indistinguishable from pairs skating, which still had not developed its dangerous throws and twists. Indeed, for a large part of its history, the ISU has had to make a habit of reining in the excesses of ice dancing, particularly when the discipline began to stray too far from its ballroom-dancing roots. During the mid-1950s, the ISU did just that: it put a halt to anything about ice dancing that started to resemble pairs skating. Lifts were out.

When Britons Diane Towler and Bernard Ford wrestled back the world championship for Britain in 1966 from Czech skaters Eva Romanova and her

Natalia Linichuk and Gennadi Karponosov continued the Soviet tradition of dance enhanced by professional choreography. They won two world titles and the 1980 Olympic gold medal before turning to coaching.

brother Pavel Roman, they tossed a dare to judges everywhere. Ford very slightly lifted Towler three to four inches (seven and a half to ten centimeters) off the ice with his elbows, wheeled around in one rotation, then set her back down again. It was a small lift, and Ford himself says it was more a move of momentum than an actual lift. They did two of them, and the judges, particularly in their own country, were not amused.

"Some judges didn't support it," says Ford, now an ice-dancing coach in Canada. "Others put us first, but gave us a stiff talking to after the competition. They told us the rules were made to be bent, not broken. They were throwing all kinds of things at us. We were only kids, sixteen, seventeen. All these people were giving us a piece of their minds." The bewildered couple looked to their coach, Gladys Hogg, for guidance. She said, simply, "Listen to them, but we'll do it anyway."

Towler and Ford used the lift when they won their first of four world titles in 1966 and astonished international judges with their speed and intricate footwork. Because of them, the ISU eventually made a rule that allowed small lifts, as long as the man's hands did not rise above his waist. Currently, the rule allows the man to raise his hands no higher than his shoulder line.

Lively dancers Krisztina Regoczy and Andras Sallay of Hungary lost the 1980 Olympic gold medal by the narrowest of margins to Soviets Natalia Linichuk and Gennadi Karponosov. The two couples finished in a virtual tie, with a British judge awarding them the very same marks. The officials had to resort to adding up the ordinals. The Hungarians lost because the Soviet judge had placed them only third.

"It was a dangerous dare," Demmy says of the couple who bravely revived ice-dancing lifts. "Ice dancing became more interesting after that. There was more a couple could do."

Towler and Ford also continued a trend that had been started by former pairs skaters Romanova and Roman, the first ice dancers to break the British stranglehold on dance. They brought in a new idea of free-dancing – with great speed, some interesting rotational moves, and a more direct way of addressing the audience.

Perhaps because they had been pairs skaters, the Romans did not copy the British model of ice dancing that was in vogue at the time. Early British skaters were more sedate than the Czechs, although quite pretty to watch, with their softly flexing knees and ballroom grace. They were most rigidly conscious of technique and timing. But although the British feet moved, their upper bodies did not. Their carriage was stiff and upright.

Before the Czechs, British skaters like Courtney Jones, who won four world championships with two different partners, skated in a closed hold, like a waltz or foxtrot, in which the man and woman face each other. But the Czechs were able to attack their routines with greater momentum and speed because they often skated in a kilian hold, in which both skaters face the same direction and are not stroking quite so closely to each other. And because they often skated together in the same direction, they could address the audience in a way that skaters in a closed hold could not.

Towler and Ford did not strictly fit the British mold either. They used a combination of holds during their free-dances, even greater speed than the Czechs, more changes of direction in every which way imaginable, awe-inspiring footwork, and a different kind of music.

They decided, one year, to skate to "Zorba the Greek," a popular piece of music during the 1960s. "Nobody had ever really used that kind of music," Ford said. "Greek music isn't really way out, but at that time to use anything other than Bert Kaempfert or any other recognized orchestra was really going off the beaten track."

Towler and Ford made "Zorba the Greek" their own in a way that the next British champions to win a world title – Jayne Torvill and Christopher Dean – made Ravel's "Bolero" their signature piece. And, in general, the British upper body was never very well used until Torvill and Dean stepped onto the scene during the early 1980s. Everything they did was incomparable.

Before they retired (the first time) from their amateur career in 1984, Torvill and Dean had earned their 136 perfect marks of 6.0, with 29 of them coming in their last (so they said at the time) performance, the world championship in Ottawa. They garnered a couple of armfuls more when they re-instated as amateurs for the 1994 season. "They're fine art," Canadian ice dancer Rob McCall, an Olympic bronze medalist in 1988, once said. "The rest of us are skate-by-numbers."

Torvill and Dean were so popular that twenty-five hundred people came to watch the couple from Nottingham skate compulsory dances at an Ottawa practice – and gave them a standing ovation. Other skaters on the same practice session stood to the side and watched in awe when those that Britain liked to call "Their Greatnesses" took to the ice. About a thousand all-event

"Watching [Britons Jayne Torvill and Christopher Dean] skate, the way they caress the ice, it's like watching God skate," fellow British world champion Bernard Ford once said. When Torvill, thirty-six, and Dean, thirty-five, reinstated as amateurs for the 1994 Olympic season, they were at their best with their intricate rumba routine. They picked the slowest beat that the rules allowed to set the mood, skating to "The History of Love." It helped them to win the European championship, but not the Lillehammer Games, where they were clearly disappointed to win bronze.

In an unprecedented ice-dancing move, Christopher Dean becomes airborne in the arms of partner Jayne Torvill during their free-skating performance at the Lillehammer Olympics. In spite of his flight, their long program, skated to "Let's Face the Music and Dance," was overshadowed in the judge's minds by the performances of two younger Russian couples. It was a sobering moment for the couple, who won bronze after they had spent six months choreographing the piece. After narrowly winning the European championship, Torvill and Dean overhauled about 80 per cent of the program and injected a string of moves they had made famous during the early 1980s. But it was all for naught. Deflated, they did not compete at the world championship in Japan a month later.

Jayne Torvill & Christopher Dean

ticket-holders showed up to watch them practice in a rink that could hold only about three hundred spectators. They were turned away. Torvill and Dean not only raised the profile of ice dancing, but they raised a tremendous interest in all skating disciplines throughout the world.

Later, as professionals, Torvill and Dean skated extensively in Australia, where the popularity of figure skating was thought to be on a par with tiddly-winks. But ninety thousand tickets for their show sold within the first half-day they were offered. Torvill and Dean originally had planned to do only nine shows in Australia, but they stayed for forty-three. Some ticket-buyers kept returning to see the same show. One intrepid fan appeared at all eighteen shows in New Zealand in 1985.

As amateurs, Torvill and Dean broke rules, some say. Others contend they broke the perception of what everybody thought the rules were. They certainly broke the intent of the rules. After Torvill and Dean sailed into the ice-dancing scene, the ISU had to scurry to redefine the rules. Their approach to dance, much of it flowing from Dean's fertile pate, was complex and strikingly imaginative.

In the relatively quiet era before Torvill and Dean, there were simple rules that forbade ice dancers, for example, to rotate more than one and a half times. But Dean would lift Torvill, rotate once, step back in another direction while making a half-turn, stop, and then twist Torvill a few times on her own, without doing a rotation himself. By the time a flabbergasted judge counted all the turns, the sum could be three or four rotations, but none were continuous. The ISU rule-makers had to stop and ask, does one count only the man's rotations? Or both? Or only the revolutions that go in the same direction?

Torvill and Dean were also known for their innovative lifts, which spawned a wild aftershock among couples who copied what was untraditional but carried it to the extreme. Before Torvill and Dean retired, a West German couple presented what skating insiders call a mini-pairs program. "They would do an entire line on the ice, with the woman on his shoulders for maybe five measures of the music," Canadian judge Ann Shaw said at the time. "That's not dancing."

"It got into people crawling up each other's backs and sitting between the shoulder blades," Ford said. "There was a lot of posing. There were some weird and wonderful things."

The post-Torvill-and-Dean rules aimed to keep skate blades on the ice rather than bodies. After all, lying on the ice makes a break with the concept of ice dancing, which is about motion and movement and continuous action,

Tracy Wilson and Robert McCall were the first Canadians to win an Olympic ice-dancing medal when they took bronze at the Calgary Olympics in 1988. Praised by Christopher Dean for their creativity, Wilson and McCall also displayed the quickest and most complex footwork in the world, coached by footwork expert Bernard Ford.

the kind of thing that makes dancers envious. With that idea in mind, the ISU sought to prevent skaters from doing body slides and excessive knee slides on the ice and from doing too many lifts in a program (now five is the limit). Under the new rules, Torvill and Dean would have been unable to have performed the "Bolero" routine with which they won an Olympic gold medal and their fourth consecutive world title. The ISU also banned the use of ballet music, because it lacks a regular beat, although classical music that has a regular tempo is acceptable.

Ballet, however, is the ultimate dance, says Dean, who decried the change.

"I don't think ballet is related to sport in any way," Demmy says. "It's a form of art."

The rules also clarified what a lift was: the body could not be used as a support to carry a partner. Many, including Rob McCall and Tracy Wilson, who were coached by Ford, found a way around this. They once did a move in which Wilson rolled over McCall's back in one continuous motion, carried by her own momentum and therefore not supported. It was legal, as long as she didn't stop for a moment in mid-roll.

Torvill and Dean themselves wandered into those murky waters in the free-dance routine they performed at the 1994 Olympics in Lillehammer.

Some considered it illegal when Torvill, hand in hand with Dean, did a flip over his head onto the ice in front of him. Others consider it a clever, legal move, because, although the two were holding hands, Torvill vaulted over his head, propelled by the force of her own body bouncing off Dean's backside. The move was in the true Torvill-and-Dean tradition, leaving ISU rule-makers to ponder whether or not they should differentiate between active and passive assistance in the future.

Just as the ISU was trying to get a handle on the excesses that followed the Torvill-and-Dean phenomenon, along came Isabelle and Paul Duchesnay, Canadians who represented France and were popular winners of the 1991 world championship. Skating to Christopher Dean's choreography, the couple also stretched the boundaries of ice dancing with unusual dance positions and a dramatic, theatrical flair – and costumes to match. The old, erect British style was hardly in their vocabulary. And that worried some.

There was certainly nothing balletic about the Duchesnays' "Jungle Rhythm" routine, presented during the 1988 Olympic season, when they first made their presence felt. Their music, which evoked African drum beats, was further from Bert Kaempfert and Demmy's ballroom waltzes than the sport had ever heard. A British couple had considered using it a few years before, but nixed it because it was too risky. Its use frightened even Paul Duchesnay. "We had a few sleepless nights, because we didn't know if it would be a total blowout or whether the judges would accept it," he says.

The program certainly had crowd appeal. The Duchesnays had clearly imparted the feeling of the dance to spectators. Canadian coach Kerry Leitch once overheard an elderly couple discussing who their dance favorites were at the 1988 Calgary Olympics. "I liked those African skaters," one said.

The judges weren't so sure. When the Duchesnays abandoned the traditionally erect posture of ice dancing and replaced it with crouching poses (as in "Jungle Rhythm") or constantly leaning poses (as in their famous "Missing" routine, depicting South American struggles for independence), some judges embraced their new style; others deducted marks for what they felt were dancing indiscretions. Marks for the Duchesnays fluctuated widely in a discipline that had been so staid at the time that marks hardly varied from the first compulsory dance to the last stroke of the free-dance.

Many international judges criticized the Duchesnays for their simple footwork, because they skated often on two feet, rather than one, but then, so did the Soviets who won the Olympic gold medal in 1988. The very theatrical Natalia Bestemianova and Andrei Bukin cleverly camouflaged the shortcomings of their footwork with elaborate choreography for the upper body.

Isabelle and Paul Duchesnay (previous page) first attracted international attention with their "Jungle Rhythm" routine (top, left) during the 1988 season, when Christopher Dean became their choreographer. Their crouched style of skating confounded judges (see p. 197). Their music for the long program, done by the Australian group Mandingo, featured African drum beats, and the Jane and Tarzan costumes started a theatrical trend in dress. Two years later, the Duchesnays did an about-face with the apparel with their famous "Missing" routine (top, right and opposite), a tale of South American political oppression. They donned simple garb, with Isabelle skating in a tattered red dress. A hastily designed sequel to "Missing" earned them their world title in 1991.

The Duchesnays left Canada because "we had many hints that we really didn't belong in the Canadian Figure Skating Association," Paul said. The couple was upset that, although they finished a very close third in the 1985 Canadian championship, the CFSA did not send them to important international events to gain exposure the next year. The French skating federation accepted the Duchesnays with open arms, paying all of their costs to train in the expensive tourist town of Oberstdorf, West Germany. The Duchesnays are still stars in France and elsewhere in Europe, where they skate professionally.

*Natalia
Bestemianova
and Andrei Bukin,
the theatrical
Russians who won
the 1988 Olympic
gold medal, were
matched together
as ice dancers late in
their careers. After
the Olympics, Bukin
was so weary,
both physically and
mentally, that
he took off a season
before he joined
in a worldwide
professional tour.*

Bestemianova, a former singles skater known to brashly toss off a double flip during a professional show, did not even start skating with her ice-dancing partner until she was seventeen. Her background was definitely not in ice dancing, with a style of movement different from singles or pairs skating. Singles skaters bend at the waist and work their body to gain speed. Ice dancers can achieve the same speed, but it is to be hidden, and the carriage is to be vertical. "It's all in the use of the knee," judge Ann Shaw once said.

Interestingly enough, the Duchesnays started their skating lives as pairs skaters, a heritage that shows up in their stroking and posture. "Their programs were really well choreographed to hide the fact that they had a lot of effort when they stroked," Ford says. "There was a lot of effort in the upper body. They really didn't have good dance posture. They broke away from the way that dancers are supposed to skate, which is very upright and vertical, but by the same token, I don't think they could have done that."

If the Duchesnays' routines were difficult, it was because the constant, deep flexing of their knees made their routines an athletic workout. "The moves are very strenuous," Paul Duchesnay says of their "Jungle Rhythm" masterpiece. "After two minutes, my sister and I are working under real stress, because we are very low on our knees for so long. Our legs take a pounding. It's like we are doing a decathlon. There is one part where I have to put my leg over Isabelle four times and turn with speed. It's really risky. By the end, we can barely walk off."

"The programs are so different, it is like learning how to write with your left hand," Isabelle adds.

The first time they presented the program, at the 1988 European championship, all but one of the judges awarded them marks in the high 5.0 range. One Polish judge gave them a mark in the 4.0 to 5.0 range, but afterward ran back in tears, saying she was sorry she had not given them higher marks.

The Duchesnays were overwhelmed with a ten-minute standing ovation, and although they finished only eighth at the Olympics that year, they were well on their way to raising the level of awareness of what was acceptable in ice dancing. Most of all, the impact of their steamy, emotional routines raised the profile of ice dancing in mainland Europe for a sport in which only skaters from Hungary, Czechoslovakia – and finally France – had interrupted the longstanding domination of the discipline by Britons and Soviets.

"They added a new dimension to ice dancing," Courtney Jones says. "That was fire, an intensity and a dramatic approach that hadn't been seen before. You can't have sex between brother and sister, so their approach had to be very different. It was very clever what they were able to do to arrange such dramatic effect under such circumstances."

The Duchesnays left yet another legacy behind them that eventually set the ISU scrambling to patch up loopholes where more excesses had slipped through. Skaters who followed the Duchesnays tried to match – or even outdo -- the Duchesnays' emotional, theatrical themes and dress (they emerged from their lair in "Jungle Rhythms" not with sequins and fluff but with earth-brown crushed velvet, chrome, and leather). But the followers of the Duchesnays sometimes carried it beyond the pale.

By the time of the 1992 world championships in Oakland, audiences began to get confused; the music did everything but oink. There were screeching sounds, bird calls, synthesized crashes, and dripping water. During the 1992 season, even the Olympic champions Marina Klimova and Sergei Ponomarenko began to set aside their delicate interpretations of classical music in favor of theatrical presentations that were sometimes so convoluted that Klimova almost wound herself into a knot about her partner-husband during their performances. Nobody understood.

"They're all ripping up the pea patch," said one disgruntled viewer.

"[The ISU was trying] to get away from deeply, heavily symbolic freedances that meant nothing to anybody except the people that were doing

Marina Klimova & Sergei Ponomarenko

Two weeks after Marina Klimova and partner-husband Sergei Ponomarenko of Russia won the 1991 European ice-dancing championship, laboratory officials in Sofia, Bulgaria, claimed that Klimova tested positive for testosterone, an anabolic steroid. However, after a second test, Klimova was cleared. The need for the cash-strapped organizing committee in Sofia to save money and use a local lab led to the mix-up, ISU president Olaf Poulsen said. The Sofia laboratory was not sanctioned by the International Olympic Committee. However, the controversy completely disrupted Klimova and Ponomarenko's preparation for the world championship in Munich. Klimova cried for three days, and the couple did not set foot on the ice for over three weeks. Had they been found to have taken drugs, they would have faced a two-year suspension that would have caused them to miss the 1992 Olympics. They did, however, win Olympic gold in 1992. "We never even take medicine for headaches," Ponomarenko said.

them," Bernard Ford says. "When you've got to give out a synopsis of the plot before you skate, you're really in trouble. Three hours of heavy and the audience just left, didn't have a good time at all."

To address the problem, the ISU tackled the rules for music choices after the 1992 season. They decided to allow only music with a rhythmic beat and a melody that could be arranged and orchestrated for use on the dance floor. "Other music such as symphonic, opera, and other classical music not originally written for the dance floor must be rearranged and reorchestrated to comply with [the above]," the rules read.

This change made ice dancers conservative during the 1994 season, which featured the most fascinating contests ever seen in skating, with the return of professionals such as Torvill and Dean. How would the innovative 1984 Olympic champions handle strict rules that did not exist when they skated previously as amateurs? Interestingly enough, two of the major contenders – Torvill and Dean and French couple Sophie Moniotte and Pascal Lavanchy – both fell onto the same idea of skating as Ginger Rogers and Fred Astaire in their free-dance routines. There was also an abundance of ethnic dances, particularly with a Russian or Hungarian flavor.

But the new change inspired praise from Betty Callaway, coach of Torvill and Dean. "I was wary of it at first," she says. "But now that I've seen some of the new free-dances, I think it is bearing in the right direction. Certainly, the French couple has a perfect program of what we really want. It's interesting and has a lot of difficulty. I don't get tired of watching it. They used their music."

Olympic champions Oksana Gritschuk and Evgeny Platov simply did a rock-and-roll routine – but with such blazing speed that it set judges on their heels during the European championships. The Russians narrowly won that free-dance, although not the championship, and used that momentum to stage an upset Olympic win over defending world champions Maia Usova and Alexander Zhulin, also from Russia, and Torvill and Dean, who were obviously disappointed to win only a bronze.

"They were stunned," said Callaway, after the British couple decided not to continue their amateur trek to the world championship in Japan. Usova and Zhulin, with their dancey, but less-inspiring and more-cautious routine, also bowed out, leaving the field wide open for Gritschuk and Platov to win their first world title. "[Gritschuk and Platov] have an enormous vitality and an approach that is immensely appealing to everybody," Courtney Jones says.

But the upstart Russians did not leave such a glowing impression behind when they won the Japan event. In fact, two of the nine judges rated Moniotte

Oksana Gritschuk and Evgeny Platov, ice-dancing champions

Sophie Moniotte and Pascal Lavanchy of France delighted audiences with their quick footwork and soft knee action when they won a silver medal at the 1994 world championship, skating to a Ginger Rogers and Fred Astaire theme.

and Lavanchy first, appreciating their intricate footwork and constant changes of hold, all done at breakneck speed and on soft knees.

By contrast, only twenty seconds into the Russians' fast-paced routine, Platov fell. Their coach, former world champion Natalia Linichuk, said the couple actually loosened up after the accident. Callaway said they loosened up all right: they got "messy" after the fall.

Gritschuk and Platov were not as good in Japan as they were at the European championships, where their footwork was as neat as a pin, some said. "The first time I saw it, I thought it was very good," says Callaway, speaking of their performance at the European championship. "The second time, I still thought it was quite good. The third time, I started to look at their feet and found they really didn't do very much with their feet. It was all top-half and body gyrations. Now I'm bored with it. Whereas, with the French and the Finns, I could go on watching it several more times and still find something interesting that I've missed before."

Susanna Rahkamo and Petri Kokko, with their bronze-medal win at the world championships in Japan, became the first Finns to win a world ice-dancing medal and the first Finns to win any kind of skating medal in sixty-one years. (Markus Nikkanen won a bronze medal in the men's event in 1933.) But wherever Rahkamo and Kokko went, controversy followed.

The flying Finns were the only dancers to dare to do a polka to music from *The Addams Family* movie. They have showed up at center ice as street-walker and sailor, as groom in tails and batty bride. At the European

Sophie Moniotte & Pascal Lavanchy

Sophie Moniotte, whose trademark is skating in long, voluminous skirts (top, left), and partner Pascal Lavanchy have benefited from the growth of ice-dancing schools in France in the wake of the Duchesnays' success during the past decade. Schools have flourished in major cities such as Paris and Lyon. The world silver medalists skate under the direction of Danielle Marotel, national coach and director of dance at the Colombes Centre in Paris, and Russian choreographer Natacha Dabadie.

Moniotte and Lavanchy got a taste of trouble during their first year as senior skaters at Skate Canada in Thunder Bay in 1988. During a lift, Moniotte's dress ripped and pieces of trim and beads scattered about the ice. They finished sixth of seven couples. On the way home, an airline hostess on their plane recognized them as the team on television with costume problems. "That was our first big competition outside Europe," said Lavanchy, wincing at the debut. Since then, life has been better. Currently, with a world silver medal to their credit, they are the heirs apparent to the Duchesnays, who won gold in 1991.

Oksana Gritschuk & Evgeny Platov

Oksana Gritschuck and Evgeny Platov, the 1994 Olympic and world champions, bring a playful and modern air to dance. "They have super talent and a very easy style. She has something inside that when you look at her, it is not possible to turn your head. All the time they give something new. He is real sportsman and really good athlete. She is absolutely rock and roll and he is absolutely gentleman." – their coach, Natalia Linichuk.

Gritschuk was at the center of a Russian drama because of her 1992 affair with Alexander Zhulin, married to Maia Usova. After coach Natalia Dubova saw Usova – a personal favorite – crying, she banished Gritschuk from her school and intended to match Platov with another skater from Lake Placid, where she trains. However, at the last minute, Platov refused to board the plane in Moscow and remained behind to stay with Gritschuk and train with Dubova's archrival coach, Natalia Linichuk.

Maia Usova and Alexander Zhulin of Russia, the 1993 world dance champions, are known for their sultry, sensual performances. One of their masterpieces was their free-skate to Vivaldi's "Four Seasons," which they used to finish third at the 1992 Olympic Games in Albertville. Zhulin made a habit of wearing tights, until the ISU ruled them out for male dancers for the 1993 season. As of July 1, 1994, no male skater in any discipline is permitted to wear tights.

Maia Usova and Alexander Zhulin shown early in their career wearing glittery garb that was so distracting it moved Toller Cranston to call for an end to the Christmas-tree look. In the past, ice dancers have been most guilty of extravagant apparel.

championships, they appeared with blackened faces, and Rahkamo with a blackened tooth, to portray tramps. "That's going too far," Ford said. The blackened faces disappeared before the Olympics and world championships on the advice of the ISU.

"[Rahkamo and Kokko] find it difficult to skate within the constraints of a competitive environment," Jones says. "If they had worked within the confines of dancing, I think they would have been on the podium long ago."

"All these years, we have wanted to develop ourselves as artists," Petri Kokko says.

The truth about the Finns, however, is that they probably have the best skating technique in the world. Callaway says she would have placed them first in one of the compulsory dances – the blues – at the Olympics, because of their flow, interpretation, and depth of blade edge as they cut into the ice with confidence at extreme angles. "They are probably the best skaters in the

Susanna Rahkamo & Petri Kokko

World bronze medalists Susanna Rahkamo and Petri Kokko of Finland have received their greatest accolades from outside the judging domain. They received a standing ovation from a British audience for their long program, skated to Vivaldi's "Four Seasons," at the 1989 European championship in Birmingham, where they finished twelfth. At the closing banquet, their competitors rose en masse to applaud when the Finns were introduced. Their best endorsements have come from Jayne Torvill and Christopher Dean, with whom they trained in Germany, who found them "new and different."

The Finns, who had no coach and little ice time in their own country, have never been boring on the world stage. One year, the couple skated a competitive comedy routine in which Rahkamo appeared as a batty bride (above, right). They rely on noted Finnish professional dance choreographer Jorma Uotinen, who "wants to bring new shapes to the body," Rahkamo explains.

In 1993, Russians Anjelika Krylova and Vladimir Fedorov surprised everybody to finish third in Prague at their world championship debut – an event marred by the brief suspension of six of the nine judges who were said to be relying too much on skaters' reputations rather than their current abilities. However, when Krylova and Fedorov resurrected the same program for the 1994 Olympics less than a year later, they finished only sixth.

world, technically, at the present moment," Jones said after the 1994 world championships, where the Finns placed third in two compulsory dances, and third throughout the rest of the competition.

Still, if they were thought to be the best technicians, the Finns were perplexed by their placings in compulsory dances, which test technical edge quality. And they remained unclear about their placings overall, even though, for the past few years, they say they have had no illegal moves in their programs. "Klimova and Ponomarenko had so many illegal moves, and they still won," Rahkamo said, suggesting that some couples can get away with breaking rules and others can't. (The Finns' comments do not necessarily suggest irregularities in judging. Faced with marking a competitor who has performed an illegal move, but also a pleasing, innovative or difficult move that should receive credit, a judge may figure the good and the bad cancel each other out.)

In fact, Gritschuk and Platov won, in spite of appearing to transgress rules about separations and lifts during their free-dance. While the rulebooks say ice dancers must not skate apart for more than five seconds, the winning Russians separated a total of eight times, once for about eight seconds. And some say that during the program Platov did a lift in which he appears to carry his partner. Carry lifts, too, are forbidden.

Gritschuk and Platov, together for less than half a dozen years, will be back, but they will have to look over their shoulders for the new stars of ice dancing. Three Russian or former Soviet teams are right at their heels, as well as a brilliant French couple; and then there are the Canadians, Shae-Lynn Bourne and Victor Kraatz.

Irina Romanova and Igor Yaroshenko of Ukraine improved at every competition they were in last year and have leaped gracefully from seventh place in the world in 1993 to fourth in 1994.

Anjelika Krylova and Vladimir Fedorov of Russia won a bronze medal at the 1993 world championships in what was only their first appearance, with a fast-stepping, dancey program that pleased the judges; but they dropped to sixth at the Olympic Games and then had to withdraw during the 1994 world championships when Krylova shattered a bone in her forearm during a fall in practice.

Tatiana Navka and Samuel Gezolian of Belarus charged from ninth at the 1993 world championships to fifth in 1994, even though Gezolian showed a lot of two-foot skating and was far overshadowed by the sparkling talent of his partner, who is only nineteen years old.

Tatiana Navka and Samuel Gezolian, rising to the top

Tatiana Navka and Samuel Gezolian learned their ice-dancing skills under the Soviet system with Moscow coach Natalia Dubova. But with the break-up of the country, they claimed Belorussian citizenship, although both were born in Ukraine. The sixteen-year-old Navka and twenty-one-year old Gezolian burst on the scene in 1991, when they won Skate America. They name Ludmila Pakhomova and Alexander Gorshkov as their favorite skaters.

Also waiting in the wings are the new couple of Marina Anissina and Gwendal Peizerat of France, tenth in their first appearance at a world championship in 1994. Anissina is a talented skater, who won two world junior titles for the Soviet Union before moving to France to skate with Peizerat, who once won a world junior silver medal with another partner.

But the most favorable talk centers around the Canadian couple, Bourne and Kraatz. "If I had to forecast a future world champion, it would be the

Shae-Lynn Bourne & Victor Kraatz

Shae-Lynn Bourne and Victor Kraatz, the unusual and highly touted ice dancers from Canada, won their junior national title in 1991 in their first season together in spite of Bourne's hairline skull fracture, which she received when she and her partner, practicing some compulsory dances, collided with another team. "The doctor said if I hit it again, I'd be a vegetable," Bourne said. She practiced with a helmet. The following season, Bourne and Kraatz won the senior title, upsetting world and Olympic competitors Jacqueline Petr and Mark Janoschak.

Bourne and Kraatz amazed the skating world with the deep angles of their blades and their low-to-the-ice positions. But their talents are more complex. "They have a glide that is developing into an endless movement," says coach Eric Gillies. "When you watch them skate and the music isn't playing, you don't hear anything. Their blades make no sound."

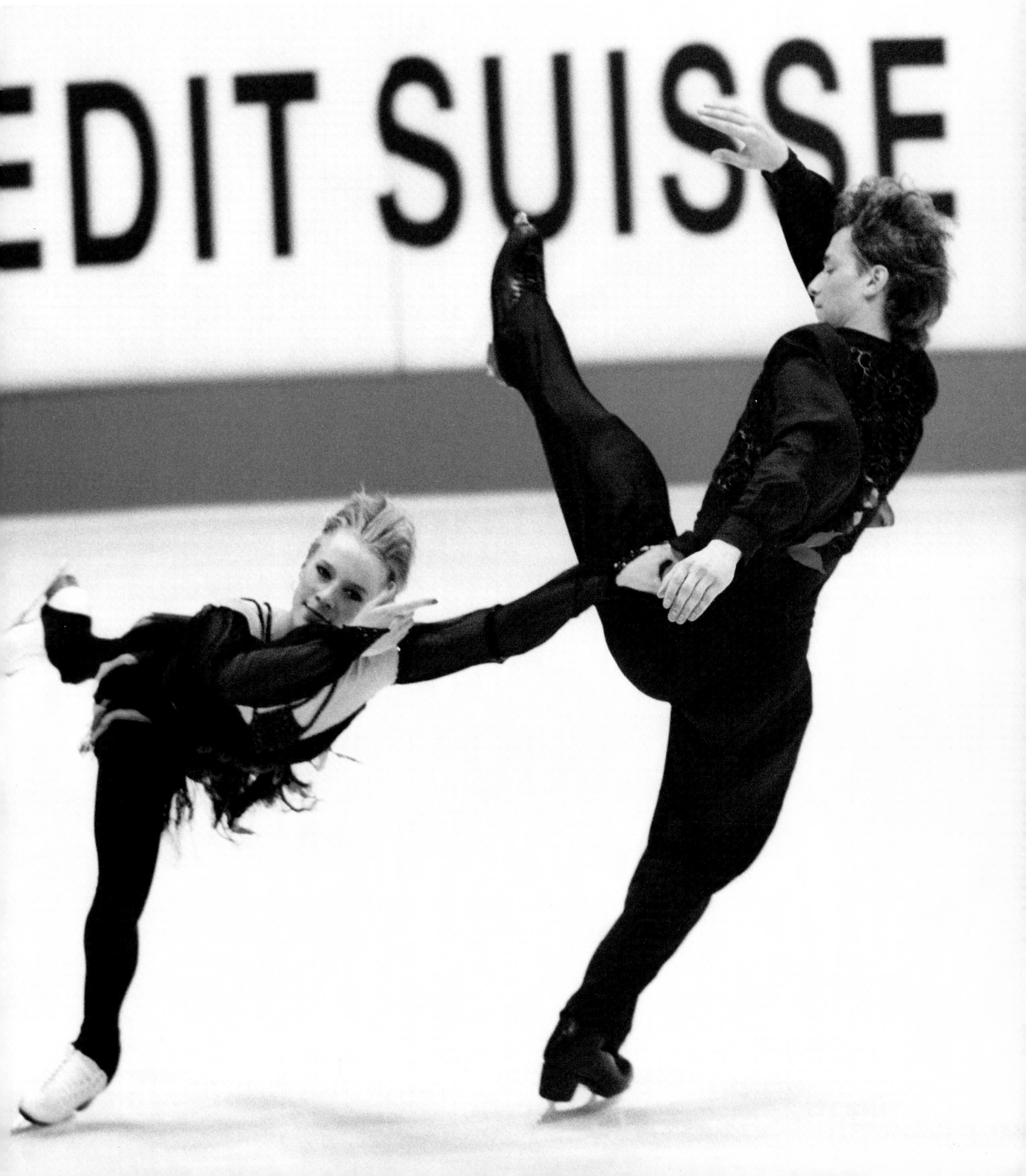
EDIT SUISSE

"Other dancers are still printing, while we're writing," says coach Eric Gillies of Canadians Shae-Lynn Bourne and Victor Kraatz.

Canadians," Courtney Jones says. "You could hear a pin drop when they did their rumba [at the 1994 world championship]."

Together Bourne and Kraatz have made one of the quickest rises ever seen in the ranks of ice dancing. In their first appearance at a world championship, they were ranked fourteenth, but then they climbed to tenth at the 1994 Olympics (with a former Soviet dance coach claiming they should have won the rumba at the Games) and, only a month later, to sixth at the world championship in Japan. Everywhere people have marveled at their easy, long glide, their knee bends, their depth of edges, their soft touch on the ice, so soft, the carving is almost silent. "They are good in so many aspects," says their coach Eric Gillies. "There's not a single direction that we're allowing to jump way ahead of everything else. When they get up there, they're not going to have any weaknesses.

"A lot of people are glad to see them come along because they are able to do many of the things that people have been saying for a long time should be in ice dancing – but that's been missing. They love the curve. They love the glide. We've seen lots of skating without it recently."

If anything, the couple's striking use of extreme knee bends and acute-angled edges and a posture that is not always so erect is apt to startle the ball-room devotees of the sport. Jones is concerned the unusual pose of their upper bodies and stance may be too "acrobatic" for ice dancing, the sport of the upright carriage. As long as Bourne and Kraatz are around, controversy in ice dancing may live on. At the very least, Bourne and Kraatz will inject a healthy dose of athleticism, technical wizardry, and lyricism into ice dancing for years to come.

Women's Singles

Barbara Ann Scott felt the pressures of winning a world title at home in Ottawa. "Tourists were beginning to visit me as though I were one of Ottawa's institutions. They were likely to come at curious hours and it was not much good refusing to go to the door. Some of them called up in the middle of the night, explaining that they didn't really want anything, that all they were calling for was to say hello." – Scott in her autobiography Skate With Me

From Madge Syers to Oksana Baiul, there always has been a bit of sparkle and dash about the women's singles event.

Syers was one of the new breed of continental skaters, even though her skirts fell ponderously to her ankles. But Sonja Henie corrected that in a hurry, with her shorter dresses. She added jewels, too, plenty of them.

Aided by her shorter outfits, Henie showed an athleticism rarely seen in women of her day. But by today's standards, her skills seem rudimentary. At the peak of her career, her highlight move was a couple of single Axels, done back to back, but each lifting only slightly off the ice. This tour de force required Henie to wind herself up like a corkscrew, pausing and hesitating in a way that loudly signaled its unleashing. This kind of preparation and execution is considered bad form today.

Barbara Ann Scott was the darling of the skating world after the Second World War, skating to "Buttons and Bows" and winning hearts with her China-blue eyes and lightning-fast spins. She was a vision; Scott was the only skater to wear a cream-colored fur skating dress, all hand sewn. It was made by Toronto furrier Jack Creed, and the women who worked on it signed their names and a good-luck message on the underside of the creamy skins. It was Scott's coronation gown, the one she wore to win the 1948 Olympics.

Scott was no hothouse flower, however. As an amateur, she practiced twenty thousand hours before her Olympic win, skating outdoors in slush, over ruts from hockey games, and in spite of howling winds and sub-zero temperatures, chilling to the bone. Sometimes she shoveled the snow off the ice herself. As a professional, Scott skated five shows a day, every day but Saturday, when she skated six shows. Her weight dropped to 98 pounds (44 kilograms) with her fifteen- to sixteen-hour work days. During training, Scott, at 5 feet, 3 inches (157.5 centimeters), considered her weight normal at 103 pounds (46 kilograms).

Even though Syers, Henie, and Scott recast the mold of female skaters by refusing to accept that they couldn't do the kind of things males do, women have physical limitations that make this task difficult.

"Girls have a much wider hip than men, and that means they have a different angle to the knee joint and also to the ankle joint," says Margarite Sweeney-Baird, a British skating coach. "That puts a lot of stress on the girls and makes it more difficult to transfer energy up through the rest of the body. That's why girls find it more difficult to do the triple jumps with any level of consistency."

Only two women – Midori Ito of Japan and Tonya Harding of the United States – have ever landed triple Axels in competition. Kristi Yamaguchi of the United States and Lisa Sargeant of Canada both flirted with them (with Sargeant actually incorporating one into her technical program as part of a combination jump) but never landed them in competition.

Surya Bonaly of France has long been determined to be the first woman to land a quadruple jump under the duress of competition, but has never achieved one. Harding practiced quadruples, too, but gave up on them because the jump was taking too heavy a toll on her ankles. During the Lillehammer Olympics, it was no surprise that Harding suffered from ankle problems. "There are stresses on the ankle, not just on the takeoff but on the landing, because if you have three or four rotations to do, you've also got to stop all that energy on the landing, to be able to hold yourself on the landing," Sweeney-Baird says.

A woman didn't land a triple Lutz in competition until Denise Biellmann of Switzerland did it at the 1978 European championship, sixteen years after Donald Jackson's breakthrough. Her performance was so impressive that a British judge gave her an extremely rare technical merit mark of 6.0. Biellmann, who is best known for her spin, in which she pulls one leg high above and behind her head, didn't land the triple Lutz again until the 1981 world championship, which she won. Even in the half-dozen years after that, only two or three women landed them, including Kay Thomson and

Sjoukje Dijkstra
of the Netherlands
reigned supreme
among postwar
women's skating
by training in
Britain and
excelling in
compulsory
figures. She won
three consecutive
world titles in
the early 1960s
and won the
Olympic gold
medal at
Innsbruck
in 1964.

Elizabeth Manley, both of Canada. Harding landed a triple Lutz when she was a novice skater, at age twelve. An extraordinary jumper, she was landing triple loops when she was only ten.

Now, a decade later, women are doing triple Lutzes in combinations, even during the technical programs, in which a fall could put them out of the running for the rest of the competition. While only five tried the triple-Lutz combination at the 1993 world championship in Prague, a year later in Japan, eleven attempted it (not counting another three, Nancy Kerrigan, Oksana Baiul, and Lu Chen, who had it in their programs but who pulled out of the Japan event). In Japan, only six achieved it without a hitch.

It wasn't always so difficult. Sjoukje Dijkstra of the Netherlands won three consecutive world titles and an Olympic gold medal in 1964 without doing anything more difficult than a double loop. She remained on the top podium because of her superiority in compulsory figures. In her day, compulsories were worth 60 per cent of the final mark.

Carol Heiss, the 1960 Olympic champion, was an intrepid competitor, a champion of compulsory figures and vivacious in her free-skating programs. She was a technocrat more than an artist, but her programs were driven by high energy. She married 1956 Olympic champion Hayes Alan Jenkins.

Indeed, in the early days after the Second World War, there was more interest in sparkle than dash in women's skating. American women took to the sport in droves, driven by their enchantment with Sonja Henie. "It's a real glamor sport in the United States for women," said Frank Carroll, who coached Linda Fratianne when she won world titles in 1977 and 1979. "It all started with Sonja Henie. Every time she went out on the ice and starred in those movies, she wore beautiful costumes."

The impressive string of American women inspired by Henie came to dominate the sport after the war. From 1953 to 1960, two American women won seven of eight world titles, the string broken only once by German Gundi Busch. Tenley Albright, a surgeon's daughter who suffered from non-paralytic polio at age eleven, won two world titles and the 1956 Olympic gold medal. Carol Heiss, an all-round skater with a happy, lively, perky personality on the ice, could not be beaten for five years, winning world titles from 1956 to 1960 as well as an Olympic gold medal in 1960.

The U.S. team, including skaters and coaches, poses for photographers just before leaving for the 1961 world championship in Prague. The plane crashed over Belgium with no survivors. Second from the left, in the front row, is promising sixteen-year-old skater Laurence Owen, the daughter of Olympian Mirabel Vinson Owen, also killed in the crash.

Then the next generation of American skaters was lost when a plane carrying the U.S. team to the 1961 world championship in Prague crashed in Belgium, with no survivors. The event was canceled.

After Dijkstra's unchallenged reign in the years after the crash, American women quickly regained their feet and again took over the sport with a vengeance. They included three-time world champion and 1968 Olympic champion Peggy Fleming; 1972 Olympic bronze medalist Janet Lynn; 1976 Olympic champion Dorothy Hamill; Linda Fratianne; 1982 world champion Elaine Zayak; 1983 world champion Rosalynn Sumners; 1986 world champion Debi Thomas; 1990 world champion Jill Trenary; and 1992 Olympic champion Kristi Yamaguchi, also a winner of two world titles.

Two of a long string of U.S. women to win world titles were Rosalynn Sumners (left) and Jill Trenary (right), who married British ice dancer Christopher Dean in early 1995.

All in all, American women have won five Olympic titles since the war, with three silvers and two bronzes in other years. And they have won ten world titles, too. Everywhere, young, talented American women seemed to be springing from the pack. At the 1991 world championship in Munich, they even swept the podium. Yamaguchi won gold, Harding won silver, and Kerrigan won bronze.

The impetus for women to attempt triple jumps began not with Americans, however, but with a Canadian, Petra Burka, who won the 1965 world championship. She became the first woman to land a triple jump, a Salchow. "She was a very good jumper," says her mother and coach, Ellen Burka. "It was a very strange time, because the big-set girls were in. Petra was heavy then, too. . . .

"Then Petra said this was ridiculous, and she decided to lose weight. She looked better. And there was more athletic-type skating. There was not good choreography, especially in Europe." The young Burka landed her triple Salchow in only her first year as a senior skater. She already had three double Axels in her program, a marvelous feat in those days. She was only fifteen when she attended her first world championship in 1962.

For the first time, U.S. women swept the podium placings at the 1991 world championships in Munich: (left to right) Tonya Harding, who finished second, Kristi Yamaguchi, the champion, and Nancy Kerrigan, third.

But Burka was soon eclipsed by an American who made her mark not with athleticism but with artistry. The United States had also lost some of its top coaches in the 1961 crash, but then Carlo Fassi, an Italian who was a European champion in 1953 and 1954, arrived, and his first famous pupil was Peggy Fleming, who defeated Burka to win the 1966 world championship. Inspired by the balletic elegance of the Protopopovs, Fleming brought artistry and a soft flow over the ice to women's skating. She was also known by a move that few seemed to copy; she would launch into a double Axel out of a spread-eagle and then resume the spread-eagle when she landed. However, she did only a single Axel when she won the Olympic gold medal in Grenoble, France, in 1968, in what was her worst performance in the four years Fassi had been training her.

Artistry and jumping, however, did not become so important until the ISU decreased the value of the compulsory figures in 1973. "They had been doing a few edges, a few spins, a few single jumps, and then they had to do all these figures," Burka says, speaking of the level of skating during the 1960s when the ISU recognized forty-one figures (at a competition, a skater would do six of them) and the compulsory event took two days to complete. "Figures held back the beauty of skating."

Others, like Maribel Vinson Owen, a ten-time U.S. champion, also predicted that the abolishment of figures would lead to "acrobatics." Perhaps she was right, for, as the emphasis on figures dimmed, along came Linda Fratianne. She could jump like a gazelle, a graceful and sure acrobat.

Peggy Fleming
was a princess
of the ice who
brought an
element of dance,
grace, and charm
to figure skating.
"Most of the
great female
skaters I have
known, like
Dorothy Hamill
or Peggy Fleming
or Linda Fratianne,
always appeared
frail on the outside,"
said U.S. coach
Frank Carroll.
"But all of them
were the opposite.
They all had
inner cores
of metal and steel."

Fratianne was by no means the first woman to do triples. Dianne de Leeuw of the Netherlands did one when she won the world title in 1975. Others would try them but would have to steady themselves with a hand on the ice after the descent. Christine Errath of the German Democratic Republic tried a triple toe-loop in her winning program at the 1974 world championship, but fell. Dorothy Hamill was the last female to win an Olympic gold medal with programs that had no triples.

Fratianne could not only do one triple jump; she could do two – and do them just as well as the male skaters. "She was the very first girl to do triple jumps easily," says her coach Frank Carroll. "Linda would land triple

Tonya Harding

Tonya Harding has had much to overcome. Aside from her connection to the Nancy Kerrigan assault, Tonya Harding's checkered past has included a mother who has been married six times; a clash with a motorist (Portland police found Harding brandishing a baseball bat at a woman whose driving etiquette she disliked); the seizure of a handgun after a neighbor of Harding's complained of hearing shots in their apartment parking lot; and an extensive use of profanities, a relaxed work ethic, and a habit of hiring, firing, and rehiring her coaches. In between all these incidents, Harding became the second woman to land a triple Axel.

Trouble follows Harding at every step. After unsettling incidents during competitions, in which Harding broke either a skate blade or a costume fastening, some observers seemed skeptical during the Lillehammer Olympics when Harding stopped her performance, complaining of a broken lace (bottom, left). She was allowed to skate in the more favorable position (for marks) near the end of her group while she fixed the problem, but Canadian Josée Chouinard was unsettled when she had to skate sooner than expected.

Kristi Yamaguchi

Kristi Yamaguchi's name aptly translates into "mountain mouse" from Japanese. Tiny, delicate, and athletic, Yamaguchi excelled both as a pairs skater and a singles skater good enough to win an Olympic gold medal and two world titles. Yamaguchi and partner, Rudy Galindo, won the world junior pairs title in 1988 in Brisbane, Australia, the same year that Yamaguchi also became the world junior women's champion. The otherwise-quiet Yamaguchi shrieked on receiving her first perfect mark of 6.0 (for artistic impression) when she won her first world title in 1991 at Munich. Coach Christy Ness has said that, although Yamaguchi was never a natural jumper, she had a dedicated work ethic that allowed her to master difficult triple Lutz–triple toe-loop combinations. "It's not hard to make a point with her," Ness said. "She listens and she does pay attention."

Nancy Kerrigan

Although Nancy Kerrigan was first profiled as the glamorous, advantaged performer in contrast to Tonya Harding's rough-edged upbringing, Kerrigan came from a blue-collar background. Her father, Dan, is a welder who took out a second mortgage in order to pay for his daughter's skating. Her mother is almost totally blind due to a virus that attacked the nerves in her eyes when her daughter was only about a year old.

Kerrigan, most elegant when she is performing a spiral (opposite), found it difficult to combine training and schooling. After four years of juggling skating and school, she was awarded a two-year "associate" degree in business studies at Emmanuel College, an all-women's college near Boston.

Linda Fratianne, the first woman to do two different triples in competition, had her nose and teeth fixed before she won two world titles. She was only fifteen when she went to the 1976 Olympics.

toe-loops and triple Salchows with great flow and ease, as if she were landing a double Axel. And after she started doing them, others had to put them in."

Fratianne was only fifteen when she went to the 1976 Olympics, which were won by Hamill, but "she had great spring in her legs, she was very quick, and she was able to get into rotation very quickly," Carroll says. "And because she was young, she had no fear. She was perfect. She was the perfect student, because she would listen and try to do exactly what she was told. If I asked her to jump off a roof, she would say 'This roof? Or that higher roof?'"

Fratianne was such a quick learner that she passed all her tests from preliminary to gold within three years, and even though her amateur skating career lasted only ten years, she won two world titles and a silver medal behind archrival Anett Poetsch of the German Democratic Republic at the 1980 Olympics. Most skaters take longer to reach their peak. The usual span of a skating career is fifteen years, perhaps even twenty.

Fratianne was a jumping trailblazer. Biellmann followed. And then along came Elaine Zayak, a jumping prodigy, who had started to skate after losing part of her foot in a lawnmower accident as a toddler. At only sixteen, Zayak won the 1982 world championship, unleashing six triple jumps, a record for a woman in a competition to that point.

236

However, she did only two different triples – four of them were triple toe-loops (two in combination with other jumps) and two were triple Salchows. Shortly afterward, the ISU, concerned that women's skating was becoming a boring contest of faltered triple jumps, set out rules that required skaters to do certain things during a long program.

One of the requirements – for the women's programs only – was the spiral, a graceful, one-foot move, trailing from one end of the ice surface to the other, aided by pushes, turns, and changes of position to gain speed. It was a move that had been neglected for years in women's competition and was included to focus more attention on artistry. Nancy Kerrigan is the champion of the spiral, with her long-limbed, exquisite lines.

The ISU also restricted the number of jumps that a skater could repeat in a long program. Some call it the Zayak rule. "I started the whole triple-jump thing," says Zayak, speaking of the current race for women to do multiple triples in their programs. "There are so many triples that the girls have to do now, it's terrible. But it's the name of the game."

Zayak faced that game when she reinstated as an amateur for the 1994 season, ten years after she retired. She had been off the ice for three or four years, was twenty pounds (nine kilograms) overweight, totally out of shape, and concerned only about having a good time. At age twenty-eight, she had to turn her life around completely.

And that she did. She skated with a glow at the U.S. nationals in Detroit, Michigan, where she finished an unexpected fourth, skating to the music she used at the 1984 Olympics. In Detroit, Zayak won the hearts of skating's avid watchers and received a standing ovation even before she took her opening pose for the long program. Sometimes the best of skating isn't about finishing first.

With all her repetitive triples, Zayak had narrowly defeated Katarina Witt of the German Democratic Republic at the 1982 world championship. But after the rule change, Zayak was at a disadvantage, and Witt's superior artistry won the day, almost every time, from 1984 to 1988.

At the best of times, Witt had only three triple jumps in her routines and didn't always land them all. Still, only the very athletic Debi Thomas upstaged Witt to win the 1986 world championship, and Elizabeth Manley, with her array of speed, flying footwork, and five different triples – everything but the triple Axel – edged her out in the free-skate at the 1988 Olympics.

Many contend that, had Biellmann continued to skate as an amateur – she retired at only eighteen, exhausted from the pressures of fame placed on her

The 1988 Olympic silver medalist, Elizabeth Manley of Canada, was of a broken army family with little financial resources. At one point her mother went $26,000 in debt to finance her daughter's skating career. When she turned professional and signed with the "Ice Capades," Manley received a $50,000 signing bonus, which she promptly used to pay off her mother's debt.

in her own country – Witt would not have won so many titles. On her heels (although felled by compulsory figures) was the whirling Midori Ito, who landed a triple toe-loop–triple toe-loop combination at age twelve and who won the 1989 world title with her high-soaring triple Axel the year after Witt retired. The tiny Ito, shy, smiling, and polite, was the first to break the Axel barrier for women, leaping as if bouncing from strings in the rafters. She was a "living phenomenon," Toller Cranston says.

When Witt returned to amateur skating in 1994, six years after her retirement, her artistry remained unquestioned, and judges told her so with their marks at the Lillehammer Olympics. However, her base mark was lower because her level of difficulty had not kept pace with the female skaters of the 1990s. But some felt that perhaps there is too much emphasis on the need for women to do triples. And perhaps the judges are reinforcing what coach Louis Stong calls a "scary" trend.

"The triple jump mania still exists," he says. "Judges are still influenced by the numbers. [During the 1994 season] a magnificently choreographed, beautifully skated technical program with a less difficult Salchow combination was placed below a brutal technical program [with falls] done by somebody who was expected to be highly placed. To me that's bad."

Stong was speaking of his own skater, Charlene Von Saher of Britain, whom judges placed sixteenth in the technical program after a strong performance at the world championship in Japan. Three of nine judges placed her behind Marie Pierre Leray of France, whose more difficult triple Lutz-combination attempt was flawed. A Polish judge went so far as to place Von Saher nineteenth, Leray ninth.

Little Michelle Kwan of the United States, whose triple-Lutz combination was even more of a disaster – she fell on the Lutz and did not complete the second part – still managed to finish eleventh in the technical program in Japan.

Stong was also puzzled that Yuka Sato won the long program with the approval of only five of the nine judges, the other four opting for Surya Bonaly. "Most of us in skating thought [Sato] was 0.5 to 0.6 points better, and she was clearly the best skater."

And therein lies one of the most fascinating arguments about the finish of the women's event at the world championship. Which skater should be ranked the best: Bonaly with her overwhelming acrobatics but jerky skating style? Or Sato with her less-dramatic triples but high speed and peerless display of edge quality?

Bonaly, clearly disappointed, didn't agree with the judges' selection of Sato. The French champion created a scene at the medal ceremony in Japan when she refused, at first, to stand on the silver-medal podium and then ripped the medal off her neck while Tanja Szewczenko of Germany was getting her bronze medal. One judge had even ranked Szewczenko, who had a less-difficult program than Sato, ahead of Bonaly in the free-skate.

Bonaly is an anomaly in figure skating, a former world tumbling champion rather than a graduate of the school of arabesques and Gillis Grafstrom edges. "Surya can't skate," says Sandra Bezic, who advised both Kurt Browning and three-time Canadian champion Josée Chouinard to set aside their spectacular jumps and concentrate on basics and the flow of edges for a while. Bonaly, on the other hand, sometimes sets up for jumps in an obvious way: she turns abruptly and thrusts herself into them. When she is not jumping, her strides are short and choppy. She once stumbled while merely stroking during a program at the 1994 European championship.

Katarina Witt

(Opposite) Katarina Witt, in her rendition of Carmen *that she used to win her second consecutive Olympic gold medal at the 1988 Calgary Games. At the competition, Witt accomplished only two different triple jumps, but her artistry was uncontested. Ironically, her main competitor, Debi Thomas of the United States, also chose to skate the music from* Carmen. *The contest was called the "Battle of the Carmens," but their interpretations were quite different. In the true tradition of Torvill and Dean, Witt "died" on the ice at the end of her program.*

Witt won her first Olympic gold medal in Sarajevo. But when she returned as an amateur to the 1994 Olympic Games ten years later, the rink in which she had won her medal had all but been destroyed by a war that devastated the former Yugoslavia. At the 1994 event, Witt chose to dedicate her Olympic performance to the Sarajevo people by skating to "Where Have All the Flowers Gone?" And for the first time, Witt's parents were able to watch her compete in Lillehammer. During her two previous Olympic triumphs, they had not been allowed to leave the former East Germany.

Midori Ito

Midori Ito of Japan was a whirling dervish who left behind three lasting memories of her amateur career: her beaming face and her utter joy as she landed difficult triple jump after jump at the Calgary Olympics in 1988; her magnificent triple Axel, a first for women, during her winning program at the 1989 world championship in Paris; and the demoralizing crashes she had at the 1991 world championship in Munich. In Munich, during the warm-up for the original program, Ito collided with French skater Laetitia Hubert. And, during her attempt at a triple Lutz combination that was squeezed too tightly into a corner, Ito tumbled right out of the rink at the feet of television cameramen. She finished fourth, and her final bow was apologetic.

Ito has rarely been seen outside of Japan since she decided to turn professional after the 1992 season. Because of the growth of skating in her country, she says she is quite busy touring the country to sold-out shows. She admits she has always suffered from a weight problem, but she was trimmer than ever when she came to Canada and the United States in late 1993 and delighted fans with her performances. She even landed a triple Axel.

Charlene Von Saher moved to the United States with her German mother and her Dutch-Austrian father when she was only a few years old, and she actually skated at the U.S. junior championships. But just before the 1992 Olympic season, she was allowed to skate for Britain, where she was born. For the 1994-95 season, she will again attempt to qualify to skate for the United States.

Marie-Pierre
Leray has come
close to winning
a major medal
only once – when
she finished fourth
at the 1993 world
junior championship –
but her exotic
looks and elegance
have landed her
modeling jobs and
even a spot in a
coffee advertisement.
Twice, the nineteen-
year-old skater
has finished second
to Surya Bonaly
at the French
championship.
She has also
tried her hand
at pairs skating.

Yuka Sato

Even Yuka Sato's mother, Kumiko Okawa (also an Olympic figure skater), did not expect her to win gold at the 1994 world championship: "When she was first after the technical program, I thought she might make an unfortunate mistake like her mother. I always made mistakes in important competitions, so I thought I may have planted some genetical problem with my daughter, and I was ready to settle for a bronze. And even if she didn't win the gold medal, I carry a gold medal, because I'm wearing a coin that I received at Innsbruck Olympics, thinking that this is my gold for her. The stage was set for Yuka to win a medal with the world championship being held in Japan. I was looking at her on the podium when the anthem was playing and I thought, how happy a child she is."

Sato is most inspired by Canadian pairs skaters Barbara Underhill and Paul Martini. (Japan has never been known for its strength in pairs.) When Sato came to Canada to train with coach Peter Dunfield, she had never been out of her country and didn't speak a word of English. At first, Dunfield put her in various skating positions to teach her. But by the end of the first summer, carrying around a dictionary wherever she went, she was able to understand basic English. She is now fluent in English.

Because Bonaly lacks skating finesse, she has to camouflage her deficiencies. In her 1994 technical program, her music, with its jarring beat, complemented her jerky style, Sweeney-Baird says. Therefore, it appeared as if she was skating with more artistry in her technical program than in her long program, skated to the same cut of Vivaldi's "Four Seasons" that the high-quality, soft-kneed Russian skaters Maia Usova and Alexander Zhulin used to compete at the 1992 Olympics in Albertville.

"The basic ability to skate across the ice with a fluidity of motion allows you to appreciate the technique," Sweeney-Baird says. "The jumps should look easy. The skating across the ice should look easy."

Sato is one skater who uses edges and flow to the ultimate. During her footwork sequences, the young skater moves across the ice at high speed, but at the same time she changes edge, steps from one foot to the other, and works with rotations that float in various directions. "She's combining two levels of energy at a very, very high level of technical difficulty, with the rotational movement and the speed across the ice," Sweeney-Baird says. "Her footwork has enormous technical quality."

Bonaly, on the other hand, does hops rather than steps, according to Sweeney-Baird. "There's very little in the way of actual true use of the skating blade, true use of rotation, counter-rotation, and speed across the ice."

"She doesn't understand," Bezic says. "Any choreographer is going to struggle with her because she doesn't have the basics. I think her choices [of music] are irrelevant. They're not going to work because she can't skate. It's too bad, because she loves to skate. Until she stops jumping to learn the basics, it's not going to work. You just need that basic flow of edge."

At only twenty, Bonaly has a long string of credits to her name. She is a junior world champion and, as of 1994, has already competed in six world championships, finishing second in two of them. She rules Europe. Four times she has been a European champion, and in 1994, Bonaly defeated Oksana Baiul, who bounced back to take the big prize away from her at the Lillehammer Olympics.

And in spite of her shortcomings, Bonaly is an exciting skater. In exhibitions, she does things with jumps that other skaters only dream about. She is the only woman to perform a back flip, a maneuver used by a handful of men at the professional level. Before Bonaly came along, the jump was considered illegal, because a skater, flipping head over heels, landed it on two feet rather than one. However, at the exhibitions in Lillehammer, Bonaly astonished the skating world when she was able to land it on one foot only.

*French coach
Didier Gailhaguet
first spotted
Surya Bonaly
at a skating
clinic in Paris.
"She was a fighter,"
he said, recalling
how she had
mastered all the
double jumps
in one month.*

The back flip has been landed only once in a world competition, when the athletic Terry Kubicka of the United States tackled it, with his knees tucked into his chest, at the 1976 Olympic Games. The ISU banned it after that. Robin Cousins does a more difficult version of it with his legs flying straight out above his head during exhibitions. But until Bonaly came along, the back flip was just not a move that women did, much less with a finish on one foot.

Bonaly was only fifteen years old when she first burst upon the world scene. She was an unknown curiosity when she finished fourth in the free-skate at the 1989 European championship in Birmingham, England. She later used that momentum to finish tenth in her world-championship debut in

Surya Bonaly

Surya Bonaly was adopted as an infant by the Bonalys; her father is a drafting engineer and her mother is a physical-education teacher. They brought her up macrobiotically, avoiding milk and anything from animal cells, and, until she was in her mid-teens, Surya never had her hair cut. Although her adoptive parents were not poor, they lived for a year in a truck with three dogs, according to former coach Didier Gailhaguet. He was later dropped as coach after a public shouting match with Surya's mother at the 1992 Olympics in Albertville.

(Above) Bonaly performs a variation of the Biellmann spin. She is best known for her jumping ability and her attempts to land a quadruple, a feat which still eludes her. Every year, Bonaly wears out several pairs of skating boots while practicing quadruple jumps and back flips. Surya means "sun" in Hindu.

Josée Chouinard

Above all, Josée Chouinard, a three-time Canadian champion, understands heartbreak. For all her athletic and artistic talent, she has never won a medal at the world championships or the Olympics. She is lucky that she had a chance to skate at all. Ten years ago, when she was fourteen, a doctor told her that a back injury she suffered during training was so serious that she would end up in a wheelchair if she didn't stop skating. She had been a precocious novice trying triple jumps, but the jarring falls developed into a dorsal-lumbar syndrome. With intense physiotherapy, she made a comeback. Although she has been close to glory several times – finishing second to Nancy Kerrigan at the pre-Olympic competition in Norway and sitting in third place after the technical program at the 1994 world championship – Chouinard's best world or Olympic finish was her fifth placing at the 1992 world championship in Oakland, California, and at the 1994 world championship.

Chouinard's programs during the 1994 season were expertly crafted by Sandra Bezic. One of Bezic's master-pieces was Chouinard's rendition of La Fille Mal Gardée *(top). "I thought that we hit on a quality of Josée that she hadn't hit on before – a playfulness and mischievousness," Bezic says. "But also she has such a sophisticated, natural beauty. I kind of wanted that angelic look with the fire underneath it, that mischievousness. Angelic beauty almost with a little bit of tongue in cheek."*

Oksana Baiul

Oksana Baiul of Ukraine reigned supreme at the 1994 Olympics, winning gold even after suffering an injury to her right ankle (shown taped, left) when she collided with Tanja Szewczenko of Germany during a practice session. Baiul became the first woman from any former Soviet republic to win a world figure-skating crown when she triumphed, at only fifteen, in 1993. But only a month before, Baiul had been such an unknown that even Lu Chen of China had never heard of her. Baiul was an orphan who benefited from the largesse of fellow Ukrainian Victor Petrenko, who paid for her skating boots and outfits. Baiul was a star of the 1994 world tour and has undertaken to train part of the season with her coach Galina Zmievskaia at a rink in Hartford, Connecticut. Both she and Petrenko are contributing money to revive their rickety home rink in Odessa that, up to last year, had no working Zamboni.

1989, in front of a home crowd in Paris. But, like Bonaly, the story of the women's event in the future is largely a story of youth. Stick your toe pick in early, the skating world seems to say.

When Oksana Baiul won the 1993 world championship in Prague, she was only fifteen years old, the youngest woman since Henie (sixty-six years earlier) to win it.

Tanja Szewczenko, showing a quality of expression rarely seen in young teens and a precocious ability to jump, made her world debut in 1993, also when she was only fifteen. Only a year later, she won a senior bronze medal at the world championship. For the past two years, Szewczenko has been young enough to compete in both the senior and junior world events.

Lu Chen followed the same path. Coming from a country that has had almost no skating history, Chen was only fourteen – the minimum age – when she competed in her first world championship in 1991. Incredibly enough, she won a bronze medal at the 1992 world junior championship the same year she won a bronze at the senior version. By eighteen, she had already taken part in two Olympic Games and three world championships. (She withdrew from a fourth in 1994 because of a foot injury.)

Baiul, on the other hand, has never competed in a world junior championship. She did not qualify for the event in 1993. She took the skating world completely by surprise when she finished second in the European championship, held only a couple of months after the world junior event, and then dusted off all the veterans to win world gold with a shake of her thin shoulders. Waiflike Baiul had come from nowhere, with all kinds of disadvantages: the death of her mother and grandparents by the time she was thirteen and poor training facilities at an Odessa rink that had a broken-down ice-cleaning machine.

A quick rise to the top has become more of a possibility since the 1990 season, when compulsory figures were dropped from world and international competitions. Without hours of tedious figures tracings, skaters have more time to devote to free-skating skills.

And it is possible to break loose from the circling crowd with a sudden understanding and feel of several different triples at once; Canadian silver medalist Susan Humphreys greatly expanded her repertoire of jumps from two to five triples in one year. In her first world championship in 1994, she finished ninth.

Only four years before that, Humphreys had finished fifteenth at the novice level in Canada and a similarly undistinguished thirteenth the

Tanja Szewczenko of Germany will be remembered for her practice crashes during the 1994 season, as well as for her world bronze medal. At the Olympics, she collided with Oksana Baiul. At the world championship, she crashed into the rink boards, hurting her arm, chin, and head. Her father, a taxi driver in Dusseldorf, had to save for a year so that he and his wife could afford to go to the world championship in Japan.

Krisztina Czako of Hungary is a young, precocious jumper who by fifteen had already competed in two Olympic Games and three world championships.

following year as a junior. She missed the 1992 season altogether, because of a recurring shoulder injury. But already, Humphreys has a collection of valuable tools to carry her to the top: an ability to do triples, a pleasing, soft flow over the ice, and Yamaguchi's coach, Christy Ness.

Many of her rivals will be younger than she. In 1994, Humphreys was eighteen years old. But Elena Liashenko of Ukraine, who has an unerring ability to do triple Lutzes in combination, was only seventeen. Rena Inoue, Sato's Japanese successor, was seventeen, too, although she looked much younger. She has seen little international competition, yet has triple-Lutz combinations in her repertoires. Kumiko Koiwai of Japan, at eighteen, was the 1993 world junior champion and shows great promise, too; at seventeen, she had finished second in the important NHK Trophy international competition in her homeland.

Krisztina Czako of Hungary gained special dispensation to skate at the world championship in 1992, when she was only thirteen years old and had

In her first world championship in Japan in 1994, tiny, graceful Michelle Kwan, all of thirteen years, finished eleventh. The skater from California is a first-generation American; her father hails from the Canton region of mainland China, while her mother is from Hong Kong.

three triples, including a loop, in her bag of tricks. When she competed at the 1992 Olympics, she was the youngest competitor entered, regardless of sport. Her father and coach, Gyoergy Czako, competed at the 1953 world championship in Davos.

Known yet only as a jumper, with little artistic quality, the muscular Czako moved from twenty-third at the 1992 Olympics to eleventh in 1994. Currently, she is ranked twelfth in the world with a program in which she rolled from one end of the rink, did a triple, rolled to the other end, and did another. Czako finished second in the 1993 world junior championship.

Unlike Czako, Natalie Krieg of Switzerland has difficulties getting around triples, but, at sixteen, she has long been known as one of the current generation's best spinners. The ability to spin has not been cultivated as fervently as the knack of jumping, but Swiss skaters seem to thrive at it. Biellmann made famous her toe-to-head spin during the late 1970s and early 1980s, but she merely expanded upon a spin invented by another Swiss skater, Karin Iten,

Nathalie Krieg, the darling of Switzerland, is the most amazing spinner in the world today. She made it into the Guinness Book of Records with a spin that lasted for three minutes, twenty seconds. She honed her craft because of a lack of ice space in her homeland and rarely strays from her centered position on the ice.

who competed at the world level in the early 1970s. Earlier versions of the spin had the skater holding the leg or foot out to the side. Biellmann's innovation was that she pulled the leg up over her head from behind. Basically, it is a variation of the layback spin.

If Ronnie Robertson was the prince of spinning, Nicole Hasler of France, third at the 1963 world championship, was its princess. "She was the fastest of spinners," Peter Dunfield says. "And pure spinning. Pure camel spin. Pure sit spin. She'd blur it, always. You could not identify anything. I've never seen anything like it. She didn't do as many positions as Nathalie Krieg. She did only the classical positions."

Kreig can do anything once she finds her spot. She honed her skills, because she had only a small patch of ice on which to practice in a country with few facilities. Once she continued to spin for three minutes, twenty-two seconds without stopping, all the time changing position with incredible flexibility and never budging from her center on the ice. From the time Krieg was a junior skater, she has been a star in Switzerland, where she passes out autographed photos. In normally quiet practice sessions, she sparks applause when she does her spins.

The ultimate in youthful female skaters is Michelle Kwan of the United States, who competed at the senior level of the U.S. championships at age twelve. Coach Frank Carroll was against it, but Kwan passed her senior competitive tests while he was away at a coaching conference in Canada. He had thought it better that she remain a junior and win the U.S. junior title.

Kwan was still only thirteen when she made her first appearance at a world championship in 1994, but she did not require special permission to attend, partly because she was to turn fourteen on July 7, 1994, a week before the deadline. Besides, Kwan also won the 1994 world junior title, and medalists at such an event are allowed to compete at the senior version of the event, regardless of age. She will, however, be eligible for world junior championships for another four years.

Currently, the sliver-slim Kwan, weighing about eighty-eight pounds (forty kilograms), lacks strength and power in her movements, although she can do triple-Lutz combinations, a feat only the top female skaters do. But everybody is looking with great curiosity at how this daughter of Chinese and Hong Kong-born parents will develop. "[Because of body changes with puberty] with a women you really can't tell what you have until they're fourteen or fifteen," says Peter Dunfield, coach of Manley and Sato. "It's just throwing the dice."

Lu Chen became the first figure skater from China to win an Olympic medal when she earned bronze at the Lillehammer Games in 1994 at age seventeen. The young skater, shown performing a spiral, is the daughter of a hockey player in northeast China and a mother who is a table-tennis coach.

Caryn Kadavy, a world bronze medalist for the United States in 1987, who had to compete against Kwan at a Pro-Am competition in April 1994, watched her childlike competitor with interest. "I worry for kids who have all the jumps too young, because what happens if they grow and they spurt," Kadavy, then twenty-six, told an American reporter. "It knocks you off a little bit, unless she doesn't change that much, like a Kristi Yamaguchi. She was like Michelle Kwan, and she just stayed the way she was.

"That's what you really hope for, that you stay in the same range that you already are [in] and that you can hold it together with all your jumps and technical ability."

Already, Kwan's body has begun to change. She has grown about six inches (fifteen centimeters) since early in the 1993-94 season. "I can see it in her timing," Carroll says. "She has a slender but strong body, and she's very quick, too."

Carroll also added that he thought the biggest factor in whether or not young girls succeed is their changing bodies and the specter of burnout. In skating, that has happened many times before. Tracey Wainman of Canada was only twelve when she was pushed to skate at the 1980 world championship (she had not been the top qualifier in her country), and she fizzled under the pressure of growing up and dealing with a changing body and the intense pressures placed on her. "Tracey Wainman was the perfect example of putting too many expectations on one so young," Carroll says. "She was really pushed.

"But Michelle is in it for the long run. She could see two more Olympics. In eight years, nobody will hold the world title every year. There will be ups and downs, and she may not be a champion all the time. My job is to keep her interested in skating. We have to give her body rest to grow. When it becomes a chore, it's time to stop."

Still, some think Kwan is being pushed too far, too fast. The Soviet machine, for all its success in spitting out top-quality pairs, ice dancers, and male figure skaters, had difficulty in producing top female skaters, with all their pushing and training. "They did not respect a women's body," Dunfield says. "They did not understand how easily you can burn out a woman. They trained women the same as men, very hard. They didn't train them through puberty with care and understanding about strengths and body differences. They'd burn them out. You'd see many good skaters come up, and then they'd just disappear.

"Women are probably the hardest to make come to fruition. They have to be trained with a very strong consciousness about what they can take at this

Lu Chen

Lu Chen of China started skating when she was five years old in Jilin, in the northeast part of China, where skating has some following. According to former skater Li Ming Zhu, who started coaching in 1985, Chen showed immediate promise and by the time she was eleven had already landed three different triple jumps. Years of ballet training have given her the grace she shows in the photos above. (Opposite) Chen, a picture of elegance during a lay-back spin, admired Midori Ito and Kristi Yamaguchi while she was developing, watching world championships, which have been shown on television in China since 1978. She has also spent time training under Carlo Fassi in Italy, who helped her with her technique in jumping, and under Frank Carroll in Lake Arrowhead, California. Her Chinese coach also makes her costumes.

time and what they can't and about their emotional drive and stability and not taxing it. Men can take less tact. Russians did not have the tact."

A worrisome example of a young female pushed to the maximum is Lu Chen, under the pressure of being the first offering of a country, China, that has had no world-class skaters, of having grown markedly over the past year, of having a drive that pushes her to practice full-out beyond pain, of having a foot injury that put her out of the world championship in Japan. Still, Chen took part in a grueling seventy-show world-champion tour winding through the United States.

Chen withdrew from the world championship when Japanese doctor Takeyuki Okazaki of the Kawatetsu Chiba Hospital diagnosed her painful foot injury as a navicular stress fracture in her right foot – a "very serious fracture," he said – and advised her that she would be unable to skate for six months, and, without surgery, perhaps for a year. Chen received eight injections of xylocain, a painkiller, while attempting to compete in the qualifying rounds earlier in the week.

However, in a news conference directly after she announced she would withdraw from the event, Chen's coach Li Ming Zhu said she would consult Chinese doctors when they returned home. But, even before consulting them, the coach said her skater may stop skating for only three months. Later she said only one month.

The injury was clearly part of the overuse syndrome. "The willpower of that girl is tremendous," Dunfield says. "The willpower of some of the top athletes is so tremendous that you have to become a watchdog, and you have to be very careful to curb them when they go too far or they can endanger their own bodies. They self-destruct."

These days, the point to the women's race to the top seems to be to get in the rink young, and only the fittest will survive.

Dancing to a New Tune: The 1994-95 Season

Elvis Stojko won his second world title the hard way — overcoming a serious and painful ligament injury with undeniable grit. "It's a sweet victory," he said. "I've been through a heck of a lot of frustration and doubt, all the roller coasters of emotions I can think of. I tested myself emotionally. Some people said it was a dumb move to try, but I knew I could do it. I proved it to myself."

For everyone in the skating world, from avid spectator to skater longing for success, the 1994-95 post-Olympic season was a watershed; the sport took unprecedented turns that would promise to change its face for years to come.

While, in general, the popularity of figure skating continued to soar, one development, in particular, tipped the applecart during the 1994-95 season: the proliferation of lucrative made-for-television professional competitions. In the recent past, pro competitions had been a line drawn in the sand for amateur skaters – skate in as many professional tours as you like, but cross the line to pro competitions unsanctioned by the International Skating Union (ISU) and amateur or "eligible" status evaporated like yesterday's excuses. But with so much money in pro competitions beckoning, crossing the line became a lot more tempting for amateurs.

The 1995 season also provided the final deadline for professionals who wanted to cross back over the line to the amateur world of Olympic events. It was also the year the ISU decided it had better fight back against the growing and powerful lure of the pro world with some enticements of its own: a Grand Prix and open competition circuit that included prize money. With all the changes, there was plenty of opportunity for viewer confusion.

❧

Frank Carroll was amused. The esteemed U.S. coach was sitting quietly one evening, watching the amateur competition Skate America in Pittsburgh, Pennsylvania, when suddenly the man behind him in the audience demonstrated that he was a new skating fan.

"He was obviously a real jock," Carroll recalls. "He was with his family, and was talking about the judges, and how they were judging, and who should have won it. He was screaming and yelling. It was like he was at a boxing match.

"He was telling his kids that they throw out the high and the low score. And I wanted to turn around and say, 'They don't throw out the high and the low score! You don't know what the hell you're talking about!'

"I thought it was so amusing, because he was so into it. This was a man who obviously knew nothing about figure skating, but he was very wrapped up in it and very gung-ho about it." Carroll's experience was symptomatic of the spirit of this new post-Olympic season. Traditionally, the year after an Olympic competition is low-key, when athletes, having met their goals, retire from the Olympic race and the members of a new, rather unknown, generation compete to carve their own niches.

It's just not that simple anymore. And the 1994-95 season certainly wasn't that quiet.

Like Carroll's raucous neighbor, people from every corner of North America, even those who perhaps had no previous interest in skating, went to rinks, even in midsummer, to catch a glimpse of an Oksana Baiul or a Scott Hamilton in full flight as the professional skating world took centre stage. Or they sat in front of television sets in record numbers to thump their fists at a judge's call. Membership in U.S. learn-to-skate programs in some clubs swelled by 300 per cent – in the country where most of the big bucks are to be found. In Florida, the land of sun and sand, new ice rinks popped up incongruously everywhere. "Skating is just going nuts in Florida," one coach said. It seemed as if everyone wanted to seize the glowing moment, to get in on a sport that became mainstream overnight. Networks, notably CBS, snapped up any kind of figure-skating property imaginable to fill their prime-time programming schedules, and were rewarded handsomely with high ratings that show few signs of letting up. Skating shows – including profiles, life stories, tours, and theatre-on-ice – proliferated on television at an unprecedented pace.

Almost every weekend from mid-November until Christmas, CBS sallied forth with its professional skating creations. One of its first made-for-TV events – "Ice Wars: U.S. vs The World" – with an elite cast of skaters such as Nancy Kerrigan and Oksana Baiul (meeting for the first time since their close battle at the Lillehammer Olympics), Kurt Browning, and Brian Boitano, hit prime-time air waves over two days. Skating helped CBS to score big during the November ratings sweeps; part one of "Ice Wars" earned a 10.8 rating share (meaning 15.2 million viewers watched at least part of the show, behind ABC'S "Roseanne" with 27 million). The finale on a Saturday night won its time slot, with 18 million American viewers.

Appearance fees became the order of the day. Although the winning team (from the United States) earned $100,000, all eight competing skaters

Kurt Browning astonished a near-capacity crowd at a "Stars on Ice" show in Toronto by spontaneously proposing to his girlfriend, Sonia Rodriguez. She said yes.

received appearance fees, as much as a reported $350,000 for Kerrigan, who is said to have pushed for team, rather than individual, scores, because she did not want to be defeated by Baiul. As it turned out, neither skated well (Kerrigan was worse), but it didn't seem to matter; CBS set about to plan another version.

Money was a lure, a tantalizing charm that drew the best skaters – and only the best would do – from around the world. The 1992 Olympic silver medalist Paul Wylie delayed his plans to attend Harvard Law School in the fall of 1995 to pursue the ice chase, noting that he could make far more as a skater – while that career lasted – than as a lawyer. It was not out of the realm of possibility to earn $100,000 in a couple of nights.

Indeed, Scott Hamilton, at thirty-six one of the oldest – but liveliest – attractions on the pro circuit, earned $260,000 in a single night by winning the new $1.3-million Gold Championship, a contest among Olympic champions, in Edmonton, Alberta. Others could command $25,000, some even $35,000, for a single appearance at a non-competitive show. Donald McPherson, a 1963 world champion who scouts talent for "Holiday on Ice" in Europe, gasps at the fiscal competition, and laments how the new money-mad business is squeezing long-established tours with fewer resources (which don't have the dollars from television backing).

Oksana Baiul, taking flight with life in a new country.

"The world of professional skating has exploded," says Kerry Leitch, president of the International Professional Skating Union (IPSU), founded in 1963 in Italy. Leitch has been busier than ever providing judges for many professional competitions, all of which are outside the domain of the ISU. He has a list of about fifty former international competitors or coaches that IPSU feels are qualified to act as professional judges.

During the 1993-94 season, IPSU fielded judges for two professional competitions organized by Dick Button's Candid Productions, based in New York. But in the following two years, the gold rush was on. For the 1995-96 season, the number of Button-produced competitions is expected to climb to as many as twelve, almost double the number from the previous year. Leitch, a Canadian who has coached world (amateur) medalists, has himself acted as judging referee for a handful of events staged by other promoters.

But the professional boom has also caused a muddle in the minds of viewers. "Our events are confusing," admits 1980 Olympic champion Robin Cousins, who still competes as a professional with an intense elegance. "The rules are different for every competition." During the post-Olympic season, some pro competitions threw out the high and low marks; some didn't. (The amateur world does not; hence the confusion of Frank Carroll's seatmate

Ekaterina Gordeeva and Sergei Grinkov moved their training base to the International Skating Center of Connecticut and proceeded to win pro competition after pro competition during the 1994-95 season.

at Skate America, which is an amateur competition.) Some pro competitions marked events out of 10; an increasing number used the amateur standard of 6.0 as a maximum mark, blurring further the worlds of amateur and professional. Some offered only one mark in a technical or an artistic program; others gave two sets of marks for both. Some offered only artistic competitions. Many didn't bother with ice dancing or pairs events. Some actually had required elements in technical programs, like amateur competitions. Others seemed to be judged entirely on – as one commentator put it – the ability to move the judges and the audience "emotionally." One event with a rock 'n roll concept (Victor Petrenko did a rap routine, but it seemed to be close enough – he almost won the competition) had some non-skating celebrities as judges. The wildest offshoot of the skating flurry was the talk of a summer beach competition in California, in which female skaters were expected to don swimsuits, with no word on what artistic impression was to be based upon. "The one thing I worry about with some of these professional things is that they don't get too gimmicky," Leitch says. "If they get into that, they'll lose it."

Sometimes the concepts and the judging results confused even the skaters themselves. Isabelle Brasseur and Lloyd Eisler were unhappy to finish second to 1994 Olympic champions Ekaterina Gordeeva and Sergei Grinkov at the Canadian Professional Skating Championship in Hamilton, Ontario, in December 1994; minutes after the results were known, they made it clear they may not compete in another professional competition, preferring instead the lucrative show circuit. "If you do a technical program, why not give the marks to ones who did everything, and not just the ones who have more medals?" Brasseur says, referring to errors Gordeeva and Grinkov made on a throw and a spin in the technical program.

"I spent seventeen years as an amateur, going through the politics," says Eisler. "I should have stayed amateur. At least I know that world better. And the money, as far as pairs skaters go, isn't that great [in pro competitions]."

Whether or not Brasseur and Eisler were left feeling confused, frustrated, and robbed, the lure of the pro world was intoxicating enough to the top level of the amateur world that ISU members felt the squeeze, particularly since fewer countries have been able to support the costs of staging major international competitions. During the post-Olympic season, only five (France, Germany, Japan, Canada, and the United States) were able to offer any kind of prize money and to pay skaters' expenses. (As it is, the United States Figure Skating Association last year spent $450,000 to send skaters to competitions in countries that cannot afford to pay transportation costs, according to then-USFSA president Claire Ferguson.) Skate America was forced to dangle a $100,000 (U.S.) purse incentive for the first time to skaters in October 1994. Still, it paled in comparison to the rewards posed by pro events.

None of it was enough to keep Oksana Baiul of Ukraine, 1993 world ice-dancing champions Maia Usova and Alexander Zhulin of Russia, U.S. silver medalist Mark Mitchell, and three-time Canadian champion Josée Chouinard in the amateur fold for the 1994-95 season. Mitchell, who had been undecided about his future, suddenly made up his mind to turn professional when, out of the blue, he received two offers to skate in pro competitions. He couldn't refuse. Baiul planned to stay out of amateur competition for only a year to take advantage of the lucrative deals, but changed her mind, and declined to reinstate after watching the world championship in Birmingham, England, preferring the freedom of professional life.

Three-time world silver medalist Surya Bonaly wanted to follow in Baiul's footsteps, then jump back into the race after the final deadline for professionals to reinstate on April 1, 1995. She had already signed twelve professional contracts early in the 1994-95 season, when the French federation told her that, if she honored them, it would not accept her application for amateur reinstatement. If it did not, Bonaly would have been unable to compete in future world championships or Olympic Games. According to her agent Michael Rosenberg, Bonaly backed down, even though it meant she forfeited $1 million and had to hope nobody would sue her for breach of contract.

Bonaly said she had signed a contract with the French federation, but thought it would extend only to the end of the 1993-94 season. Under her

Philippe Candeloro's new exhibition routine – sans chemise.

current contract, she is obligated to stay amateur until the end of the 1998 season. Had she turned professional, she would have been unable to service a contract her French federation had already set up with a television network to broadcast an amateur competition; the contract included financial support for Bonaly and for her countryman, Philippe Candeloro.

"The French federation went bazookas," Rosenberg says. "They were trying to persuade her to stay amateur, and, at the same time, they were threatening. They were holding a carrot in one hand and a knife in the other."

Candeloro had been tempted by the same idea, but retained his eligibility after the Bonaly incident. "I didn't want to make trouble for my amateur career," he says. "If you leave, the federation makes trouble to you."

Finally, the ISU took the issue by the skate blades. During the world championship in Birmingham, it agreed to set up a $1.7-million U.S. Grand Prix circuit to coax amateur skaters to retain their status. And it promised to allow up to eight open (or pro-am) competitions. "It's going to be a battleground for the next twelve months [the 1995-96 season]," says David Dore, director-general of the Canadian Figure Skating Association, whose Skate Canada International event will be part of the Grand Prix circuit. "But at least it's good news that the ISU has decided to get in it."

In the circuit, Canada, France, Germany, Japan, and the United States will combine their existing international competitions (Skate Canada, Trophée de France, Nations Cup, NHK Trophy, and Skate America) into a series that is almost entirely invitational. Each competition will have the same prize money: a total of $232,000 U.S., culminating in a final worth $466,000 U.S. The ISU hopes to attract the top six skaters in men's and women's events, and the top four couples from each of the pairs and ice-dancing events for the final.

"They're trying to show that there's as much money inside of the [amateur] sport as outside," Dore says. "They're trying to go head-to-head with the promoters. Skaters could earn $300,000 to $400,000 by skating in these events. I think the long-term goal is for these skaters to stay until the 1998 Olympic Games. They're worried that [eligible] skaters will slowly be enticed out of the sport this year, and that, next year, they're not going to have them."

Although Usova and Zhulin, Mitchell, and Chouinard did reinstate for the 1995-96 season (as well as Midori Ito of Japan, who has been a professional since 1992), the move was not enough to entice Baiul back to the ice wars. "Coming back is not a financial decision," says Kevin Albrecht, agent for Browning, Hamilton, and Kristi Yamaguchi. "It's a lifestyle decision. And

Josée Chouinard defeated four world champions to win a pro event in Hamilton, Ontario, in December 1994.

Finnish ice dancing pioneers Susanna Rahkamo and Petri Kokko bowed out of amateur competition after the 1994-95 season and married each other on July 1, 1995. After a third-place finish at the 1994 world championship, the couple, always at odds with amateur rules, decided to skate only to the end of the 1995 season. They have vowed to stretch their imaginations to the limit in their new career as professional ice dancers.

the only people it affects financially are ice dancers, who do not get appearance fees for professional championships. It's the only area [in which it] is financially best to stay amateur."

Ironically, 1995 world champions Oksana Gritschuk and Evgeny Platov of Russia and silver medalists Susanna Rahkamo and Petri Kokko of Finland said they had skated their last amateur competition the week the ISU decision was announced. Usova and Zhulin, who are making the opposite move, appeared to have made the best financial decision. Few professional competitions staged dance events last year.

But at the eleventh hour, Usova and Zhulin decided to remain professional. Few professionals appear willing to jump back into the amateur world as it currently exists, because they dislike its rules and restrictions. Although the first ISU-sanctioned international open (formerly called pro-am) competition took place in Los Angeles in March 1995, only one professional, Caryn Kadavy, took part. Kadavy, who retired from amateur competition in 1989, finished fifth of five women in the event, won by Michelle Kwan, who was only fourteen years old. The event used strict ISU rules. The ice dancers in the event even had to perform a compulsory dance. The Grand Prix requires one compulsory.

If the Grand Prix circuit is meant to keep the amateur (or eligible) world intact, it may not necessarily provide the final solution to ISU problems. Dore is concerned that the Grand Prix final may end up competing with the world championship. "It could be possible that before January [when they intend to hold the final in the future] you could have blown your wad.... And it's really dependent on those ten skaters agreeing to [take part]. I hope [the ISU] realizes to get into this, there's a lot more to announcing that we're in this business.... The ISU hasn't had to do very much in order to be successful.... I just hope they haven't gone too fast into these open international events and will sort of dilute their marketplace as well."

Singularly unruffled by all the talk of money was Elvis Stojko, who won his second consecutive world title in 1995 against all odds – a very painful ligament injury that would have felled any other skater. With the same kind of pluck, focus, and clear thinking that helped him overcome various drawbacks during the year, Stojko decided to follow the star of the Gillis Grafstroms and the Barbara Ann Scotts before him. He was never tempted, he said, to turn professional to take advantage of the sudden opportunity.

"I would never stop because of money, because those are not the ideals of sport," Stojko says. "A lot of different sports are starting to lose the whole idea of it. . . . . It's good that we're able to make money [as amateurs] and put it in our trust fund to be able to pay for our skating. That enables us to search for our dreams, reach for our dreams. By no means would I ever end it because someone gave me an offer of so much money. I don't think there's anyone in the world who can give me enough money to get me to stop and become a professional."

Still, Stojko is one of the lucky skaters at the top who benefited from the post-Olympic boom and the relatively new rules that allow him to make money as an amateur – a world that Barbara Ann Scott never envisaged. After Stojko's first world-championship win, he took part in more than forty stops of the Tom Collins tour of world champions throughout the United States in 1994, conducted his own eight-stop Canadian tour in the fall of 1994, and enjoyed fruitful support from a bevy of corporate sponsors.

*Elvis Stojko.
A look of anguish,
just before pulling
out of the Canadian
championship.*

276

But what the sport is really about, says Stojko, is meeting challenges and testing your limits. And in 1995, he explained what he meant in very concrete terms: a day before he was to compete in the Nations Cup in Germany, a bedridden Stojko courageously chucked the intravenous needed to battle his violent flu, and went on to win the event. In fact, ill as he was, he even pushed himself to try a quadruple jump.

Worse problems developed at an early practice for the Canadian championship in Halifax when he slipped off an edge, rammed the toe pick of his right skate into the boards, and turned his knee in a contorted way. He tore an anterior ligament between the two bones of his lower leg, and pulled and strained soft tissue behind the Achilles' tendon. He could feel the effects of the injury all the way up his leg, at the back of his knee, and into the lower back, Stojko said. Doctors estimated it could take eight to twelve weeks to heal completely. But Stojko wasn't finished.

After withdrawing about a minute into his short program at the Canadian championship in Halifax, Stojko embarked over the next seven weeks on a frustrating road to recovery that sparked doubts about his ability to compete at the world championship in Birmingham. In fact, one skating magazine announced prematurely that he had withdrawn from the event. Even though he suffered daily setbacks in his training, Stojko had other plans. "We didn't do it because we had to. We did it because we knew we could," says Stojko's coach, Doug Leigh, who admitted that even he thought his charge was "superhuman" after landing a triple Axel–triple toe-loop combination in the short program at Birmingham. Stojko was one of only two men to do it in the event. It was equally amazing that he had even tried such a difficult maneuver; before that display of mettle, he had skated the program only about four times in two months and only two or three times without a hitch. Three weeks before the world event, his best effort was landing a double-loop jump.

Even more miraculous was his performance in the long program, done fittingly to the soundtrack from the Christopher Columbus movie, *1492, Conquest of Paradise*. The idea of the program, Stojko said, was to depict the story of his life in the past year: leaving shore in search of new horizons, believing in himself to move on. Many of his positions and stances were symbolic, but no move was more trusting than the unprogrammed triple Lutz–triple toe-loop combination he stuck in at the four-minute, fifteen-second mark of his four-and-a-half-minute program, when fatigue usually sets in. Stojko added the triple toe-loop, he said, because he had fallen on a quadruple attempt earlier. It was a gutsy move, also, because Lutzes gave his ailing foot the most trouble. Stojko said his mind was so set that he did not feel the effects of his deeds until he was finished, the adrenaline had dropped, and a dull throb wrapped his lower leg. He convinced six of the nine judges in that program – enough for the victory.

Stojko said he went through every emotion in the book – frustration, depression, happiness – in the weeks leading up to the world championship, but he did not corner the market on them. Todd Eldredge of the United States had felt them all, too, but over a longer period of time. His comeback in the season of 1994-95 was unparalleled; at age twenty-three, he proved to be a tough veteran, with a new sensibility to music and an unflappable attitude that ignored disaster. It hadn't always been that way; Eldredge hadn't even been to a world championship in three years, and was forced to go through the qualifying rounds, but his performances in Birmingham revealed the stuff of champions. Although he finished second, he graciously said that he was disappointed, but that Stojko had simply skated better.

Eldredge had defeated Stojko in the short program, showing more spark and aggression, and it was that same mind-set that pushed him to ignore his choreography and add a triple Axel at the end of his long program after having fallen on an earlier attempt. "I thought, okay, this is your only shot," Eldredge said afterward. Taking such a risk hardly ever works in programs under pressure, but Eldredge made it work – somehow.

In the past, the old Eldredge would have floundered under pressure, and, from the moment in 1990 when he became the youngest man to win the U.S. senior title in twenty-four years (he was eighteen), the hubbub started. It

Todd Eldredge was the comeback story of the 1994-95 season, although he had shown brilliance in winning two international competitions the previous year. Eldredge was almost unbeatable in 1994-95 and actually defeated Elvis Stojko in the short program at the world championship. Eldredge left home at age nine to pursue his skating dreams and lived with other skaters in a house run by the mother-in-law of his coach, Richard Callaghan.

Nicole Bobek found relative peace under the wing of Detroit coach Richard Callaghan, who seemed to be able to turn her from a wayward teen into a focused, fit athlete who came within a breath of winning the world title. Although there was unfavorable publicity hanging over her head (she was accused of home invasion; the sentence was later dropped), Bobek won the short program in Birmingham.

continued unabated when he won a world bronze medal in 1991, and pressures multiplied when he developed a back problem, caused by one of his legs being slightly shorter than the other. He had to withdraw from the U.S. championship in 1992, the qualifying event for the Albertville Olympics, but his country gave him a medical bye, allowing him to bypass the event and qualify for the Games anyway. The bye came at the expense of his countryman, Mark Mitchell, who had to sit at home and watch the Olympics on TV. Eldredge felt even more guilty when he was able to finish only tenth at the Games.

The following year, Eldredge finished only sixth at the U.S. nationals, and skated as if the sun would never shine again, limp, listless, and seemingly uninterested in his task. He then took two months off.

"I told him to quit unless he learned to love the sport again," says coach Richard Callaghan. "He lost his focus. He got caught up with what people were seeing. When he got up to the top so fast, people just wanted more, and it turned negative."

Eldredge did make a comeback, with the 1994 Olympics in mind, but misfortune struck when he developed a flu bug, and his temperature rose to 104 degrees, at the U.S. nationals. The flu caused him to faint in his hotel bathroom one night and hit his head on the sink. He finished only fourth, frustrated that nobody was able to see what he could do, and he failed to make the Olympic and world-championship teams. Many people wrote him off.

Eldredge's comeback was symbolic of what is happening to the U.S. skating team in general; after a couple of years of dismal performances, it has again become a major force, and promises to continue with strength and depth that reaches down into the junior ranks in singles skating.

Before the 1994-95 season, many had also dismissed Nicole Bobek, a charismatic child of misadventure who was a last-minute replacement for Tonya Harding at the 1994 world championship in Japan. Bobek, whose training habits had not always been exactly ardent, flopped miserably and failed to advance out of the qualifying rounds. But a year later, having settled on Eldredge's coach, Richard Callaghan (her third coach in one season), Bobek, too, was a different skater, more trained, more focused, more consistent. With all the power and speed of a condor, she swept to victory at the U.S. championship in Providence, Rhode Island, flashing difficult triple jumps and one of the most spectacular spiral sequences ever seen. Bobek, all of seventeen, and – strangely – considered an old veteran in U.S. ranks, carried the momentum with her to win the short program at the world championship in Birmingham, although a couple of falls in the long program placed her third

Michelle Kwan was touted to win the U.S. championship, but her coach reminded everyone that the smiling fourteen-year-old sprite was still not champion of anything. With a few faux pas in her long program, Kwan finished second to Nicole Bobek in the U.S. nationals, but was nearly perfect at the world championship in Birmingham. Only weeks later, she delivered a stunning upset to win the International Figure Skating Challenge, a pro-am event.

over all. "One good thing that I saw [at the world championship] is that you can be out one year and back in the next," Dore said. "It's very healthy. It's not like in the old days when, if skaters didn't place well, you were never going to get back. It does mean, though, that you have to be good to get back."

Her efforts last season will make Bobek a major contender for an Olympic gold medal in Nagano, Japan, in 1998, but she knows she will have to be glancing over her shoulder at her younger competition. Half of the thirty-six competitors at the event at Birmingham were younger than she was, most notably Michelle Kwan, who will always be remembered for her flawless, exquisitely choreographed long program in Birmingham. Kwan finished third in the long program, skimming over the ice surface as if barely touching it, barreling into the most difficult of triple jumps with the best of them, and actually defeating

Bobek. All of this in spite of the fact that, in eight months, Kwan gained 14 pounds (6 kilograms) and grew about 4 inches (10 centimeters). Her body changes forced her to adjust the timing in her jumps. Even though Kwan has been under intense media scrutiny since the Olympic season, she insists she feels no pressure. "She's not champion of anything," says coach Frank Carroll, speaking of the fact that, when Harding was stripped of her 1994 title, the USFSA did not hand it over to Kwan, who finished second. Kwan again finished second in 1995. "It's a lot easier fighting for a title than defending," Carroll adds.

If the world was all aflutter about Kwan's accomplishments at such a young age, it focused even more intensely, at least in the United States, on little Tara Lipinski, who, at 4 feet, 6 inches (135 centimeters) and 69 pounds (31 kilograms), was already becoming a media celebrity at age twelve. When Lipinski landed a triple flip at the U.S. nationals – a jump she had been practicing for only two-and-a-half weeks – and finished second over all in the junior women's event, everyone all but forgot about the winner, Sydne Vogel, a spectacular young skater who landed a triple Lutz. Lipinski's coach, Jeff Di Gregorio, boldly claimed that his young charge does triples so easily, in spite of her age, that his goal is for her to do all the quadruple jumps. (No woman has ever landed a quad in competition, and few have even tried one.) "That is what the sport is leading to," he said, making no mention of the changes young women go through at puberty. "I see her as the first woman with several quads."

Indeed, to be competitive at the 1995 world championships, women – and the younger, the better – had to do five or six triples. Irina Slutskaia, a tiny Russian who won the world junior title last year, was sixteen by the time she went to Birmingham and fired off six triples (she had intended seven) in the long program after fumbling a very difficult combination jump in the short program. She finished seventh over all.

Still, although Lu Chen, the eventual winner of the women's event, did one fewer triple than the gamine-like Slutskaia, she did it with style and maturity. At eighteen, Chen became China's first world figure-skating champion, with her completely new look and elegant costumes and choreography, which were both designed by Toller Cranston. "Total impression wins the day," Cranston says.

"I tried to make her more consistent with who she was, where she came from, and to put her in touch with her culture," says Cranston of Chen's long program to music from the movie *The Last Emperor*. "She's not like Michelle Kwan, who is an Oriental girl but who is much more Californian. [Chen] had started to emulate the glitter dolls from California, but I tried to make her

Irina Slutskaia, 1994-95 world junior champion from Russia.

more of what she was. She's not going to outjump Bonaly and she's not going to have greater strength than other skaters. Her clothes are almost *haute couture*, with no sequins, completely the opposite to everyone else. She was completely 180 degrees away from her No. 1 competitor, Bonaly, who is dipped in glitter. I wanted to go for the total picture, where you do everything right, like Kristi Yamaguchi."

As it was, four of nine judges rated the athletic Bonaly ahead of Chen in the long program. For the third consecutive year, Bonaly finished second at a world championship, this time after a slow start in the short program, in which she made a slight mistake in her triple-Lutz combination.

Youth was also the order of the day in the men's events. Ilia Kulik, age seventeen, of Russia, the world junior champion, shocked everybody when he won the European championship, defeating Olympic champion Alexei Urmanov with the ultimate weapon: landing the most difficult of jumps – even triple-Axel combinations – with astonishing ease, sureness, and grace. However, by the time Kulik arrived in Birmingham, his resolve was already flagging under the new weight of media pressure, the inexperience of his youth, and a dizzying schedule, which had included an eight-day trip to Mexico in February, where a group of Russians did five exhibitions just before the world championship. His energy was sapped. In Birmingham, everything unraveled when Kulik landed only a single Axel–single toe-loop combination in the short program. "I expected that this would happen here," said coach Victor Kudryavtsev. "He is young, and it is not normal for such a young sportsman to skate without faults. It is a normal development, and we do not worry about it." Kulik finished only eleventh in that portion, ninth over all, but he promises to be a major threat at the 1998 Olympics.

In the men's event, the threats will come from both young and old in the next few years. Urmanov, who is still only twenty-one, failed to get onto the world podium for the second year in a row, and was not invited to the lucrative world tour of champions in the United States. But the quality of his skating is high, and his biggest drawback is the difficulty of finding training time in an economically stressed Russia, as rinks close down everywhere. On at least one occasion, Urmanov has lived up to his Olympic-champion mantle; he graciously told Briton Stephen Cousins – who was placed only sixth in the short program at Birmingham after a flawless effort – that Cousins deserved to be placed higher than he. He was ranked fourth after rough landings in his jump combination.(Cousins constantly fields questions about whether he is related to 1980 Olympic champion Robin Cousins of England. He is not.)

Lu Chen, China's
first world
figure-skating
champion.

Olga Markova made a lasting impression during the 1994-95 season. Unlike many Russians, she skates to contemporary North American music, and used it to finish second at the 1994 Goodwill Games and earn a silver medal at the 1995 European championship in Dortmund, Germany.

If 1994-95 was not Urmanov's year in the end, neither was it completely Philippe Candeloro's, although he won the bronze medal at the world championship. Beseiged by offers to skate exhibitions around the world, Candeloro had little time to prepare for the European championships, where he did not skate well, finishing fourth. He was better prepared when he showed up at Birmingham, but his use of *The Godfather* theme for both short and long programs for the second consecutive year became wearisome. By contrast, the 1994-95 season was a breakthrough year for his countryman Eric Millot, who mastered the triple Axel just before he turned twenty-six, and, with his superior attention to foot detail and his heartfelt interpretations of sophisticated music, finished fifth at the world championships. A Japanese judge rated him second-best in the long program, in which he landed two triple Axels, one in combination, while Finnish, French, and Norwegian judges ranked him third.

With new rule changes for the 1994-95 season allowing triple jumps in the short program, the pairs event became a race to see who could land triple toe-loops. In the risky short programs, eleven out of the twenty-three teams competing included the jump. Of those who attempted the jump in the long program, only four were successful. Notably, the champions, Radka Kovarikova and Rene Novotny of the Czech Republic, missed the triple in the long program, although they landed it with perfection in the short. However, some doubted that they should have won; their performance in the long program seemed strained and marred by minor mistakes – although it was winsome, romantic, and beautiful. Some speculated that the win was perhaps a tradeoff for having lost the European championship by the vote of one judge; many thought they should have defeated eventual European champions Mandy Woetzel and Ingo Steuer of Germany, whose routines are often contemporary, introverted, and detached. Whatever the result, the Czechs had already decided to make Birmingham their last stop as amateurs.

The career of Steven Cousins took a marked upswing when he moved to Canada to train with Elvis Stojko's coach, Doug Leigh, after the 1993 season, when he finished only eighteenth at the world championship. Under the positive atmosphere of the club, Cousins won his first medal in international competition at Skate Canada in late 1993, landed a triple Axel combination in a competition for the first time in the short program at the 1994 Olympics (in which he was ninth overall), and was even landing quadruple Salchows in practice at the world championships in Birmingham, in his home country.

Most disappointed to win silver at the world championship were defending pairs champions Evgenia Shishkova and Vadim Naumov of Russia, who never put a foot wrong in their difficult long program, which was, nevertheless, a bloodless routine skated without emotion. "Nothing can surprise me again," said Naumov, who appeared in shock at losing. Shishkova and Naumov had much to overcome in the season leading up to the Birmingham event. An

Eric Millot of France almost completely severed a ligament in his left foot in an accident at Skate Canada in Ottawa in late 1993, and missed two months of training, but he came back and, at age twenty-six, landed his first triple Axel in competition at Skate America in Pittsburgh, Pennsylvania, in late 1994. He married another skater, Valerie, and became a father just before the world championship in Birmingham.

illness that Shishkova picked up before the European championship caused the pair to miss two weeks of preparation; their training was also hampered by the closing of their rink in St. Petersburg, which forced their federation to incur additional expenses by sending them to Moscow to train. Their training mates, Marina Eltsova and Andrei Bushkov, world bronze medalists in 1994, missed the podium ceremony with a fourth-place finish in Birmingham after encountering similar problems. Bushkov was also ill the week of the world championship.

Perhaps the most riveting pairs performances in Birmingham were those of Jenni Meno and Todd Sand, who won the U.S. title with six (out of nine)

U.S. champions Jenni Meno and Todd Sand came to pairs skating late in their careers (at nineteen and twenty respectively) with different partners. The couple, who are romantically linked off the ice, caused a major stir in U.S. skating circles when they dropped their previous partners for each other after the 1992 season. The decision proved profitable; they won the bronze medal at the 1995 world championship, and wed in the summer of 1995.

perfect marks of 6.0 for artistic impression in the long program. However, when they decided the week of the world championship to drop an attempt at triple toe-loops and do double Axels instead, they finished third with their lyrical, exquisite routines, even drawing an artistic mark of 5.9 from an Austrian judge. The pairs event was so closely contested, with a mixture of placings throughout the competition, that Meno and Sand did not know they had won bronze until the last skater had left the ice. They expected only fifth. The U.S. judge placed them behind Russians Eltsova and Bushkov.

Other than Meno and Sand, who drew a standing ovation for the long program, the pairs event could have used the dramatics usually provided by Artur Dmitriev of Russia, who was forced to miss the European championship because of a back injury brought on, according to coach Tamara Moskvina, by having to lift his Olympic-champion partner Natalia Mishkuteniok. Shortly afterward, Mishkuteniok, known for her flexibility and ability to do novel

moves, suddenly decided to leave the skating world behind to get married, and the rush was on to find Dmitriev a new partner. Moskvina even raided the pairs trained by her husband, Igor Moskvin; Bushkov sat helpless by the sidelines, while his partner, Eltsova, skated for a week with Dmitriev. Finally, the choice rested on Oksana Kasakova, who had finished fourth at the 1991 world junior pairs championship in Hull, Quebec (actually finishing second in the original program), with another partner. The new pair missed the event in Birmingham, but are committed to remaining amateur, or eligible, until the 1998 Olympics.

The story in ice dancing is in who remains in the chase for the 1998 Games, after the retirement of the entertaining Susanna Rahkamo and Petri

Kokko of Finland, who became the 1995 European champions when Russian Evgeny Platov (and his partner, Oksana Gritschuk) was on the sidelines with a knee that had troubled him for four years. There are plenty of skaters racing to take their place: the French team of Sophie Moniotte and Pascal Lavanchy, who won world silver in 1994, but slid back to a bronze in 1995, and received the unusual suggestion from judges that their work is too difficult (they have responded by coyly promising "big changes" for the 1995-96 season, including a greater concentration on presentation); the arresting Canadian champions Shae-Lynn Bourne and Victor Kraatz, whose style, flair, and vastly improved compulsories brought them a fourth-place finish in 1995; the new Russian couple, Anjelika Krylova and Oleg Ovsiannikov, who turned heads

Marina Anissina and Gwendal Peizerat of France proved they were major forces in the ice-dancing scene by moving their world ranking from tenth in 1994 to sixth in 1995 and winning two major international competitions in a busy season. Anissina is the daughter of pairs skater Irina Chernieva, who finished sixth at the 1972 Olympics in Sapporo, Japan, with partner Vassili Biagov. Anissina's father was a hockey player in the former Soviet Union.

immediately after they were matched in May 1995 and won the European bronze medal, adding a fifth placing at Birmingham; and the fast-rising French couple, Marina Anissina and Gwendal Peizerat, who placed sixth in only their second appearance at a world championship, with speedy, effortless movement across the ice. All of them will have to respond to the apparent return of the two-time world-championship team from Russia, Oksana Gritschuk and Evgeny Platov, who had announced their retirement in March but are scheduled for two Grand Prix competitions, open only to eligible skaters.

Gritschuk and Platov, Tara Lipinski, and Scott Hamilton are all part of a new age of skating, one in which vistas will open up in ways that Jackson Haines never dreamt of. It hardly seems real, this world of blades and ice and performances that thaw hearts. But every powerful move, every artistic nuance of light and shade, is a celebration of an uncommon sport that is, indeed, magic.

A P P E N D I X

1990 WORLD CHAMPIONSHIPS, HALIFAX, NOVA SCOTIA: TOP TEN FINISHERS

	Men	Women	Pairs	Ice Dancing
1.	Kurt Browning CAN	Jill Trenary USA	Gordeeva–Grinkov URS	Klimova–Ponomarenko URS
2.	Victor Petrenko URS	Midori Ito JPN	Brasseur–Eisler CAN	Duchesnay–Duchesnay FRA
3.	Christopher Bowman USA	Holly Cook USA	Mishkuteniok–Dmitriev URS	Usova–Zhulin URS
4.	Grzegorz Filipowski POL	Kristi Yamaguchi USA	Selezneva–Makarov URS	Wynne–Druar USA
5.	Todd Eldredge USA	Natalia Lebedeva URS	Yamaguchi–Galindo USA	Gritschuk–Platov URS
6.	Petr Barna CZE	Lisa Sargeant CAN	Hough–Ladret CAN	Rahkamo–Kokko FIN
7.	Richard Zander FRG	Patricia Neske FRG	Woetzel–Rauschenbach GDR	Borlase–Smith CAN
8.	Viacheslav Zagorodniuk URS	Evelyn Grossman GDR	Kovarikova–Novotny	Sargent–Witherby USA
9.	Elvis Stojko CAN	Surya Bonaly FRA	Landry–Johnston CAN	McDonald–Mitchell CAN
10.	Paul Wylie USA	Marina Kielmann FRG	Schwarz–Koenig GDR	Calegari–Camerlengo ITA

1991 WORLD CHAMPIONSHIPS, MUNICH: TOP TEN FINISHERS

	Men	Women	Pairs	Ice Dancing
1.	Kurt Browning CAN	Kristi Yamaguchi USA	Mishkuteniok–Dmitriev URS	Duchesnay–Duchesnay FRA
2.	Victor Petrenko URS	Tonya Harding USA	Brasseur–Eisler CAN	Klimova–Ponomarenko URS
3.	Todd Eldredge USA	Nancy Kerrigan USA	Kuchiki–Sand USA	Usova–Zhulin URS
4.	Petr Barna CZE	Midori Ito JPN	Bechke–Petrov URS	Gritschuk–Platov URS
5.	Christopher Bowman USA	Surya Bonaly FRA	Shishkova–Naumov URS	Engi–Toth HUN
6.	Elvis Stojko CAN	Josée Chouinard CAN	Kovarikova–Novotny CZE	Calegari–Camerlengo ITA
7.	Michael Slipchuk CAN	Joanne Conway GRB	Schwarz–Koenig FRG	Rahkamo–Kokko FIN
8.	Alexei Urmanov URS	Marina Kielmann FRG	Ball–Bombadier CAN	Yvon–Palluel FRA
9.	Erik Millot FRA	Patricia Neske FRG	Urbanski–Marval USA	Sargent–Witherby USA
10.	Masakazu Kagiyama JPN	Yulia Vorobieva URS	Meno–Wendland USA	Petr–Janoschak CAN

1992 WORLD CHAMPIONSHIPS, OAKLAND, CALIFORNIA: TOP TEN FINISHERS

	Men	Women	Pairs	Ice Dancing
1.	Victor Petrenko CIS	Kristi Yamaguchi USA	Mishkuteniok–Dmitriev CIS	Klimova–Ponomarenko CIS
2.	Kurt Browning CAN	Nancy Kerrigan USA	Kovarikova–Novotny CZE	Usova–Zhulin CIS
3.	Elvis Stojko CAN	Lu Chen CHN	Brasseur–Eisler CAN	Gritschuk–Platov CIS
4.	Christopher Bowman USA	Laetitia Hubert FRA	Bechke–Petrov CIS	Calegari–Camerlengo ITA
5.	Mark Mitchell USA	Josée Chouinard CAN	Shishkova–Naumov CIS	Rahkamo–Kokko FIN
6.	Petr Barna CZE	Tonya Harding-Gillooly USA	Schwarz–Koenig FRG	Moniotte–Lavanchy FRA
7.	Todd Eldredge USA	Alice Sue Claeys BEL	Urbanski–Marval USA	Yvon–Palluel FRA
8.	Alexei Urmanov CIS	Yuka Sato JPN	Kuchiki–Sand USA	Mrazova–Simecek CZE
9.	Philippe Candeloro FRA	Karen Preston CAN	Hough–Ladret CAN	Sargent-Thomas–Witherby USA
10.	Viacheslav Zagorodniuk CIS	Patricia Neske FRG	Ball–Wirtz CAN	Stergiadu–Razgouliaev LAT

1993 WORLD CHAMPIONSHIPS, PRAGUE: TOP TEN FINISHERS

	Men	Women	Pairs	Ice Dancing
1.	Kurt Browning CAN	Oksana Baiul UKR	Brasseur–Eisler CAN	Usova–Zhulin RUS
2.	Elvis Stojko CAN	Surya Bonaly FRA	Woetzel–Steuer GER	Gritschuk–Platov RUS
3.	Alexei Urmanov RUS	Lu Chen CHN	Shishkova–Naumov RUS	Krylova–Fedorov RUS
4.	Mark Mitchell USA	Yuka Sato JPN	Kovarikova–Novotny CZE	Rahkamo–Kokko FIN
5.	Philippe Candeloro FRA	Nancy Kerrigan USA	Meno–Sand USA	Moniotte–Lavanchy FRA
6.	Scott Davis USA	Marina Kielmann GER	Eltsova–Bushkov RUS	Calegari–Camerlengo ITA
7.	Eric Millot FRA	Tanja Szewczenko GER	Menzies–Bombardier CAN	Romanova–Yaroshenko UKR
8.	Masakazu Kagiyama JPN	Karen Preston CAN	Urbanski–Marval USA	Mrazova–Simecek CZE
9.	Cornel Gheorghe ROM	Josée Chouinard CAN	Monod–Monod SWI	Navka–Gezolian BLS
10.	Marcus Christensen CAN	Lenka Kulovana CZE	Higgins–Rice CAN	Stergiadu–Razgouliaev UZB

1994 WORLD CHAMPIONSHIPS, CHIBA, JAPAN: TOP TEN FINISHERS

	Men	Women	Pairs	Ice Dancing
1.	Elvis Stojko CAN	Yuka Sato JPN	Shishkova–Naumov RUS	Gritschuk–Platov RUS
2.	Philippe Candeloro FRA	Surya Bonaly FRA	Brasseur–Eisler CAN	Moniotte–Lavanchy FRA
3.	Viacheslav Zagorodniuk CIS	Tanja Szewczenko GER	Eltsova–Bushkov RUS	Rahkamo–Kokko FIN
4.	Alexei Urmanov CIS	Marina Kielmann GER	Woetzel–Steuer GER	Romanova–Yaroshenko UKR
5.	Erik Millot FRA	Josée Chouinard CAN	Kovarikova–Novotny CZE	Navka–Gezolian BLS
6.	Masakazu Kagiyama JPN	Elena Liashenko UKR	Meno–Sand USA	Bourne–Kraatz CAN
7.	Scott Davis USA	Marie Pierre Leray FRA	Berezynana–Shliakhov LAT	Goolsbee–Schamberger GER
8.	Sebastien Britten CAN	Michelle Kwan USA	Petrova–Sikharulidze RUS	Mrazova–Simecek CZE
9.	Igor Pashkevich RUS	Susan Humphreys CAN	Schwarz–Koenig FRG	Drobiazko–Vanagas LIT
10.	Stephen Cousins GRB	Olga Markova RUS	Carr–Carr AUS	Anissina–Peizerat FRA

PHOTO CREDITS